Rick Steves'
ITALY
1998

John Muir Publications
Santa Fe, New Mexico

Other JMP travel guidebooks by Rick Steves
Asia Through the Back Door (with Bob Effertz)
Europe 101: History, Art, and Culture for the Traveler
    (with Gene Openshaw)
Europe Through the Back Door
Mona Winks: Self-Guided Tours of Europe's Top Museums
    (with Gene Openshaw)
Rick Steves' Best of Europe
Rick Steves' France, Belgium & the Netherlands (with Steve Smith)
Rick Steves' Germany, Austria & Switzerland
Rick Steves' Great Britain & Ireland
Rick Steves' Russia & the Baltics (with Ian Watson)
Rick Steves' Scandinavia
Rick Steves' Spain & Portugal
Rick Steves' Phrase Books: German, Italian, French,
    Spanish/Portuguese, and French/Italian/German

John Muir Publications, P.O. Box 613, Santa Fe, NM 87504
Copyright © 1998, 1997, 1996, 1995 by Rick Steves
Cover copyright © 1998 by John Muir Publications
All rights reserved.

Printed in the United States of America
First printing January 1998

Previously published as *2 to 22 Days in Italy* (1993, 1994)

For the latest on Rick Steves' lectures, guidebooks, tours, and public television series, contact Europe Through the Back Door, Box 2009, Edmonds,
WA 98020, tel. 425/771-8303, fax 425/771-0833, web site: www.rick-
steves.com, or e-mail: rick@ricksteves.com.

ISSN 1084-4422
ISBN 1-56261-388-X

Europe Through the Back Door Editor Risa Laib
John Muir Publications Editors Krista Lyons-Gould, Marybeth Griffin
Production Mladen "Milo" Baudrand
Design Linda Braun
Cover Design Janine Lehmann
Typesetting Ruth Anne Velasquez
Maps David C. Hoerlein
Printer Banta Company
Cover Photo Colloseum; Rome, Italy; copyright © Blaine Harrington III

Distributed to the book trade by Publishers Group West
Emeryville, California

CONTENTS

Europe

500 KM
300 MI

ITALY'S BEST DESTINATIONS

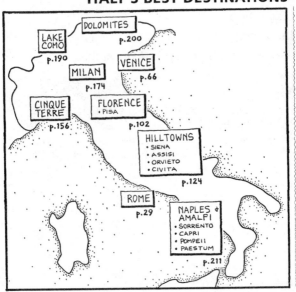

DOLOMITES p.200

LAKE COMO p.190

VENICE p.66

MILAN p.174

CINQUE TERRE p.156

FLORENCE • PISA p.102

HILLTOWNS
• SIENA
• ASSISI
• ORVIETO
• CIVITA
p.124

ROME p.29

NAPLES & AMALFI
• SORRENTO
• CAPRI
• POMPEII
• PAESTUM
p.211

INTRODUCTION

This book breaks Italy into its top big-city, small-town, and rural destinations. It then gives you all the information and opinions necessary to wring the maximum value out of your limited time and money in each of these destinations.

If you plan a month or less in Italy and have a normal appetite for information, this lean and mean little book is all you need. If you're a travel info fiend (like me), this book sorts through all the superlatives and provides a handy rack upon which to hang your supplemental information.

Italy is my favorite country. Experiencing its culture, people, and natural wonders economically and hassle-free has been my goal for over 20 years of traveling, researching, and tour guiding. With this book, I pass on to you the lessons I've learned, updated (personally in mid-1997) for 1998.

Rick Steves' Italy is a tour guide in your pocket. Places covered are balanced to include a comfortable mix of big cities and cozy small towns, from brutal but *bello* Rome to *tranquillo* and traffic-free Riviera villages. It covers the predictable biggies and mixes in a healthy dose of "Back Door" intimacy. Along with marveling at the masterpieces of Michelangelo, you'll enjoy a *bruschetta* snack as a village boy pours oil and rubs fresh garlic on your toast. I've been selective, including only the most exciting sights. For example, after visiting dozens of hill towns, I recommend just the best four.

The best is, of course, only my opinion. But after two busy decades of travel writing, lecturing, and tour guiding, I've developed a sixth sense for what tickles the traveler's fancy.

This Information Is Accurate and Up-to-Date

This book is updated every year. Most publishers of guidebooks that cover a country from top to bottom can afford an update only every two or three years (and even then, it's often by letter). Since this book is selective, covering only the places I think make the top month or so in Italy, I'm able to get it personally updated each summer. Even with an annual update, things change. But if you're traveling with the current edition of this book, I guarantee you're using the most up-to-date information available. This book will help you have an inexpensive, hassle-free trip. Use this year's edition. I tell you, you're crazy to save a few bucks by traveling on old information.

If you're packing an old book, you'll learn the seriousness of your mistake . . . in Italy. Your trip costs about $10 per waking hour. Your time is valuable. This guidebook saves lots of time.

Planning Your Trip

This book is organized by destinations. Each destination is a mini-vacation on its own, filled with exciting sights and homey, affordable places to stay. In each chapter, you'll find:

Planning Your Time, a suggested schedule with thoughts on how to best use your limited time.

Orientation, including tourist information, city transportation, and an easy-to-read map designed to make the text clear and your arrival smooth.

Sights with ratings: ▲▲▲—Don't miss; ▲▲—Try hard to see; ▲—Worthwhile if you can make it; no rating—Worth knowing about.

Sleeping and Eating, with addresses and phone numbers of my favorite budget hotels and restaurants.

Transportation Connections to nearby destinations by train and route tips for drivers.

The **Appendix** is a traveler's tool kit, with telephone tips, a climate chart, public transportation routes, and survival phrases.

Browse through this book, choose your favorite destinations, and link them up. Then have a great trip! You'll travel like a temporary local, getting the absolute most out of every mile, minute, and dollar. You won't waste time on mediocre sights because, unlike other guidebooks, I cover only the best. Since your major financial pitfalls are lousy, expensive hotels, I've worked hard to assemble the best accommodations values for each stop. And as you travel the route I know and love, I'm happy you'll be meeting some of my favorite Italian people.

Trip Costs

Six components make up your trip cost: airfare, surface transportation, room and board, sightseeing, shopping/entertainment/miscellany, and gelato.

Airfare: Don't try to sort through the mess. Find and use a good travel agent. A basic round-trip U.S.A.-to-Milan (or Rome) flight should cost $700 to $1,000, depending on where you fly from and when. Always consider saving time and money in Europe by flying "open jaws" (flying into one city and out of another).

Surface Transportation: For a three-week whirlwind trip of all my recommended destinations, allow $300 per person for public transportation (train and buses), or $500 per person (based on two people sharing car) for a three-week car rental, tolls, gas, and insurance. Car rental is cheapest if arranged from the U.S.A. Some train passes are available only outside of Europe. You might save money by getting an Italian railpass or buying tickets as you go (see below).

Room and Board: You can thrive in Italy on $60 a day for room and board. With good information, even Rome is affordable. This budget allows $10 for lunch, $15 for dinner, and $35 for lodging (based on two people splitting the cost of a $70 double room that includes breakfast). That's doable. Students and tightwads do it on $40 ($20 for a bed, $20 for meals and snacks). But budget sleeping and eating require the skills covered later in this chapter (and in much more depth in my book *Rick Steves' Europe Through the Back Door*).

Sightseeing: In big cities, figure $7 to $10 per major sight (Vatican Museum, Roman Forum), $2 for minor ones (climbing church towers), and $25 for splurge experiences (e.g., tours or gondola rides). An overall average of $15 a day works for most. Don't skimp here. After all, this category directly powers most of the experiences all the other expenses are designed to make possible.

Shopping/Entertainment/Miscellany: This can vary from nearly nothing to a small fortune. Figure $1 per postcard, $2 per gelato, $1 for coffee and soft drinks, and $10 to $30 for evening entertainment. Good budget travelers find that this category has little to do with assembling a trip full of lifelong and wonderful memories.

Exchange Rate
I've priced things in lire (L) throughout the book. L1,600 = about $1. To figure lire quickly and easily, cover the last three digits and cut what's left by a third (e.g., a L24,000 dinner costs $16).

Prices, Times, and Discounts
The prices in this book, as well as the hours and telephone numbers, are accurate as of mid-1997—but once you pin Italy down, it wiggles. I know you'll understand that this, like any other guidebook, starts to yellow even before it's printed.

Italy's Best Three-Week Trip

Day	Plan	Sleep in
1	Arrive and see Milan	Milan
2	See Milan	Milan
3	Milan to the Riviera	Vernazza
4	Beach day in Cinque Terre	Vernazza
5	Riviera to Florence via Pisa	Florence
6	See Florence	Florence
7	To Siena via San Gimignano	Siena
8	Free day in Siena	Siena
9	Free day for hill towns or Assisi	Assisi or ?
10	To Civita di Bagnoregio	Bagnoregio
11	To Rome, see Rome	Rome
12	See Rome	Rome
13	See Rome	Rome
14	Survive Naples	Sorrento
15	Pompeii, Amalfi Coast	Sorrento
16	Amalfi Coast, Paestum	night train
17	Venice	Venice
18	Venice	Venice
19	To Bolzano, into Dolomites	Castelrotto
20	Free day in mountains	Castelrotto
21	To Lake Como via Verona	Varenna
22	Relax on Lake Como	Varenna

Note: While you can fly easily into either Milan or Rome, I'd start in Milan (less crazy) and consider either starting or finishing the trip easy in Varenna on Lake Como (a quick hour by train from Milan).

By train, consider seeing everything but Venice on the way south and sleeping through everything you've already seen by catching the night train from Rome (or Naples) to Venice. This saves you a day, gives you a late night in Rome, and an early arrival in Venice.

Route-specific travel strategies (such as home-basing in Siena to do Florence, and drivers parking in Orvieto and catching the train into Rome) are covered in the individual chapters.

Whirlwind Three-Week Tour of Italy

In Italy—and in this book—you'll use the 24-hour clock. It's the same through 12:00 noon, then keep going—13:00, 14:00 . . . For anything over 12, subtract 12 and add p.m. (14:00 is 2:00 p.m.).

This book lists peak-season hours for sightseeing attractions (July and August). Off-season, roughly October through April, expect shorter hours, more lunchtime breaks, and fewer activities. Confirm your sightseeing plans locally, especially when traveling between October and May.

While discounts for sights and transportation are not listed in this book, seniors (60 and over), students (with International Student Identity Cards), and youths (under 18) may snare a deal—although these days many discounts are limited to European residents.

When to Go

Italy's best travel months are May, June, September, and
October. November through April usually has pleasant
weather with generally none of the sweat and stress of the
tourist season. Peak season (July and August) offers the
longest hours and the most exciting slate of activities—but
terrible crowds and, at times, suffocating heat. During peak
times, many resort area hotels maximize business by requiring
that guests buy dinner in their restaurants. August, the local
holiday month, isn't as bad as many make it out to be, but big
cities tend to be quiet (with discounted hotel prices), and
beach and mountain resorts are jammed (with higher hotel
prices). If you anticipate crowds, arrive early in the day or call
hotels in advance (call from one hotel to the next; your
fluent-in-Italian receptionist can help you).

Summer temperatures range from the 70s in Milan to the
high 80s and 90s in Rome. In the winter it often drops to the
30s and 40s in Milan and the 40s and 50s in Rome. Spring and
fall can be cold and many hotels do not turn on their heat. (See
climate chart in the Appendix.)

Sightseeing Priorities

Depending on the length of your trip, here are my recommended priorities.

3 days: Florence, Venice
5 days, add: Rome
7 days, add: Cinque Terre
10 days, add: Civita di Bagnoregio and Siena
14 days, add: Sorrento, Naples, Pompeii, Amalfi, Paestum
18 days, add: Milan, Lago di Como, Varenna, Assisi
21 days, add: Dolomites, Verona, Ravenna

(This includes everything on the "Whirlwind Three-
Week Tour" map.)

Considering how you're likely to go both broke and
crazy driving in Italian cities, and how handy and affordable
Italy's trains and buses are, I'd do most of Italy by public
transportation. If you want to drive, consider doing the
big intense stuff (Rome, Naples area, Milan, Florence,
and Venice) by train or bus and renting a car for the hill
towns of Tuscany and Umbria and for the Dolomites.
A car is a worthless headache on the Riviera and in the
Lake Como area.

Red Tape, Business Hours, and Banking

You need a passport, but no visa or shots, to travel in Italy.

Business Hours: Traditionally, Italy uses the siesta plan: people work from 8:00 or 9:00 to 13:00 and from 15:30 to 19:00, six days a week. Many businesses have adopted the government's new recommended 8:00–14:00 workday. In tourist areas, shops are open longer. If you're buying more than $200 worth of souvenirs, ask in the shops about getting the 10 to 19 percent tax back at the airport upon departure.

Banking: You'll want to spend local hard cash. To get it, use traveler's checks or plastic: your ATM, credit, or debit card.

Regular banks have the best rates for cashing traveler's checks. For a large exchange, it pays to compare rates and fees. Bank of Sicily consistently has good rates. Banking hours are generally Monday–Friday 8:30–13:30 and 15:30–16:30, but can vary wildly. Post offices and train stations usually change money if you can't get to a bank.

To get a cash advance from a bank machine you'll need a four-digit PIN (numbers only, no letters) with your bankcard. Before you go, verify with your bank that your card will work. While many rely successfully on their PIN numbers, I'd bring some traveler's checks as a backup.

Visa and MasterCard are more commonly accepted than American Express. Just like at home, credit or debit cards work easily at larger hotels, restaurants, and shops, but smaller businesses prefer payment in hard lire.

Use a money belt. Thieves target tourists. A money belt (call 425/771-8303 for our free newsletter/catalog) provides peace of mind and allows you to carry lots of cash safely.

Don't be petty about changing money. The greatest avoidable money-changing expense is having to waste time every few days returning to a bank. Change a week's worth of money, get big bills, stuff it in your money belt, and travel!

Travel Smart

Many people travel through Italy thinking it's a chaotic mess. Any attempt at organization is seen as futile and is put off until they get to Switzerland. This is dead wrong—and expensive. Italy, which seems as orderly as spilled spaghetti, actually functions quite well. Only those who understand this and travel smart can enjoy Italy on a budget.

Upon arrival in a new town, lay the groundwork for a smooth departure. Reread this book as you travel and visit local tourist information offices. Buy a phone card and use it for reservations, reconfirmations, and to double-check hours. Enjoy the friendliness of the local people. Ask questions. Most locals are eager to point you in their idea of the right direction. Learn the currency and develop a simple formula to quickly estimate rough prices in dollars. Keep a notepad in your pocket for organizing your thoughts, and practice the virtue of simplicity. Those who expect to travel smart, do.

As you read this book, note the days when most museums are closed. (Mondays are bad in Milan, Florence, and Rome.) Museums and sights, especially large ones, usually stop admitting people 30 to 60 minutes before closing time. Sundays have the same pros and cons as they do for travelers in the U.S.A. Sightseeing attractions are generally open but with shorter hours, shops and banks are closed, and minor transportation connections are more frustrating (e.g., no bus service to or from Civita). City traffic is light. Rowdy evenings are rare on Sundays. Saturdays are virtually weekdays with earlier closing hours. Hotels in tourist areas are often booked up at Easter, in August, and on Fridays and Saturdays.

Plan ahead for banking, laundry, post-office chores, and picnics. Mix intense and relaxed periods. Every trip (and every traveler) needs at least a few slack days. Pace yourself. Assume you will return. Drink your water *con gas*.

Tourist Information

During your trip, your first stop in each town should be the tourist office (abbreviated TI in this book, and turismo, EPT, and "i" in Italy). While Italian tourist offices are about half as helpful as those in other countries, their information is twice as important. Prepare. Have a list of questions and a proposed plan to double-check. If you're arriving late, telephone ahead (and try to get a map for your next destination from a TI in the town you're departing from).

Be wary of the travel agencies or special information services that masquerade as tourist information offices, but serve fancy hotels and tour companies. They are crooks and liars selling things you don't need.

While the TI is eager to book you a room, use their room-finding service only as a last resort. Across Europe room-finding services are charging commissions from hotels, taking fees from travelers, and blacklisting establishments that buck their materialistic rules. They are unable to give hard opinions on the relative value of one place over another. The accommodations stakes are too high to go potluck through the TI. You'll do better going direct with the listings in this book.

Italian Tourist Offices in the U.S.A.

Before your trip, contact the nearest Italian TI and briefly describe your trip and request information. You'll get the general packet, and if you ask for specifics (individual city maps, a calendar of festivals, good hikes around Lake Como, wine-tasting in Umbria, and so on), you'll get an impressive amount of help. If you have a specific problem, they're a good source of sympathy.

Write, call, or fax: 630 Fifth Avenue, #1565, New York, NY 10111, tel. 212/245-4822, fax 212/586-9249; 12400 Wilshire Boulevard, #550, Los Angeles, CA 90025, tel. 310/820-0098, fax 310/820-6357.

Recommended Guidebooks

Especially if you'll be traveling beyond my recommended destinations, you may want some supplemental information. When you consider the improvements they'll make in your $3,000 vacation, $30 for extra maps and books is money well spent. Especially for several people traveling by car, the weight and expense are negligible. One simple budget tip can easily save the price of an extra guidebook.

Lonely Planet's *Italy* is thorough, well-researched, and packed with good maps and hotel recommendations for low-to-moderate-budget travelers, but it's not updated very often. Use it only with a one- or two-year-old copyright. The hip *Rough Guide to Italy* (British researchers, more insightful), and the highly opinionated *Let's Go: Italy* (by Harvard students, better hotel listings) are great for students and vagabonds. If you're a low-budget train traveler interested in the youth and night scene (which I have basically ignored), get *Let's Go: Italy*. The Italy section in *Let's Go: Europe* is skimpy.

Cultural and Sightseeing Guides: The tall green Michelin guides to Italy and Rome have nothing on room and board, but do have great maps for drivers and lots on sights,

customs, and culture (sold in English in Italy). Loved by
overachievers, the slick and user-friendly *Eyewitness Guides*,
among several good series specializing in Venice, Florence,
and Rome, are packed with art and historical background.
The Cadogan guides to various parts of Italy offer an insightful look at the rich and confusing local culture. Those heading for Florence or Rome should read Irving Stone's *The
Agony and the Ecstasy* for a great—if romanticized—rundown
on Michelangelo, the Medici family, and the turbulent times
of the Renaissance.

Rick Steves' Books and Videos

Rick Steves' Europe Through the Back Door (John Muir
Publications, 1998) gives you budget travel skills on minimizing
jet lag, packing light, planning your itinerary, traveling by car or
train, finding budget beds without reservations, changing money,
avoiding rip-offs, outsmarting thieves, hurdling the language bar-
rier, staying healthy, taking great photographs, using your bidet,
and much more. The book also includes chapters on 37 of my
favorite "Back Doors," five of which are in Italy.

Rick Steves' Country Guides are a series of eight
guidebooks covering Europe; Britain & Ireland; France,
Belgium, & the Netherlands; Spain & Portugal; Germany,
Austria, & Switzerland; Russia & the Baltics; and Scandinavia
just as this one covers Italy. These are updated annually and
come out each January.

Europe 101: History and Art for the Traveler (co-written
with Gene Openshaw, John Muir Publications, 1996), which
gives you the story of Europe's people, history, and art, is
heavy on Italy's ancient, Renaissance, and modern history.
Written for smart people who were sleeping in their history
and art classes before they knew they were going to Europe,
101 helps resurrect the rubble.

Mona Winks: Self-Guided Tours of Europe's Top Museums
(co-written with Gene Openshaw, John Muir Publications,
1996) gives you one- to three-hour self-guided tours through
Europe's 20 most exhausting and important museums. Nearly
half of the book is devoted to Italy, with tours covering Venice's
St. Mark's, the Doge's Palace, and Accademia Gallery;
Florence's Uffizi Gallery, Bargello, Michelangelo's *David*,
and a Renaissance walk through the town center; and Rome's
Colosseum, Forum, Pantheon, Vatican Museum, and St. Peter's

Basilica. If you want to enjoy the great sights and museums of Italy, *Mona* will be a valued friend.

In Italy, a phrase book is as fun as it is necessary. My *Rick Steves' Italian Phrase Book* (John Muir Publications, 1997) is the only book of its kind, designed to help you meet the people and stretch your budget. It's written by a monoglot who, for 20 years, has fumbled happily through Italy struggling with all the other phrase books. This is a fun and practical communication aid to help you make accurate hotel reservations over the telephone, tell your cabbie if he doesn't slow down you'll throw up, ask at the gelato shop for a free taste of cantaloupe-flavored gelato, and have the man in the deli make you a sandwich.

My public television series, *Travels in Europe with Rick Steves*, with an all-new fourth season in 1998, includes six half-hour shows on Italy. All 52 shows are run throughout the U.S.A. on public television stations and on the Travel Channel. Each episode is also available in information-packed home videos, along with my two-hour slideshow lecture on Italy (call us at 425/771-8303 for our free newsletter/catalog).

Maps

The maps in this book, drawn by Dave Hoerlein, are concise and simple. Dave, who is well-traveled in Italy, designed the maps to help you locate recommended places and the tourist offices, where you can pick up more in-depth maps of the city or region (cheap or free).

Train travelers can do fine with a simple rail map (such as the one that comes with your train pass) and city maps from the TI as you travel. But drivers shouldn't skimp on maps. Excellent maps are available throughout Italy at bookstores, newsstands, and gas stations. Get a good 1:200,000 map to get the most out of your miles, and study the key to get the most sightseeing value out of your map.

Transportation

By Car or Train?

Each mode of transportation has pros and cons. Public transportation is one of the few bargains in Italy. Trains and buses are inexpensive and good. City-to-city travel is faster, easier, and cheaper by train than by car. Trains give you the

Cost of Public Transportation

1998 ITALY RAIL CARD

	1st class	2nd class
8 consec. days	$281	$192
15 consec. days	347	236
21 consec. days	401	272
30 consec. days	480	325
Any 4 days in 1 month flexi	224	154
Any 8 days in 1 month flexi	308	210
Any 12 days in 1 month flexi	390	265

Note: Flexi versions of the Italy Card are sold only in the USA. Prices above include an extra $15 per pass tacked on by the CIT folks in New York. Passes cover all supplements and surcharges except for the fast-n-classy "Pendolino" trains. Passes are retailed in the USA through travel agents, direct from CIT in NYC (800/248-7245 or 800/223-7987), or cheaper and easily in Italy at CIT travel agencies and major train stations. Nearly-half-off kids' versions are available, too.

Italy: Point-to-point 1-way 2nd class rail fares in $US. Add up fares for your itinerary to see whether a railpass will save you money.

ITALIAN KILOMETRIC TICKET

Also known as the "Biglietto Chilometrico," this features coupons for up to 20 trips totaling up to 3,000 kilometers that can be split by up to 5 people for $264 first class and $156 second class (e.g., a group of five could go the 570 km from Venice to Rome on a Kilometric Ticket for $34 each vs. the normal $45 regular ticket price). Supplements charged for fast intercity trains. Like the Italy Rail Card, this is sold in the USA through CIT (see above), or cheaper and easily in Italy at CIT travel agencies and major train stations.

convenience and economy of doing long stretches overnight. By train I arrive relaxed and well-rested—not so by car.

Parking, gas (about $4 per gallon), and tolls are expensive in Italy. But drivers enjoy more control, especially in the countryside. Cars carry your luggage for you, generally from door to door—especially important for heavy packers (such as chronic shoppers and families traveling with children). And groups know that the more people you pack into a car or minibus, the cheaper it gets per person.

Trains

To travel by train cheaply in Italy simply buy tickets as you go and avoid the more expensive express trains. A second-class Rome-to-Venice ticket costs about $50 (with express supplement). But Italy's train ticket system confounds even the locals, and for convenience alone, I'd go with the Italian State Railway's Italy Rail Card (see box, above). Unlike the Rail Card, Italy's Kilometric pass is a headache because it doesn't cover fast-train supplements. For travel exclusively in Italy, a Eurailpass is a bad value (though consider a cheaper Europass).

You'll encounter several types of trains in Italy. Along with the various milk-run trains there are the slow *IR—Inter-regional* and *directo* trains, the medium *expresso*, the fast *IC (Intercity)*, and the *Pendolino/ATR 500* (Italy's bullet train; costs L20,000 supplement even with train passes). *IC* or *Intercity* trains are the sleek, air-conditioned, top-of-the-line trains. While schedules say these require a reservation and a supplement, those with train passes can hop on and grab unreserved seats and pay no extra.

First-class tickets cost 50 percent more than second-class tickets. While second-class cars go exactly as fast as their first-class neighbors, Italy is one country where I would consider the splurge of first class. The easiest way to upgrade a second-class ticket once on board an impossibly crowded train is to nurse a drink in the snack car. If you anticipate a crowd, you can get a firm seat reservation in advance for about L5,000. Newsstands sell up-to-date regional and all-Italy timetables (L6,000). There is now a single all-Italy toll-free telephone number for train information—1478-88088 (7:00–21:00 daily, English generally spoken). On the web, check mercurio.iet.unipi.it.

Italian trains are famous for their thieves. Never leave a bag unattended. There have been cases of bandits gassing an entire car before looting the snoozing gang. I've noticed that police now ride the trains and things seem more controlled. Still, for an overnight trip, I'd feel safe only in a *cuccetta* (a berth in a special sleeping car with an attendant who keeps track of who comes and goes while you sleep—L19,000 in a six-bed compartment, L25,000 in a less cramped four-bed compartment). Avoid big-city train station lines whenever you can. For about L4,000, you can buy tickets and reserve a *cuccetta* at a travel agency.

Because of the threat of bombs, you won't find storage lockers in train stations. But each station has a *deposito* (or *bagagli*) where you can safely leave your bag for L5,000 per 12-hour period (payable when you pick up the bag).

Finally, strikes are common. Strikes generally last a day, and train employees will simply say, "*Sciopero*," (no train). But in actuality, sporadic trains, following no particular schedule, lumber down the tracks during most strikes.

Car Rental

Research car rental before you go. It's cheaper to arrange for car rentals through your travel agent while still in the U.S.A. Rent by the week with unlimited mileage. If you need a car for three or more weeks, it's cheaper to lease (saving money on insurance and taxes). Explore your drop-off options (south of Rome can be a problem).

For peace of mind, I spring for the CDW insurance (Collision Damage Waiver, about $14 per day), which gives a zero-deductible rather than the standard value-of-the-car "deductible." A few "gold" credit cards cover CDW insurance; quiz your credit-card company on the worst-case scenario.

Theft insurance (separate from CDW insurance) is mandatory when you're renting a car for use in Italy. The insurance usually costs about $10 to $15 a day, payable when you pick up the car.

A rail-and-drive pass (such as a EurailDrive or Europass Drive) can be put to thoughtful use. Certain areas (like the Dolomites and the hill towns of Tuscany and Umbria) are great by car, while most of Italy is best by train.

Driving

Driving in Italy is frightening—a video game for keeps and you only get one quarter. All you need is a U.S.A. driver's license and a car. According to everybody but the Italian police, international driver's licenses are not necessary. The police fine you if they can't read your license.

Autostradas: Italy's freeway system is as good as our interstate system, but you'll pay about a dollar for every ten minutes of use. (I paid L37,000 for the four-hour drive from Bolzano to Pisa.) While I favor the autostradas because I feel they're safer, cheaper (saving time and gas), and less nerve-wracking than smaller roads, savvy local drivers know which toll-free "superstradas" are actually faster and more direct than the autostrada (e.g., Florence to Pisa).

Gas: Most cars take unleaded (green pumps, available everywhere). Autostrada rest-stops are self-service stations open daily without a siesta break. Small-town stations are usually cheaper, offering full service, but shorter hours. Many 24-hour-a-day stations are entirely automated with machines that trade gas for paper money.

Metric: A liter is about a quart, four to a gallon; a kilo-meter is .6 of a mile. Figure kilometers to miles by cutting them in half and adding back 10 percent of the original (120 km: 60 + 12 = 72 miles, 300 km: 150 + 30 = 180 miles).

Parking: White lines generally mean parking is free. Blue lines mean you'll have to pay—usually L1,500 per hour. If there's no meter, there is probably a roving attendant who will take your money. Study the signs. Many free zones are cleared out (by car owners or tow trucks) one day a week for street cleaning. Often, the free zones have a 30- or 60-minute time limit. *Zona disco* has nothing to do with dancing. Cars have a time disc which you set at your arrival time and lay on the dashboard so the attendant knows how long you've been parked. This is a fine system which all drivers should take advantage of. Garages are safe, save time, and help you avoid the stress of parking tickets. Take the parking voucher with you to pay the cashier before you leave.

Theft: Cars are routinely vandalized and stolen. Try to make your car look locally owned: hide the "tourist-owned" rental company decals and put a local newspaper in your back window.

Telephones and Mail

Smart travelers use the telephone every day—especially in Italy—to make hotel reservations, call tourist information offices, and phone home. The key to dialing long distance is understanding city codes and having an Italian phone card. When spelling out a proper noun on the phone, "i" and "e" are confusing. Say "i, Italia" and "e, Empoli" to clear up that problem.

Italy's phone cards aren't credit cards, just handy cards you insert in the phone instead of coins. The L5,000, L10,000, or L15,000 phone cards are much easier to use than coins for long-distance calls. Buy a phone card at post offices, tobacco shops, and machines near phone booths (many phone booths indicate where the nearest phone-card sales outlet is located). Rip off the corner to "activate" the card. Insert it into the phone. Dial slowly and deliberately, as if the phone doesn't understand numbers very well. Repeat as needed.

Dialing Direct: To call long-distance within Italy, dial the city code (which starts with zero), then dial the local number. For example, Venice's city code is 041, and the number of my favorite Venice hotel is 522-7131. To call it from Rome, dial 041/522-7131. When dialing internationally, dial the international access code (of the country you're calling from), the country code (of the country you're calling to), the city code (without the initial zero), and the local number. To call the Venice hotel from the U.S.A., dial 011 (the U.S.A.'s international access code), 39 (Italy's country code), 41 (Venice's area code without the zero), then 522-7131 (local number). To call my office from Italy, I dial 00 (Italy's international access code), 1 (U.S.A.'s country code), 425 (Edmonds' area code), and 771-8303. In this book, city codes are listed with phone numbers (e.g., 041/522-7131). For international access codes and country codes, see the Appendix.

Orange SIP public telephones are everywhere and take coins or cards. Hotel-room phones are reasonable for calls within Italy (the faint beeps stand for L200 phone units), but a terrible rip-off for calls to the U.S.A. Never call home from your hotel room unless your hotel allows toll-free access to your USA Direct Service.

USA Direct Services: Calling the U.S.A. from any kind of phone is easy if you have an AT&T, MCI, or Sprint calling card. Each card company has a toll-free number in each European country which puts you in touch with an English-speaking operator who takes your card number and the number you want to call, puts you through, and bills your home phone number for the call (at the cheaper U.S. rate of about $3 for the first minute and $1.25 per additional minute, plus a $2.50 service charge). You'll save money on calls of three minutes or more. Hanging up when you hear an answering machine is expensive ($5.50). First use a coin or an Italian phone card to call home for five seconds—long enough to say "call me," or to make sure an answering machine is off so you can call back, using your USA Direct number to connect with a person. European time is six/nine hours ahead of the east/west coast of the U.S.A. For a list of AT&T, MCI, and Sprint calling card operators, see the Appendix. Avoid using USA Direct for calls between European countries; it's much cheaper to call direct using coins or an Italian phone card.

Mail: Mail service is miserable in Italy. Postcards get last priority. If you must have mail stops, consider a few pre-reserved hotels along your route or use American Express offices. Most American Express offices in Italy will hold mail for one month. This service is free to anyone using an AmexCo card or traveler's checks (and available for a small fee to others). Allow 14 days for U.S.A.-to-Italy mail delivery, but don't count on it. Federal Express makes pricey two-day deliveries. Phoning is so easy that I've completely dispensed with mail stops. If possible, mail nothing precious from Italy.

Sleeping

For hassle-free efficiency, I favor hotels and restaurants handy to your sightseeing activities. Rather than list hotels scattered throughout a city, I describe two or three favorite neighborhoods and recommend the best accommodations values in each, from $15 bunks to fancy-in-my-book $200 doubles.

Sleeping in Italy is expensive. Cheap big-city hotels can be depressing and dangerous. Tourist information services cannot give opinions on quality. A major feature of this book is its extensive listing of good value hotels with doubles ranging from $50 to $150 a night. I like places that are clean, small, central, quiet at night, traditional, inexpensive, friendly, with firm beds—and those not listed in other guidebooks. (In Italy, for me, six out of nine is a keeper.)

Sleep Code

To pack maximum information into minimum space, I use this code to describe accommodations in this book. When there is a range of prices in one category, the price will fluctuate with the season, size of room, or length of stay. Prices listed are per room, not per person.

S = Single room or price for one person using a double.

D = Double or twin room. "Double beds" are often two twins sheeted together and are usually big enough for non-romantic couples.

T = Three-person room (often a double with a single bed moved in).

Q = Four-adult room (an extra child's bed is usually cheaper).

b = Private bathroom with a toilet and shower or tub.

t = Private toilet only. (The shower is down the hall.)

s = Private shower or tub only. (The toilet is down the hall.)

CC = Accepts credit cards (V = Visa, M = MasterCard, A = American Express). Many places also accept Diners' (which I don't note). If CC isn't mentioned, assume you'll need to pay cash.

SE = Speaks English. This code is used only when it seems predictable that you'll encounter English-speaking staff.

NSE = Does not speak English. Used only when it's unlikely you'll encounter English-speaking staff.

According to this code, a couple staying at a "Db-L95,000, CC:V, SE" hotel would pay a total of 95,000 lire (about $60) for a double room with a private bathroom. The hotel accepts Visa or Italian cash. The staff speaks English.

Hotels

Double rooms listed in this book will range from about $40 (very simple, toilet and shower down the hall) to $200 (maximum plumbing and more), with most clustering around $80 (with private bathrooms). Prices are higher in big cities and heavily touristed cities and lower off the beaten path. Three or four people economize by requesting larger rooms. Solo travelers find that the cost of a *camera singola* is often only 25 percent less than a *camera doppia*. Most listed hotels have rooms for anywhere from one to five people. If there's room for an extra cot, they'll cram it in for you. Prices are often soft—especially if you are arriving direct. If there's no middleman, you're in a stronger position to bargain. Consider the supply-and-demand situation. Breakfasts are legally supposed to be optional, but initial prices quoted often include breakfast and a private bathroom. Use breakfast as a bargaining chip.

Prices are pretty standard, and you normally get close to what you pay for. Shopping around earns you a better location and more character but rarely a cheaper price.

All rooms have sinks with hot and cold water. Rooms with bathrooms are often bigger and renovated, while cheaper rooms without bathrooms will often be unrefurbished and on the upper floors. Any room lacking a private bathroom has access to a bathroom on the corridor (free unless otherwise noted).

You'll save $10 to $20 if you ask for a room without a shower and just use the shower down the hall. Generally rooms with a bath or shower also have a toilet and a bidet (which Italians use for quick "sponge baths"). Tubs usually come with a frustrating "telephone shower." If a shower has no curtain, the entire bathroom showers with you. The cord that dangles over the tub or shower is not a clothesline. You pull it when you've fallen and can't get up.

Double beds are called *matrimoniale*, even though hotels aren't interested in your marital status. Twins are *due letti singoli*. A few places have kept the old titles, *locanda* or *pension*, indicating they offer budget beds. The Italian word for "hotel" is *albergo*.

When you check in, the receptionist will normally ask for your passport and keep it for a couple of hours. Hotels are legally required to register each guest with the local police. Relax. Americans are notorious for making this chore more difficult than it needs to be.

Ancient Romans ate no breakfast at all, and the breakfast scene has improved only marginally. Except for the smallest places, a very simple continental breakfast is normally available. If you like juice and protein for breakfast, supply it yourself. I enjoy a box of juice in my hotel room and often supplement the skimpy breakfasts with a piece of fruit and a separately wrapped small piece of cheese. (A zip-lock baggie is handy for petite eaters to grab an extra breakfast roll and slice of cheese, when provided, for a fast and free light lunch.) The hotel breakfast, while convenient, is usually a bad value—$6 to $8 for a roll, jelly, and usually unlimited *caffè latte*. You can always request cheese or salami (L5,000 extra). I enjoy taking breakfast at the corner café. It's OK to supplement what you order with a few picnic goodies.

Rooms are safe. Still, zip cameras and keep money out of sight. More pillows and blankets are usually in the closet or available on request. In Italy towels and linen aren't always replaced every day—drip dry and conserve.

While bed and breakfasts (*affitta camere*) and youth hostels (*ostello della gioventù*) are not as common in Italy as elsewhere in Europe, I've listed many in this book. While big-city hostels are normally overrun with the *Let's Go* crowd, small-town hostels can be a wonderfully enjoyable way to save money and make friends.

Making Reservations

It's possible to travel at any time of year without reservations, but given the high stakes, erratic accommodations values, and the quality of the gems I've found for this book, I'd recommend making reservations in advance. You can call long in advance from home or grab rooms a day or two in advance as you travel. (If you have difficulty, ask the fluent-in-Italian receptionist at your current hotel to call your next hotel.) You might make a habit of calling between 9:00 and 10:00 on the day you plan to arrive, when the hotel clerk knows who'll be checking out and just which rooms will be available. I've taken great pains to list telephone numbers with long distance instructions (above; also in Appendix). Use the telephone and the convenient telephone cards. Most hotels listed are accustomed to English-only speakers. A hotel receptionist will trust you and hold a room until 17:00 (5:00 p.m.) without a deposit, though some will ask for a credit-card number. Honor (or cancel by phone) your reservations. Long distance is cheap and easy from public phone booths. Don't let these people down—I promised you'd call and cancel if for some reason you won't show up. Don't needlessly confirm rooms through the tourist office; they'll take a commission.

If you know where you want to stay each day (and you don't need or want flexibility), reserve your rooms a month or two in advance from home. To reserve from home, telephone first to confirm availability, then fax your formal request. Phone and fax costs are reasonable, and simple English is usually fine. To fax, use the handy form in the Appendix. If you don't get an answer to your fax request, consider that a "no." If you're writing, add the zip code and confirm the need and method for a deposit. A two-night stay in August would be "2 nights, 16/8/98 to 18/8/98"— European hotel jargon uses your day of departure. You'll often receive a letter back requesting one night's deposit. A credit card will usually be accepted as a deposit, though you may need to send a personal check, signed traveler's check, or a bank draft in the local currency. If your credit card is the deposit, you can pay with your card or cash when you arrive; if you don't show up, you'll be billed for one night. Always reconfirm your reservations a day in advance by phone.

Eating Italian

The Italians are masters of the art of fine living. That means eating . . . long and well. Lengthy, multi-course lunches and dinners and endless hours sitting in outdoor cafés are the norm. Americans eat on their way to an evening event and complain if the check is slow in coming. For Italians, the meal is an end in itself, and only rude waiters rush you. When you want the bill, mime-scribble on your raised palm or ask for it: *"Il conto?"*

Even those of us who liked dorm food will find that the local cafés, cuisine, and wines become a highlight of our Italian adventure. Trust me, this is sightseeing for your palate, and even if the rest of you is sleeping in cheap hotels, your taste buds will relish an occasional first-class splurge. You can eat well without going broke. But be careful; you're just as likely to blow a small fortune on a disappointing meal as you are to dine wonderfully for $20.

Restaurants

When restaurant-hunting, choose places filled with locals, not the place with the big neon signs boasting, "We speak English and accept credit cards." Look for menus posted outside. For unexciting but basic values, look for a *menù turistico*, a three- or four-course set-price menu. Galloping gourmets order à la carte with the help of a menu translator. (The *Marling Italian Menu Master* is excellent. *Rick Steves' Italian Phrase Book* has enough phrases for intermediate eaters.)

A full meal consists of an appetizer (*antipasto*, L5,000 and up), a first course (*primo piatto*, pasta or soup, L5,000–14,000), and a second course (*secondo piatto*, expensive meat and fish dishes, L10,000–20,000). Vegetables (*contorni, verdure*) may come with the *secondo* or cost extra (L5,000) as a side dish. Restaurants normally pad the bill with a cover charge (*pane e coperto*, about L2,000) and a service charge (*servizio*, 15 percent); these charges are listed on the menu. Italian waiters are paid well and tipping is not expected.

As you will see, the lire adds up in a hurry. Light- and budget-eaters get by with a *primo piatto*. Hungry paupers can even get two: a minestrone and a pasta. Self-service places and lower-class eateries feed you without the add-ons. Family-run places operate without hired help and can offer cheaper meals.

The word *osteria* (normally a simple local-style restaurant) gets me salivating.

Many modern Italian fast food places slam-dunk pasta, rather than burgers, cheap and fast. A *tavola calda* (literally, "hot table") serves Italian-style fast food. A *rosticceria* is like a deli with great cooked food to go. American-style fast food is just like you know it—but with better salad bars and beer.

Pizza is cheap and everywhere. Key pizza vocabulary: *capricciosa* (the house specialty), *funghi* (mushrooms), *margherita* (tomato sauce and mozzarella), *marinara* (tomato sauce, oregano, garlic, no cheese), *quattro formaggi* (four different cheeses), *quattro stagioni* (different toppings on each of the four quarters for those who can't choose just one menu item). Pizza-to-go places (often called *pizza rustica*) sell fresh pizza by the weight. Two hundred grams with a beer or soft drink make a good, cheap lunch.

The Italian bar is not just a place to drink. It is a local hangout serving coffee, mini-pizzas, sandwiches, cartons of milk from the cooler, and plates of fried cheese and vegetables under the glass counter, ready to reheat. This is my budget choice, the Italian equivalent of English pub grub. Don't be limited by what you can see. If you'd like a salad with a slice of cantaloupe and a hunk of cheese, they'll whip that up for you in a snap. Belly up to the bar and with these key words and a pointing finger, you can get a fine *piatto misto di verdure* (mixed plate of vegetables). *"Scaldari, per favore"* means "Heated, please." Ask for *carciofo* (artichoke), *asparagi* (asparagus), *fagioli* (beans), *fagiolini* (string beans), *broccoli, carote, funghi* (mushrooms), *patate* (potato), *spinaci, zucchine, pomodoro* (tomato), *verdure miste* (mixed vegetables), *mozzarella*, or *grissini* (bread sticks). If something's a mystery, ask for *un assaggio* (a little taste). *Panini* and *tramezzini* are sandwiches.

Bar procedure can be frustrating: 1) decide what you want; 2) check the price list on the wall or find out from the barman; 3) pay the cashier; and 4) give the receipt to the barman (whose clean fingers handle no dirty lire), and tell him what you want.

Coffee: While there's nothing wrong with this, only a tourist would order a *caffè latte* or *cappuccino* after about 11:00 a.m. That's when Italians shift into espresso gear, using these words: *alto* (tall), *basso* (short or stronger), *doppio* (a double shot), *macchiato* (with a little milk), *freddo* (cold and black), or *corretto* (with a shot of alcohol). If you order *caffè*, you'll get espresso. American-style coffee (probably just watered-down espresso) is *caffè Americano*. Decaf is *hag* or *caffè hag* and easily available. Italians like their cappuccino only lukewarm. You can ask, *"Più caldo, per favore"* ("Hotter, please"). You'll notice a two-tiered price system. Drinking a cup of coffee while standing at the bar is cheaper than drinking it at a table. If on a budget, don't sit without checking out the financial consequences. *Da portar via* is "for the road."

Picnics

In Italy picnicking saves lots of lire and is a great way to sample local specialties. In the process of assembling your meal, you get to deal with the Italians in the local market scene. On days you choose to picnic, gather supplies early. You'll probably visit several small stores or market stalls to put together a complete meal, and many close around noon. While it's fun to visit the small specialty shops, a local *alimentari* is your one-stop corner grocery store. *Supermercatis* give you decent quality with less color, less cost, and more efficiency.

Juice lovers can get a liter of o.j. for the price of a Coke or coffee. Look for "100% *succo* (juice)" on the label or suffer through a sickly-sweet orange drink. Hang onto the twist-top half-liter mineral water bottles (sold everywhere for about L1,000). Buy juice in less-expensive liter boxes, and store it in your reusable water bottle for nipping between sights.

Picnics can be an adventure in high cuisine. Be daring. Try the fresh mozzarella, presto pesto, shriveled olives, and any UFOs the locals are excited about. Shopkeepers are happy to sell small quantities of produce and will even slice and stuff a sandwich for you. In a busy market, a merchant may not want to weigh and sell small, three-carrot-type quantities. In this case, estimate generously what you think it should cost, and hold out the lire in one hand and the produce in the other. Wear a smile that says, "If you take the money, I'll go." He'll grab the money. A typical picnic for two might be fresh rolls, 100 grams of cheese, 100 grams of meat (100 grams = about a quarter-pound, called an *etto* in Italy), two tomatoes, three carrots, two apples, yogurt, and a liter box of juice. Total cost—$10.

Culture Shock—Accepting Italy as a Package Deal

We travel all the way to Italy to enjoy differences—to become temporary locals. You'll experience frustrations. Certain truths that we find "God-given" or "self-evident," like cold beer, ice in drinks, bottomless cups of coffee, hot showers, body odor smelling bad, and bigger being better, are suddenly not so true. One of the benefits of travel is the eye-opening realization that there are logical, civil, and even better alternatives. A willingness to go local ensures that you'll enjoy a full dose of Italian hospitality.

If there is a negative aspect to the image Italians have of Americans, it is that we are big, loud, aggressive, impolite, rich, and a bit naive. While Italians look bemusedly at some of our Yankee excesses—and worriedly at others—they nearly always afford us individual travelers all the warmth we deserve.

Back Door Manners

While updating this book, I heard over and over again that my readers are considerate and fun to have as guests. Thank you for traveling as temporary locals who are sensitive to the culture. It's fun to follow you in my travels.

Send Me a Postcard, Drop Me a Line

If you enjoy a successful trip with the help of this book and would like to share your discoveries, please fill out and send the survey at the end of this book to me at Europe Through the Back Door, Box 2009, Edmonds, WA 98020. I personally read and value all feedback. Thanks in advance—it helps a lot.

For our latest travel information on Italy, tap into our web site at www.ricksteves.com. Our e-mail address is rick@ricksteves.com. Anyone is welcome to request a free issue of our Back Door quarterly newsletter (it's free anyway).

Judging from all the positive feedback and happy postcards I receive from travelers who have used this book, it's safe to assume you're on your way to a great vacation—independently, inexpensively, and with the finesse of an experienced traveler. Thanks, and *buon viaggio!*

BACK DOOR TRAVEL PHILOSOPHY
As Taught in *Rick Steves' Europe Through the Back Door*

Travel is intensified living—maximum thrills per minute and one of the last great sources of legal adventure. Travel is freedom. It's recess, and we need it.

Experiencing the real Europe requires catching it by surprise, going casual . . . "Through the Back Door."

Affording travel is a matter of priorities. (Make do with the old car.) You can travel—simply, safely, and comfortably—anywhere in Europe for $60 a day plus transportation costs. In many ways, spending more money only builds a thicker wall between you and what you came to see. Europe is a cultural carnival, and time after time, you'll find that its best acts are free and the best seats are the cheap ones.

A tight budget forces you to travel close to the ground, meeting and communicating with the people, not relying on service with a purchased smile. Never sacrifice sleep, nutrition, safety, or cleanliness in the name of budget. Simply enjoy the local-style alternatives to expensive hotels and restaurants.

Extroverts have more fun. If your trip is low on magic moments, kick yourself and make things happen. If you don't enjoy a place, maybe you don't know enough about it. Seek the truth. Recognize tourist traps. Give a culture the benefit of your open mind. See things as different but not better or worse. Any culture has much to share.

Of course, travel, like the world, is a series of hills and valleys. Be fanatically positive and militantly optimistic. If something's not to your liking, change your liking. Travel is addicting. It can make you a happier American, as well as a citizen of the world. Our Earth is home to nearly 6 billion equally important people. It's humbling to travel and find that people don't envy Americans. They like us, but with all due respect, they wouldn't trade passports.

Globetrotting destroys ethnocentricity. It helps you understand and appreciate different cultures. Travel changes people. It broadens perspectives and teaches new ways to measure quality of life. Many travelers toss aside their hometown blinders. Their prized souvenirs are the strands of different cultures they decide to knit into their own character. The world is a cultural yarn shop. And Back Door Travelers are weaving the ultimate tapestry. Come on, join in!

ITALY

- 116,000 square miles (the size of Arizona)
- 60 million people (477 people per square mile)
- 800 miles long, 100 miles wide
- 1,600 lire = about U.S. $1; 1,000 lire = about 65 cents
- Country telephone code: 39; international access code: 00

Bella Italia! It has Europe's richest, craziest culture. If I had to choose just one, Italy's my favorite. If you take it on its own terms and accept the package deal, Italy is a cultural keelhauling that actually feels good.

Some people, often with considerable effort, manage to hate it. Italy bubbles with emotion, corruption, stray hairs, inflation, traffic jams, body odor, strikes, rallies, holidays, crowded squalor, and irate ranters shaking their fists at each other one minute and walking arm in arm the next. Have a talk with yourself before you cross the border. Promise yourself to relax and soak in it; it's a glorious mud puddle.

With so much history and art in Venice, Florence, and Rome, you'll need to do some reading ahead to maximize your experience. There are two Italys: the north is industrial, aggressive, and "time-is-money" in its outlook. The Po River basin and the area between Milan, Genoa, and Torino have the richest farmland and the heavy-duty industry. The south is crowded, poor, relaxed, farm-oriented, and traditional. Families here are very strong and usually live in the same house for many generations. Loyalties are to the family, city, region, soccer team, and country—in that order. The Apennine Mountains give Italy a rugged north-south spine, while the Alps divide Italy from France, Switzerland, and Austria in the north.

Economically, Italy has had its problems, but somehow things work out. Today Italy is the Western world's seventh-largest industrial power. Its people earn more per-capita than the British. Italy is the world's leading wine producer. It is sixth in cheese and wool output. Tourism (as you'll find out) is also big business in Italy. Cronyism, which complicates my work, is an integral part of the economy.

Italy, home of the Vatican, is Catholic, but the dominant religion is life—motor scooters, soccer, fashion, girl-watching, boy-watching, good coffee, good wine, and *la dolce far niente* ("the sweetness of doing nothing"). The Italian character shows itself on the streets with the skilled maniac drivers and the classy dressers who star in the ritual evening stroll, or *passeggiata*.

The language is fun. Be melodramatic and move your hand with your tongue. Hear the melody, get into the flow. Fake it, let the farce be with you. Italians are outgoing characters. They want to communicate, and they try harder than any other Europeans. Play with them.

Italy, a land of extremes, is also the most thief-ridden country you'll visit. Tourists suffer virtually no violent crime—but plenty of petty purse-snatchings, pickpocketings, and shortchangings. Wear your money belt! The scruffy-looking women and children loitering around the major museums aren't there for the art.

Sightseeing hours are always changing in Italy. By the time you travel, many of the hours in this book will be wrong (especially because of the expected new austerity programs promised by the new right-wing government). Use the local tourist offices to double-check your sightseeing plans.

For extra sightseeing information, take advantage of the cheap, colorful, and dry-but-informative city guidebooks sold on the streets all over. Also use the information telephones you'll find in most historic buildings. Just set the dial on English, pop in your coins, and listen. The narration is often accompanied by a brief slide show. Many dark interiors can be brilliantly lit for a coin. Whenever possible, let there be light.

Some important Italian churches require modest dress: no shorts or bare shoulders on men or women. With a little imagination (except at the Vatican), those caught by surprise can improvise something—a jacket for your knees and maps for your shoulders. I wear a super-lightweight pair of long pants for my hot and muggy big-city Italian sightseeing.

While no longer a cheap country, Italy is still a hit with shoppers. Glassware (Venice), gold, silver, leather, and prints (Florence), and high fashion (Rome) are good souvenirs, but do some price research at home so you'll recognize the good values.

Many tourists are mind-boggled by the huge prices: 16,000 lire for dinner! L42,000 for the room! L126,000 for the taxi ride! That's still real money—it's just spoken of in much smaller units than a dollar. Since there are roughly L1,600 in a dollar, figure Italian prices by covering the last three zeros with your finger and taking about two-thirds of the remaining figure. That L16,000 dinner costs $10 in U.S. money; the L42,000 room, $28; and the taxi ride . . . uh-oh!

Beware of the "slow count." After you buy something, you may get your change back in batches. The salesperson (or bank teller) hopes you're confused by all the zeros and that you'll gather up your money and say *"grazie"* before he or she finishes the count. Always do your own rough figuring beforehand and understand the transaction. Only the sloppy are ripped off. Try to enforce the local prices. It's only natural for them to inflate prices or assume you don't know what's a fair rate. Be savvy, firm, and friendly.

La dolce far niente is a big part of Italy. Zero in on the fine points. Don't dwell on the problems. Accept Italy as Italy. Savor your cappuccino, dangle your feet over a canal (if it smells, breathe through your mouth), and imagine what it was like centuries ago. Ramble through the rubble of Rome and mentally resurrect those ancient stones. Look into the famous sculpted eyes of Michelangelo's *David*, and understand Renaissance man's assertion of himself. Sit silently on a hilltop rooftop. Get chummy with the winds of the past. Write a poem over a glass of local wine in a sun-splashed, wave-dashed Riviera village. If you fall off your moral horse, call it a cultural experience. Italy is for romantics.

ROME (ROMA)

Rome is magnificent and brutal at the same time. Your ears will ring, your nose will turn your hankie black, the careless will be run down or pickpocketed, you'll be frustrated by chaos that only an Italian can understand. You may even come to believe Mussolini was necessary. But Rome is required. If your hotel provides a comfortable refuge; if you pace yourself, accept and even partake in the siesta plan; if you're well-organized for sightseeing; and if you protect yourself and your valuables with extra caution and discretion, you'll do fine. You'll see the sights and leave satisfied.

Rome at its peak meant civilization itself. Everything was either civilized (part of the Roman Empire, Latin- or Greek-speaking) or barbarian. Today Rome is Italy's political capital, the capital of Catholicism, and a splendid . . . "junkpile" is not quite the right word . . . of western civilization. As you peel through its fascinating and jumbled layers, you'll find its buildings, people, cats, laundry, and traffic endlessly entertaining. And then, of course, there are its magnificent sights.

Tour St. Peter's, the greatest church on earth, and scale Michelangelo's 100-yard-tall dome, the world's largest. Learn something about eternity by touring the huge Vatican Museum. You'll find paradise—bright as the day it was painted—in the newly restored Sistine Chapel. Do the "Caesar shuffle" walk through ancient Rome's Forum and Colosseum. Take an early evening "Dolce Vita Stroll" down the Via del Corso with Rome's beautiful people. Enjoy an after-dark walk from

Rome Area

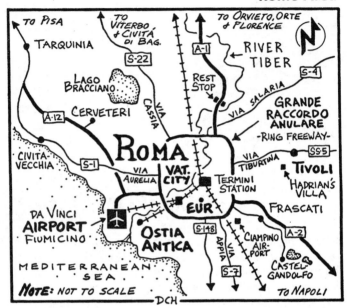

Trastevere to the Spanish Steps, lacing together Rome's
Baroque and bubbling night spots.

Planning Your Time

For most, Rome is best done quickly. It's great, but exhausting.
Time is normally short, and Italy is more charming elsewhere.
To "do" Rome in a day, consider it as a side trip from Orvieto
or Florence and maybe before the night train to Venice. Crazy
as that sounds, if all you have is a day, it's a great one.

Rome in a day: Vatican (two hours in the Museum and
Sistine Chapel, and one hour in St. Peter's), taxi over the river to
the Pantheon (munch a bar snack picnic on its steps), then hike
over Capitoline Hill, through the Forum, and to the Colosseum.
Have dinner on Campo dei Fiori and dessert on Piazza Navona.

Rome in two days (the optimal first visit): Do the
"Caesar Shuffle" from the Colosseum and Forum, over the
Capitoline Hill to the Pantheon. After a siesta, join the locals
strolling from Piazza del Popolo to the Spanish Steps. Have
dinner near your hotel. On the second day, see the Vatican
City (St. Peter's, climb the dome, tour the Vatican Museum).

Spend the evening walking from Trastevere to Campo dei Fiori (atmospheric place for dinner) to the Spanish Steps. With a third day, consider adding another museum and a side trip to Ostia.

Orientation (tel. code: 06)

The modern sprawl of Rome is of no interest to us. Our Rome actually feels small when you know it. It's the old core—within the triangle formed by the train station, Colosseum, and Vatican. Get a handle on Rome by considering it in these chunks:

The ancient city had a million people. Tear it down to size by walking through just the core. The best of the classical sights stand in a line from the Colosseum to the Pantheon.

Medieval Rome was a little more than a hobo-camp of 50,000—thieves, mean dogs, and the pope, whose legitimacy required a Roman address. The medieval city, a colorful tangle of lanes, lies between the Pantheon and the river.

Window-shoppers' Rome twinkles with nightlife and ritzy shopping near medieval Rome, on or near Rome's main drag, the Via del Corso.

Vatican City is a compact world of its own with two great sights: a huge basilica and the museum.

Trastevere, the seedy/colorful wrong-side-of-the-river neighborhood-village, is Rome at its crustiest—and perhaps most "Roman."

Baroque Rome is an overleaf that embellishes great squares throughout the town with fountains and church facades.

Since no one is allowed to build taller than St. Peter's dome, the city has no modern skyline. And the Tiber River is ignored. It's not navigable and after the last floods (1870), the banks were built up very high and Rome turned its back on its naughty river.

Tourist Information

Few cities offer less tourist information per capita than Rome. There are three tourist information offices: airport, train station (near track #1, very crowded, the only one open on Sunday), and central office (open Monday–Friday 8:15–19:15, Saturday 8:15–13:45, next to the SAAB dealership, Via Parigi 5, tel. 06/488-99255 or 06/488-99253).

The central TI office, near Piazza della Republica's huge fountain, is a five-minute walk out the front of the train station.

Rome

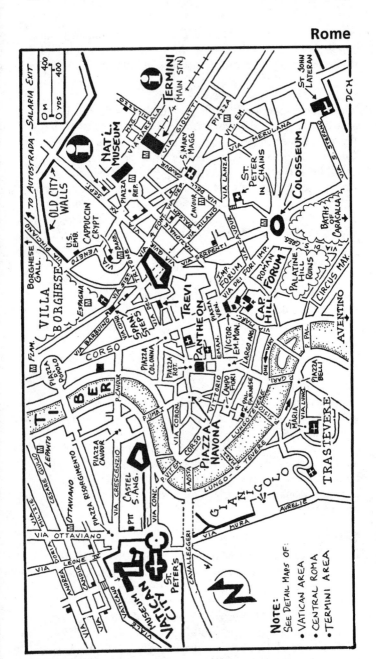

It's air-conditioned, less crowded and more helpful than the other TIs, and has comfortable sofas and a desk to plan on—or sit at to overcome your frustration. Ask for the better "long stay" city map and a quarterly periodical entertainment guide for evening events and fun. (If all you need is a map, forget the TI and pick one up at your hotel.) All hotels list an inflated rate to cover the hefty commission any TI room-finding service charges. Save money by booking direct.

Romanc'e is a cheap little weekly entertainment guide sold at newsstands with a helpful English section on musical events and the pope's schedule for the week. Fancy hotels carry a free English monthly, *Un Ospite a Roma* (A Guest in Rome).

Enjoy Rome is a free and friendly information service providing maps, museum hours, a useful city guide (free), and a room-finding service, but you'll get better prices by going direct (8:30–13:30, 15:30–18:30, closed Saturday afternoon and on Sunday, 3 blocks northeast of the station at Via Varese 39, tel. 06/445-1843, fax 06/445-0734, English-speaking). They offer several English-only city walking tours daily (L30,000 per three-hour tour, L25,000 for those under 26, children under 15 go free, tel. 06/397-28728).

Guided Walks Through Rome: Several companies do guided walks through Rome. Tom Rankin (an American in love with Rome and his Roman wife) runs **Scala Reale**, a small company committed to sorting out the rich layers of Rome for small groups of three to six people (with a longer-than-normal attention span). His excellent three-hour tours run around L50,000 per person and are well-explained on his web site (tel. & fax 06/447-00898, e-mail: scalareale@mail.nexus.it, web site: www.scalareale.org). You can book tours with Tom or one of his associates in advance or call upon arrival in Rome to see what's planned.

Helpful Hints

General Museum Hours: Most museums close on Monday (except the Vatican) and at 13:00 on Sunday. Outdoor sights like the Colosseum, Forum, and Ostia Antica are open 9:00 to 19:00 (or one hour before sunset). There are absolutely no absolutes in Italy. These hours will vary. Confirm sightseeing plans each morning with a quick L200 telephone call asking, "Are you open today?" (*"Aperto oggi?"*) and "What time do you close?" (*"A che ora chiuso?"*). I've included telephone numbers for this purpose. The last pages of the daily *Messaggero* newspaper list current events, exhibits, and hours.

Churches: Churches open early, close for lunch, and reopen from about 16:00 to 19:00. Modest dress means no bare shoulders, miniskirts, or shorts (men or women). Kamikaze tourists maximize their sightseeing hours by visiting churches before 9:00 and seeing the major sights that stay open during the siesta (St. Peter's and the Forum) while all good Romans are taking it cool and easy.

Shop Hours: Usually 9:00 to 13:00 and 16:00 to 20:00. Groceries are often closed on Sunday. In the holiday month of August, many shops and restaurants close up for vacation and *"Chiuso per ferie"* signs decorate locked doors all over town.

Theft Alert: With sweet-talking con artists, pickpockets on buses and at the station, and thieving gangs at the ancient sights, Rome is a gauntlet of rip-offs. Other than getting run down, there's no great physical risk. But green tourists will be ripped off. Thieves strike when you're distracted. Don't trust kind strangers. Keep nothing important in your pockets. Assume you're being stalked. (Then relax and have fun.)

Buyer Beware: I carefully understand the final price before I order *anything* and I deliberately count my change. Expect the "slow count." Wait for the last bits of your change to straggle over to you. There are legitimate extras (café prices skyrocket when you sit down, taxis get L5,000 extra after 22:00, and so on) to which paranoid tourists wrongly take offense. But the waiter who charges you L70,000 for the pizza and beer assumes you're too polite to involve the police. If you have any problem with a restaurant, hotel, or taxi, get a cop to arbitrate. Rome is trying to civilize itself.

Staying Healthy: The siesta is a key to survival in summertime Rome. Lie down and contemplate the extraordinary power of gravity in the eternal city. I drink lots of cold, refreshing water from Rome's many drinking fountains (the Forum has three). If you get sick, call the International Medical Center (tel. 06/884-0113).

Arrival in Rome

By Train: The Termini train station is a minefield of tourist services: a late-hours bank, a day hotel, luggage lockers, 24-hour thievery, the city bus station, and a subway stop. Handy multilingual charts make locations very clear. The place is crawling with sleazy sharks with official-looking cards.

Generally, avoid anybody selling anything at the station if you
can. La Piazza, however, is a bright and cheery self-service
restaurant (daily 11:00–22:30).

Most of my hotel listings are easily accessible by foot (near
the train station) or by Metro (Colosseum and Vatican neighborhoods). The train station has its own Metro stop (Termini).

By Plane: If you arrive at the airport, catch a train (hourly,
30 min, L13,000) to Rome's train station or take a taxi to your
hotel. For details, see Transportation Connections below.

Getting Around Rome

Sightsee on foot, by city bus, or by taxi. I've grouped your
sightseeing into walkable neighborhoods. Public transportation
is efficient, cheap, and part of your Roman experience.

By Subway: The Roman subway system (Metropolitana)
is simple, with two clean, cheap, fast lines. While much of
Rome is not served by its skimpy subway, these stops are helpful:
Termini (central train station, several recommended hotels,
National Museum), Republica (main tourist office, several
recommended hotels), Barberini (Cappuccin Crypt, Trevi
Fountain), Spagna (Spanish Steps, Villa Borghese, classy shopping area), Flaminio (Piazza del Popolo, start of the Via del
Corso Dolce Vita stroll), OttaViano (the Vatican, recommended
hotels), Colosseo (the Colosseum, Roman Forum, recommended
hotels), and E.U.R. (Mussolini's futuristic suburb).

By Bus: Bus routes are clearly listed at the stops. Bus #64
is particularly useful, connecting the station, my recommended
Via Nazionale hotels, Victor Emanuel Monument (near the
Forum), Largo Argentina (near the Pantheon) and the Vatican.
Ride it for a city overview and to watch pickpockets in action.

Buses and subways use the same ticket. You can buy tickets
at newsstands, tobacco shops, or at major stations or bus stops
but not on board (L1,500, good for 75 minutes—one Metro ride
and unlimited buses, punch them yourself as you board—or you
are cheating). Buy a bunch so you can hop a bus without search-
ing for an open tobacco shop. (Riding without a ticket, while relatively safe, is stressful. Inspectors fine even innocent-looking
tourists L50,000 if found on a bus or subway without a ticket
that has been stamped.) If you hop a bus without a ticket, locals
who use tickets rather than a monthly pass can sell you a ticket
from their wallet bundle. All-day bus/Metro passes cost L6,000.
Learn which buses serve your neighborhood.

Metropolitana: Rome's Subway

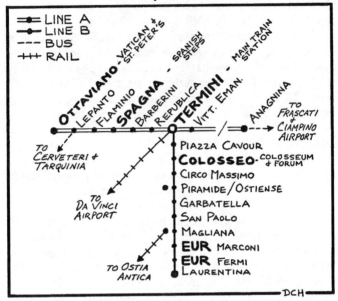

Buses, especially the touristic #64, and the subway, are havens for thieves and pickpockets. Assume any commotion is a thief-created distraction. Bus #64 gets extremely crowded.

By Taxi: Taxis start at about L5,000 (L2,000 surcharge on Sunday and L5,000 surcharge after 22:00). Sample fares: train station to Vatican, L12,000; train station to Colosseum, L8,000; Colosseum to Trastevere, L10,000. Three or four companions with more money than time should taxi almost everywhere. Rather than wave and wave, ask in local shops for the nearest taxi stand (*"Dové [DOH-vay] una fermata dei tassi?"*). Taxis with their telephone number on the door have fair meters—use them.

Sights—Rome, Near Forum
▲**St. Peter-in-Chains Church (San Pietro in Vincoli)**— The original chains and Michelangelo's able-to-stand-and-toss-those-tablets *Moses* are on exhibit in an otherwise unexceptional church, just a short walk uphill from the Colosseum (free, daily 6:30–12:30, 15:30–19:00, modest dress required).

▲▲**Colosseum**—This is the great example of Roman engineering, 2,000 years old. Using concrete, brick, and their
trademark round arches, Romans constructed much larger
buildings than the Greeks. But in deference to the higher
Greek culture, notice how they finished their no-nonsense
mega-structure by pasting all three orders of Greek columns
(Doric, Ionic, and Corinthian) as exterior decorations. The
Flavian Amphitheater's popular name "Colosseum" comes
from the colossal statue of Nero that once stood in front of it.

Romans were into "big." By putting two theaters
together, they created a circular amphitheater. They could
fill and empty its 50,000 numbered seats as quickly and effi-
ciently as we do our super-stadiums. Teams of sailors hoisted
canvas awnings over the stadium to give fans shade. This was
where ancient Romans, whose taste for violence was the
equal of modern America's, enjoyed their Dirty Harry and
Terminator. Gladiators, criminals, and wild animals fought
to the death in every conceivable scenario. They even waged
mock naval battles (L10,000 gets you inside and upstairs,
Sunday and Wednesday 9:00–13:00, all other days 9:00–19:00,
less off-season, tel. 06/700-4261).

▲▲▲**Roman Forum (Foro Romano)**—Ancient Rome's
birthplace and civic center, the Forum was the common ground
between Rome's famous seven hills (L12,000, Monday–Saturday
9:00–18:00, Sunday 9:00–13:00, off-season 9:00–15:00, last
tickets sold an hour before closing, tel. 06/699-0110). Just past
the entry, there's a WC and a handy headless statue for you to
pose behind. To help resurrect this confusing pile of rubble,
study the before-and-after pictures in the cheap city guidebooks sold on the streets. (Check out the small red *Rome, Past
and Present* books with plastic overlays to un-ruin the ruins.
They're priced at L25,000—pay no more than L15,000.)
Follow this basic walk:

1. Start at the Basilica Aemilia (second century B.C., on
your right as you walk down the entry ramp). Study the floor
plan of the ancient palace. This pre-Christian "basilica" design
was later adopted by medieval churches.

2. From the Basilica Aemilia, step out onto the Via Sacra
(the Sacred Road), the main street of ancient Rome. It runs
from the Arch of Septimus Severus on your right, past
Basilica Aemilia, up to the Arch of Titus and the Colosseum
on your left.

The Forum Area

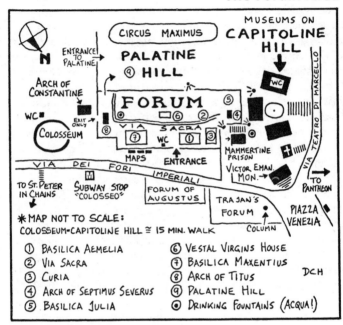

3. The plain, intact brick building near the Arch of Septimus Severus was the Curia where the Roman senate sat. (Peek inside.) Roman buildings were basically brick and concrete, usually with a marble veneer, which in this case has been long lost.

4. The Arch of Septimus Severus, from about A.D. 200, celebrates that emperor's military victories. In front of it, a stone called the Lapis Niger covers the legendary tomb of Romulus. To the left of the arch, the stone bulkhead is the Rostra or speaker's platform. It's named for the ship's prows which used to decorate it as big shots hollered, "Friends, Romans, countrymen. . . "

5. The grand Basilica Julia, a first-century law court, fills the corner opposite the Curia. Ancient backgammon-type game boards are cut into the pavement.

6. Climb up toward the Palatine Hill, past the semi-circular Temple of Vesta to the House of the Vestal Virgins. Here, the VVs kept the eternal flame lit. A set of ponds and a marble chorus line of Vestal Virgins mark the courtyard of the house.

7. Climb down to the Via Sacra and turn right toward the Colosseum. A path on the left leads to up to the remains of the mammoth Basilica Maxentius. Only the giant barrel vaults remain, looming crumbly and weed-eaten. As you stand in the shadow of the Bas Max, reconstruct it in your mind. The huge barrel vaults were just side niches. Extend the broken nub of an arch out over the vacant lot and finish your imaginary Roman basilica with rich marble and fountains. People it with plenty of toga-clad Romans. Yeow.

8. Back on Via Sacra, continue climbing to the small Arch of Titus (drinking fountain opposite). The arch is carved with propaganda celebrating the A.D. 70 defeat of the Jews, beginning the Diaspora that ended with the creation of Israel in 1947. Notice the gaggle of soldiers carrying the menorah.

9. From the Arch of Titus, walk up the Palatine Hill to the remains of the Imperial palaces. We get our word "palace" from this hill, where the emperors chose to live. The pleasant garden overlooks the Forum. On the far side, look down into an emperor's private stadium and then beyond at the dusty old Circus Maximus.

▲Thief Gangs—If you know what to look out for, the gangs of children picking the pockets and handbags of naive tourists are no threat but an interesting, albeit sad, spectacle. Gangs of city-stained children, too young to prosecute but old enough to rip you off, troll through the tourist crowds around the Forum, Colosseum, and train and Metro stations. Watch them target tourists distracted with a video camera or overloaded with bags. The kids look like beggars and use newspapers or cardboard signs to confuse their victims. They scram like stray cats if you're onto them. A fast-fingered mother with a baby is often nearby.

▲Mammertine Prison—The 2,500-year-old converted cistern that once imprisoned Saints Peter and Paul is worth a look. On the walls are lists of prisoners (Christian and non-Christian) and how they were executed: *strangolati, decapitato, morto di fame* . . . (donation requested, daily 9:00–12:00, 14:30–18:00). At the top of the stairs leading to Capitoline Hill, you'll find a refreshing water fountain. Block the spout with your fingers; it spurts up for drinking.

Sights—Rome's Capitoline Hill
▲▲Capitoline Hill (Campidoglio)—This hill was the religious and political center of ancient Rome. It's still the home of the

city's government. Michelangelo's Renaissance square is
bounded by two fine museums and the mayoral palace. Its
centerpiece is a famous equestrian statue of Marcus Aurelius,
a copy of the original (behind glass in the adjacent museum).
There's a fine view of the Forum from the terrace just past
the mayor's palace on the right.

The two **Capitoline Museums** (Musei Capitolino) are in
two buildings (one L10,000 ticket is good for both museums,
free for those over 60 and under 18, Tuesday–Saturday 9:00–
19:00, Sunday 9:00–13:00, closed Monday, tel. 06/671-02071).
The **Palazzo dei Conservatori** (the building nearest the river,
on Marcus Aurelius' left side) is the world's oldest museum
(500 years old). Outside the entrance, notice the marriage
announcements (and, very likely, wedding-party photo ops).
Inside the courtyard, have some photo fun with chunks of a
giant statue of Emperor Constantine. (A rare public toilet hides
near the museum ticket-taker.) The museum is worthwhile, with
lavish rooms housing several great statues. Tops is the original
(500 B.C.) Etruscan Capitoline Wolf (the little statues of
Romulus and Remus were added in the Baroque age). Don't
miss the *Boy Extracting a Thorn* or the enchanting *Commodus
as Hercules*. The painting gallery (second floor) is forgettable
except for one Carravagio.

Across the square, the **Palazzo Nuovo**, houses mostly
portrait busts of forgotten emperors. But it has two must-sees:
the *Dying Gaul* (first floor) and the restored gilded bronze
equestrian statue of Marcus Aurelius (behind glass in the
museum courtyard). This greatest surviving equestrian statue
of antiquity was the original centerpiece of the square. While
most such statues were destroyed by Dark Age Christians,
Marcus was mistaken as Constantine (the first Christian
emperor) and therefore spared.

To approach the great square the way Michelangelo
wanted you to, walk halfway down the grand stairway toward
Piazza Venezia, spin around, and walk back up. At the bottom
of the stairs, look up the long stairway to your right (which pilgrims climb on their knees) for a good example of the earliest
style of Christian church. While pilgrims find it worth the
climb, sightseers can skip it.

From the bottom of the stairs, way down the street on
your left, you'll see a condominium actually built around surviving ancient pillars and arches—perhaps the oldest inhabited

building in Europe. Farther ahead (toward Piazza Venezia), look down into the ditch on your right, and see how everywhere modern Rome is built on the forgotten frescoes and mangled mosaics of ancient Rome.

Piazza Venezia—This vast square is the focal point of modern Rome. The Via del Corso, starting here, is the city's axis, surrounded by Rome's classiest shopping district. From the Palazzo Venezia's balcony above the square (to your left with back to Victor Emanuel Monument), Mussolini whipped up the nationalistic fervor of Italy. Fascist masses filled the square screaming, "Four more years!" or something like that. (Fifteen years later, they hung him from a meat hook in Milan.)

Victor Emanuel Monument—This oversized monument to an Italian king loved only by his relatives and the ignorant is known to most Romans as "the wedding cake," "the typewriter," or "the dentures." It wouldn't be so bad if it weren't sitting on a priceless acre of Ancient Rome. Soldiers guard Italy's Tomb of the Unknown Soldier as the eternal flame flickers. Stand directly in front of it and see how Via del Corso bisects Rome.

▲**Trajan's Column**—This is the grandest column and best example of "continuous narration" from antiquity. Study the propaganda which winds up the column like a scroll, trumpeting Trajan's wonderful military exploits. You can view this close-up for free across Mussolini's busy Via dei Fori Imperiali from the Victor Emanual Monument. In its day, for easier viewing, Trajan fans could study the scenes from the balconies of buildings which stood tall on either side.

Sights—Heart of Rome

▲▲▲**Pantheon**—For the greatest look at the splendor of Rome, antiquity's best-preserved interior is a must (free, normally open 9:00–18:30, Sunday 9:00–13:00, less in winter, tel. 06/683-00230). Since it became a church dedicated to the martyrs just after the fall of Rome, the barbarians left it alone and the locals didn't use it as a quarry. The portico is called Rome's umbrella—a fun local gathering in a rainstorm. Walk past its one-piece granite columns (biggest in Italy, shipped from Egypt) and through the original bronze doors. Sit inside under the glorious skylight and study it.

The dome, 140 feet high and wide, was Europe's biggest until the 20th century. Michelangelo's dome at St. Peter's,

Heart of Rome

❶ Hotel Campo dei Fiori   ❹ Casa di Santa Brigida
❷ Albergo del Sole   ❺ Il Delfino Rest.
❸ Hotel Navona   ❻ Volpetti

while much higher, is 1 meter smaller. The brilliance of its construction astounded architects through the ages. During the Renaissance, Brunelleschi was given permission to cut into the dome (see the little square hole above and to the right of the entrance) to analyze the material. The concrete dome gets thinner and lighter with height—the highest part is of volcanic pumice.

This wonderfully harmonious architecture greatly inspired the artists of the Renaissance, particularly Raphael. Raphael, along with Italy's first two kings, chose to be buried here. As you walk around the outside of the Pantheon, notice the "rise of Rome"—about 15 feet since it was built.

▲▲**Curiosities near the Pantheon**—The only Gothic church you'll see in Rome is **Santa Maria sopra Minerva**. On a little square behind the Pantheon to the east, past the

Bernini statue of an elephant carrying an Egyptian obelisk, this Dominican church was built *sopra* (over) a pre-Christian temple of Minerva. Before stepping in, notice the high-water marks on the wall (right of door). Inside, you'll see that the lower parts of the frescos were lost to these floods.

Rome was at its low ebb, almost a ghost town, through much of the Gothic period. Little was built from this time. (And much of what was, was redone Baroque.) This church is a refreshing exception. St. Catherine's body lies under the altar (her head is in Siena). The patron saint of Italy, she convinced the pope to return from France to Rome, thus saving Italy from untold chaos.

Left of the altar stands a little-known Michelangelo statue, *Christ Bearing the Cross*. Michelangelo gave Jesus an athlete's or warrior's body (a striking contrast to the more docile Christ of medieval art) but left the face to one of his pupils. Fra Angelico's simple tomb is farther to the left, on the way to the back door. Before leaving, head over to the right (south transept), pop in a L500 coin for light and enjoy a fine Filippo Lippi fresco showing scenes from the life of St. Thomas Aquinas—founder of the Dominicans.

Exit the church via its rear door (behind the Michelangelo statue), walk down Fra Angelico lane (spy any artisans at work), turn left, and walk to the next square. On your right you'll find the **Chiesa di St. Ignazio** church, a riot of Baroque illusions. Study the fresco over the door and the ceiling in the back of the nave. Then stand on the yellow disk on the floor between the two stars. Look at the central (black) dome. Keeping your eyes on the dome, walk under and past it. Church building project runs out of money? Hire a painter to paint a fake (and flat) dome. (Both churches stay open until 19:00, take a 12:30–16:00 siesta, and welcome modestly dressed visitors.)

A few blocks away, back across Corso Vittorio Emanuele, is the very rich and Baroque **Gesu Church**, headquarters of the Jesuits in Rome. The Jesuits powered the Church's Counter-Reformation. With Protestants teaching that all roads to heaven didn't pass through Rome, the Baroque churches of the late 1500s were painted with spiritual road maps that said they did.

Walk out the Gesu Church and 2 blocks down Corso V. Emanuele to the **Sacred Area** (Largo Argentina), an excavated square facing the boulevard, 2 blocks from the Pantheon. Walk around this square looking into the excavated pit at some of

the oldest ruins in Rome. It was here that Caesar was assassi-
nated. Today, this is a refuge for cats. Some 250 cats are cared
for by volunteers. You'll see them (and their refuge) at the far
(west) side of the square.

Self-guided Walks—Rome

▲▲▲The Dolce Vita Stroll down Via del Corso—
This is the city's chic and hip "cruise" from the Piazza del
Popolo (Metro: Flaminio) down a wonderfully traffic-free
section of the Via del Corso and up Via Condotti to the
Spanish Steps each evening around 18:00. Shoppers, take a
left on Via Condotti for the Spanish Steps and Gucci (shops
open after siesta, 16:30–19:30). Historians, start with a visit
to the Baroque Church of Santa Maria del Popolo (with
Raphael's Chigi Chapel and two Caravaggio paintings, on
the far side of Piazza del Popolo), and continue down the
Via del Corso to the Victor Emanuel Monument. Climb
Michelangelo's stairway to his glorious Campidoglio Square,
and catch the lovely view of the Forum (from past the mayor's
palace on right) as the horizon reddens and cats prowl the
unclaimed rubble of ancient Rome.

▲▲▲Floodlit Rome Hike: Trastevere to the Spanish
Steps—Rome can be grueling. But a fine way to enjoy this
historian's fertility rite is an evening walk lacing together
Rome's floodlit night spots. Fine urban spaces, real-life theater
vignettes, sitting close enough to the Bernini fountain to hear
no traffic, water flickering its mirror on the marble, jostling with
local teenagers to see all the gelato flavors, enjoying lovers straddling more than the bench, jaywalking past flak-vested *polizia*,
marveling at the ramshackle elegance that softens this brutal city
for those who were born here and can imagine living nowhere
else—these are the flavors of Rome best tasted after dark.

Taxi or ride the bus (#23 from the Vatican area, #75 or
#170 from Via Nazionale or Victor Emanuel) to Trastevere,
the colorful neighborhood across (*tras*) the Tiber (*tevere*). Start
your hike at Santa Maria in Trastevere. Trastevere offers the
best look at medieval-village Rome. The action all marches to
the chime of the church bells. Go there and wander. Wonder.
Be a poet. This is Rome's Left Bank.

Santa Maria in Trastevere (free, daily 7:30–13:00, 15:00–
19:00), one of Rome's oldest churches, was made a basilica in
the fourth century when Christianity was legalized. It was the

first church dedicated to the Virgin Mary. Most of what you see today is from around the 12th century, but the ancient basilica floor plan (and ambiance) survives and the portico (covered area just outside the door) is decorated with fascinating ancient fragments filled with early Christian symbolism. The 12th-century mosaics behind the altar are striking and notable for their portrayal of Mary—the first showing her at the throne with Jesus in Heaven. The ahead-of-their-time paintings (by Cavallini, from 1300) below scenes from the life of Mary predate the Renaissance by 100 years.

Don't leave Trastevere until you've wandered the back streets. From the square (see Eating, below), Via del Moro leads to the river and Ponte Sisto, a pedestrian bridge with a good view of St. Peter's dome. Cross the bridge and continue straight ahead for 1 block. Take the first left, which leads down Via di Capo di Ferro through the scary and narrow darkness to Piazza Farnese, with the imposing Palazzo Farnese. Michelangelo contributed to the facade of this palace, now the French embassy. The fountains on the square feature huge one-piece granite hot tubs from the ancient Roman Baths of Caracalla.

One block from there (opposite the palace) is **Campo dei Fiori** (Field of Flowers), which is my favorite outdoor dining room after dark (see Eating, below). The statue of Giordano Bruno, a heretic who was burned in 1600 for believing the world was round and not the center of the universe, marks the center of this great and colorful square. Bruno overlooks a busy produce market in the morning and strollers after dark. This neighborhood is still known for its free spirit. When the statue of Bruno was erected in 1889, local riots overcame Vatican protests against honoring a heretic. Bruno faces his executioner, the Vatican Chancellory (the big white building in the corner a bit to his right), while on the pedestal the words say "and the flames rose up." The square is lined and surrounded by fun eateries. Bruno also faces La Carbonara, which gave birth to pasta Carbonara. The Forno, next door, is a popular place for hot and tasty take-out *pizza bianco*.

If Bruno did a hop, step, and jump forward and turned right, he'd cross the busy Corso Vittorio Emanuele and find **Piazza Navona**. Rome's most interesting night scene features street music, artists, fire-eaters, local Casanovas, ice cream, outdoor cafés (splurge-worthy if you've got time to sit and enjoy the human river of Italy), and three fountains by

Bernini, the father of Baroque art. Its Tartufo "death by chocolate" ice cream (L5,000 to go, L11,000 at a table) made the Tre Scalini café world-famous among connoisseurs of ice cream and chocolate alike. This oblong square is molded around the long-gone stadium of Domitian, an ancient chariot racetrack that was often flooded so the masses could enjoy major water games.

Leave Piazza Navona directly across from the Tre Scalini café, go past rose peddlers and palm readers, jog left around the guarded building, and follow the yellow sign to the Pantheon straight down Via del Salvatore (cheap pizza place on left just before the Pantheon). Sit for a while under the flood- and moon-lit Pantheon's portico.

With your back to the Pantheon, head right, passing Bar Pantheon on your right. A blue-and-white arrow points down the street past the Tazza d'Oro Casa del Caffè. The Tazza d'Oro, one of Rome's top coffee shops, dates back to the days when this area was licensed to roast coffee beans. Look back at the fine view of the Pantheon from here.

Ahead is Piazza Capranica with the Florentine Renaissance-style Palazzo Capranica. Big shots, like the Capranica family, built stubby towers on their palaces—not of any military use . . . just to show off. Leave the piazza to the right of the palace, following another white arrow. (These arrows, which I put here for this tour in the late 1980s, are now accepted by local traffic.) Via in Aquino leads to another arrow pointing to a sixth-century B.C. Egyptian obelisk (taken as a trophy by Augustus after his victory in Egypt over Mark Antony and Cleopatra). Approaching the obelisk you'll find two arrows. Detour to the left for some of Rome's best gelato. **Gelateria Caffè Pasticceria Giolitti** (just behind Albergo Nazionale, Via Uffici del Vicario 40, open daily until very late) is cheap to go or elegant and splurge-worthy for a sit among classy locals. Or head right, walking down Via della Colonna Antonina to the big noisy main drag of downtown Rome, Via del Corso.

Piazza Colonna features a huge second-century column honoring Marcus Aurelius. The big important-looking palace is the prime minister's residence. While pink, this is the closest thing in Italy to a "White House." Cross the street, and take the right branch of the Y-shaped shopping gallery (1928) and exit, continuing straight down Via de Crociferi (or, if closed, head down Via dei Sabini) to the roar of the water, light, and people of the Trevi fountain.

Vatican City, St. Peter's, and the Museum

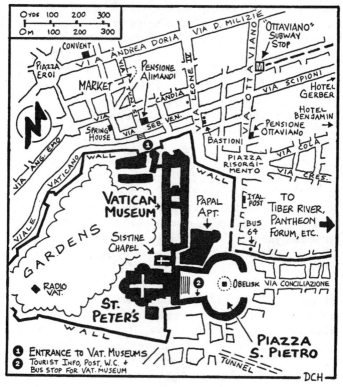

The **Trevi fountain** is an example of how Rome took full advantage of the abundance of water brought into the city by its great aqueducts. This watery Baroque avalanche was built in 1762. Romantics toss two coins over their shoulder thinking it will give them a wish and assure their return to Rome. That may sound silly, but every year I go through this touristic ritual . . . and it actually seems to work.

Take some time to people-watch (whisper a few breathy *bellos* or *bellas*) before leaving. Facing the fountain, go past it on the right down Via delle Stamperia to Via del Triton. Cross the busy street and continue to the Spanish Steps (ask, *"Dové Piazza di Spagna?"*) a few blocks and thousands of dollars of shopping opportunities away.

The **Piazza di Spagna** (rhymes with "lasagna"), with the very popular Spanish Steps, got its name 300 years ago when this was the site of the Spanish Embassy. It's been the hangout of many romantics over the years (Keats, Wagner, Openshaw, Goethe, and others). The Boat Fountain at the foot of the steps was done by Bernini's father, Bernini. This is a thriving night scene.

Facing the steps, walk to your right about a block to tour one of the world's biggest and most lavish McDonald's. About a block on the other side of the steps is the subway, or Metropolitana, which (until 23:30) will zip you home.

Sights—Vatican City

This tiny independent country of just over 100 acres, contained entirely within Rome, has its own postal system, armed guard, helipad, mini-train station, and radio station (KPOP). Politically powerful, the Vatican is the religious capital of 800 million Roman Catholics. If you're not one already, become a Catholic for your visit. There's a helpful tourist office just to the left of St. Peter's Basilica (Monday–Saturday 8:30–19:00, tel. 06/698-84466). Check out the glossy L5,000 guidebooklet (crowded piazza on cover), which doubles as a classy souvenir. Telephone the Vatican TI if you're interested in their sporadic but very good tours of the Vatican grounds or the church interior, or the pope's schedule (see below). If you don't care to see the pope, minimize crowd problems by avoiding these times. Handy buses shuttle visitors between St. Peter's (in front of the tourist office) and the Vatican Museum (L2,000, twice an hour, 8:45 until 13:45, or 12:45 when museum closes early). This is far better than the exhausting 15-minute walk around the Vatican wall as it gives you a pleasant peek at the garden-filled Vatican grounds, and you bypass the line outside the Vatican Museum.

▲▲▲St. Peter's Basilica—There is no doubt: this is the richest and most impressive church on earth. To call it vast is like calling God smart. Marks on the floor show where the next largest churches would fit if they were put inside. The ornamental cherubs would dwarf a large man. Birds roost inside, and thousands of people wander about, heads craned heavenward, hardly noticing each other. Don't miss Michelangelo's *Pietà* (behind bulletproof glass) to the right of the entrance. Bernini's altar work and seven-story tall bronze canopy (*baldacchino*) are brilliant.

For a quick self-guided walk through the basilica, follow these points:

St. Peter's Basilica

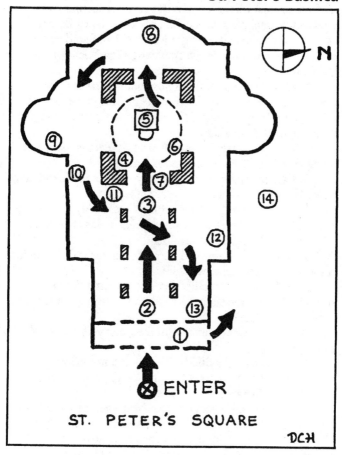

ST. PETER'S SQUARE

DCH

1. The atrium is larger than most churches. Notice the historic doors (the Holy Door, on the right, will be opened in the year 2000—see point 13 below). Guided tours depart from the desk nearby.

2. The purple circular porphyry stone marks the site of Charlemagne's coronation in A.D. 800. From here get a sense of the immensity of the church, which can accommodate 95,000 worshippers standing on its 6 acres.

3. Michelangelo planned to build a Greek Cross church plan. A Greek cross, symbolizing the perfection of God,

and by association the goodness of man, was important
to the humanist Michelangelo. But accommodating large
crowds was important to the Church in the fancy Baroque
age, so the original nave length was doubled. Stand halfway
up the nave and imagine the stubbier design Michelangelo
had in mind.

4. View the magnificent dome from the statue of St.
Andrew. Check out the lofty vision of heaven above the windows: Jesus, Mary, a ring of saints, rings of angels, and on the
very top, God the Father.

5. The main altar sits directly over St. Peter's tomb and
under Bernini's 70-foot-tall bronze canopy.

6. Take the stairs down to the crypt to see the foundation
of St. Peter's chapels and tombs of popes.

7. The statue of St. Peter, with an irresistably kissable toe,
is one of the few pieces of art which predate this church. It
adorned the first St. Peter's church.

8. St. Peter's Throne and Bernini's star-burst dove window
is the site of a daily Mass at 17:00.

9. St. Peter was crucified here (at the time the middle
spot of a Roman race course) when this location was simply
"the Vatican Hill."

10. For most, the treasury (in the sacristy) is not worth
the admission.

11. The church is filled with mosaics, not paintings.
Notice the mosaic version of Raphael's Transfiguration.

12. Blessed Sacrament Chapel.

13. Michelangelo sculpted this *Pietà* when he was 24 years
old. A pietà is a work showing Mary with the dead body of
Christ taken down from the cross. Michelangelo's mastery of
the body is obvious in this powerfully beautiful masterpiece.
Jesus is believably dead and Mary, the eternally youthful
"handmaiden" of the Lord, still accepts God's will. . . even if it
means giving up her son.

The Holy Door (piled high with plaster with a cross in its
center, just to the right of the *Pietà*) will be opened in 2000,
symbolizing the "Jubilee Year." Every 25 years the Church celebrates an especially festive year derived from the Old Testament
idea of the Jubilee Year (originally every 50 years) which encour-
ages new beginnings. Sins and debts are forgiven. The pope is
tirelessly calling for this particularly monumental Jubilee year to
be one in which the World Bank and the world's rich countries

will usher in the new millennium by forgiving or relieving the crippling debt burden which keeps much of the Third World in squalor.

14. An elevator leads to the roof and the stairway up the dome. The dome, Michelangelo's last work, is (you guessed it) the biggest anywhere. Taller than a football field is long, it's well worth the sweaty climb for a great view of Rome, the Vatican grounds, and the inside of the Basilica—particularly heavenly while there is singing. Look around—Rome has no modern skyline. No building is allowed to exceed the height of St. Peter's. The elevator (just outside the church to the right as you face it) takes you to the rooftop of the nave. From there a few steps bring you to a balcony at the base of the dome looking down into the church interior. After that the one-way 300-step climb (for some people, claustrophobic) to the cupola begins. The rooftop level (below the dome) has a gift shop, bathroom, drinking fountain, and a commanding view (L6,000 elevator, allow an hour to go up and down, closes 18:30).

The church strictly enforces its dress code. Dress modestly—a dress or long pants, shoulders covered (men and women). You are usually required to check any bags at a free cloakroom near the entry. St. Peter's is open daily 7:00–19:00, until 18:00 in winter; ticket booths to the treasury and dome close an hour early. All are welcome to join in the mass at the front altar (60 minutes, Monday–Saturday 17:00, Sunday 17:45).

The church is particularly moving at 7:00 while tourism is still sleeping. Volunteers who want you to understand and appreciate St. Peter's give free and excellent 90-minute "Pilgrim Service" tours in English at 15:00 (and occasionally at 10:00). Check for the day's schedule at the desk just after the dress code check as you're entering. Seeing the *Pietà* is neat; understanding it is divine.

▲▲▲The Vatican Museum—Too often the immense Vatican Museum is treated as an obstacle course, with 4 nagging miles of displays, separating the tourist from the Sistine Chapel. Even without the Sistine, this is one of Europe's top three or four houses of art. It can be exhausting, so plan your visit carefully, focusing on a few themes. Allow two hours for a quick visit, three or four for time to enjoy it. The museum uses a nearly-impossible-not-to-follow, one-way system.

You'll start as civilization did, in Egypt and Mesopotamia. Next, the Pio Clementino collection features Greek and

Roman statues. Decorating its courtyard are some of the very best Greek and Roman statues in captivity, including the Laocoon group (first century B.C., Hellenistic) and the *Apollo Belvedere* (a second-century Roman copy of a Greek original). The centerpiece of the next hall is the *Belvedere Torso* (just a 2,000-year-old torso, but one which had a great impact on the art of Michelangelo). Finishing off the classical statuary are two fine fourth-century porphyry sarcophagi (royal, purple stones for the coffins of Constantine's mother and daughter). Crafted in Egypt at a time when a declining Rome was unable to do such fine work, the details are fun to study.

After long halls of tapestries, old maps, broken penises, and fig-leaves, you'll come to what most people are looking for: the Raphael *stanza*, or rooms, and Michelangelo's Sistine Chapel.

These outstanding works are frescoes. A *fresco* (meaning "fresh" in Italian) is not actually a painting. The color is mixed into wet plaster and when the plaster dries, the painting is actually part of the wall. This is a durable but difficult medium requiring speed and accuracy as the work is built slowly, one patch at a time.

After fancy rooms illustrating the "immaculate conception of Mary" (a hard-to-sell, 19th-century Vatican doctrine) and the triumph of Constantine (with divine guidance which led to his conversion to Christianity), you enter the first room completely done by Raphael and find the newly-restored *School of Athens*. This is remarkable for its blatant pre-Christian Classical orientation wallpapering the apartments of Pope Julius II. Raphael honors the great pre-Christian thinkers—Aristotle, Plato, and company—who are portrayed as the leading artists of Raphael's day. The bearded figure of Plato is Leonardo da Vinci. Diogenes, history's first hippie, sprawls alone in bright blue on the stairs reading a ripped-out chapter of *Mona Winks*, while Michelangelo broods in the foreground—supposedly added late. Apparently Raphael snuck a peek at the Sistine Chapel and decided that his arch-competitor was so good he had to put their personal differences aside and include him in this tribute to the artists of his generation. Today's St. Peter's was under construction as Raphael was working. In the *School of Athens*, he gives us a sneak preview of the unfinished church.

Next (unless you detour through the refreshingly modern Catholic art section) is the brilliantly restored Sistine Chapel. The Sistine Chapel, the pope's personal chapel, is where, upon the death of the ruling pope, a new pope is elected. The College of Cardinals meet here and vote four times a day until a two-thirds-plus-one majority is reached and a new pope is elected.

The Sistine is famous for Michelangelo's pictorial culmination of the Renaissance, showing the story of Creation with a powerful God weaving in and out of each scene through that busy first week. This is an optimistic and positive expression of the High Renaissance and a powerful example of the artistic and theological maturity of the 33-year-old Michelangelo who spent four years at this work.

Later, after the Reformation wars had begun and after the Catholic army of Spain had sacked the Vatican, the reeling church began to fight back. As part of its Counter-Reformation, a much-older Michelangelo was commissioned to paint the *Last Judgment* (behind the altar). Newly restored, the message is as brilliant and clear as the day Michelangelo finished it: Christ is returning, some will go to hell and some to heaven, and some will be saved by the power of the rosary.

In the recent (and controversial) restoration project no paint was added. Centuries of dust, soot (from candles used for lighting and Mass), and glue (added to make the art shine) were removed, revealing the bright original colors of Michelangelo.

The Vatican's small but fine collection of paintings, the Pinacoteca (with Raphael's *Transfiguration* and Caravaggio's *Entombment*), is near the entry/exit. The underrated early Christian art section is the final possible side trip before exiting via the souvenir shop.

Vatican Museum nitty-gritty: Just inside the entrance two huge elevators *(ascensore)* zip you past mobs climbing the fancy staircase. (Museum admission L15,000, open late March, April, May, early June, September, and October hours: 8:45–16:45, Saturday 8:45–14:00, closed Sunday, except last Sunday of month when museum is free; the rest of the year it's open 8:45–13:45. Last entry 45 minutes before closing. Many minor rooms close 13:45–14:45 or from 13:30 on. The Sistine Chapel is closed 30 minutes before the rest of the museum.) The museum clearly marks out four color-coded visits of different lengths. The rentable CD-ROM tour (L8,000) is a great new system, letting you dial whichever piece of art you'd like commentary on as you come across numbered pieces in the museum. It offers a fine coverage of the Raphael rooms and Michelangelo's Sistine masterpiece. A small door at the rear of the Sistine Chapel allows tour groups and speedy individuals (without CD-ROM) to escape directly to St. Peter's basilica (ignore sign saying "Tour Groups Only"). If you squirt out here you're done with the museum. The Pinacoteca is the only important part left. Consider doing it at the start. Otherwise, it's a ten-minute heel-to-toe slalom through tourists from the Sistine to the entry/exit, tel. 06/698-83333. Closed May 1, June 29, August 15, November 1, December 8, and on church holidays.

The museum's excellent book-and-card shop offers a priceless (L12,000) black-and-white photo book (by Hupka) of the *Pietà*—great for gifts. The Vatican post, with an office in the museum and one on Piazza San Pietro (comfortable writing rooms, Monday–Friday 8:30–19:00, Saturday 8:30–18:00), is the only reliable mail service in Italy. The stamps are a collectible bonus (Vatican stamps are good throughout Rome, Italian stamps are not good at the Vatican). The Vatican bank has sinful rates. The modern cafeteria is handy but comes with long lines and mediocre food.

To see the pope: The pope reads a prayer and blesses the gathered masses from his library window overlooking Piazza San Pietro each Sunday at noon. During the summer (when he's in town), the Holy Father blesses the masses from St. Peter's Square each Wednesday morning at 11:00 (10:00 if it's really hot). In the winter this is done in the 7,000-seat Aula Paola VI Auditorium (free, Wednesday 11:00, call 06/698-83017 for reservations and details). Smaller ceremonies celebrated by the pope require reservations. The weekly entertainment guide *Romanc'e* always has a "Seeing the Pope" section.

More Sights—Rome
▲**National Museum of Rome (Museo Nazionale Romano delle Terme)**—Directly in front of the train station, the Palazzo Massimo houses much of the greatest ancient Roman sculpture (L12,000, 9:00–14:00, Sunday until 13:00, closed Monday, tel. 06/488-0530).
▲**Baths of Diocletian**—At the far side of the National Museum, facing Piazza Republica, the Aula Ottagona (or Rotunda of Diocletian, free, daily 10:00–19:00, borrow the English description booklet) is an impressive octagonal hall

from A.D. 300 decorated with fine ancient statues and worth a quick peek.

▲**Cappuccin Crypt**—If you want bones, this is it: below Santa Maria della Immaculata Concezione on Via Veneto, just off Piazza Barberini, are thousands of skeletons, all artistically arranged for the delight—or disgust—of the always-wide-eyed visitor. The monastic message on the wall explains that this is more than just a macabre exercise. Pick up a few of Rome's most interesting postcards (L1,000 donation, daily 9:00–12:00, 15:00–18:30). A bank with long hours and good exchange rates is next door, and the American Embassy and Federal Express are just up the street.

▲**Villa Borghese**—Rome's unkempt "Central Park" is great for people-watching (plenty of modern-day Romeos and Juliets). Take a row on the lake or visit its fine museums. The Borghese Gallery has some world-class Baroque art, including Bernini's *David* and his excited statue of Apollo chasing Daphne (L10,000, Tuesday–Saturday 9:00–19:00, Sunday 9:00–13:00, closed Monday, tel. 06/854-8577). The gallery's great painting collection (including works by Caravaggio, Giorgioni, Titian, and Rubens) is temporarily in the Complesso Monumentale San Michele a Ripa (L4,000, in Trastevere at Via de San Michele 22, Tuesday–Saturday 9:00–19:00, Sunday 9:00–13:00, closed Monday, tel. 06/581-6732). Also in the Villa Borghese, the **Museo di Villa Giulia** is a fine Etruscan museum (L8,000, Tuesday–Saturday 9:00–19:00, Sunday 9:00–13:30, closed Monday, tel. 06/320-1951).

▲**E.U.R.**—Mussolini's planned suburb of the future (65 years ago) is a ten-minute subway ride from the Colosseum to Metro: Magliana. From the Magliana subway stop, walk through the park uphill to the Palace of the Civilization of Labor (Pal. d. Civilta d. Concordia), the essence of Fascist architecture, with its giant, no-questions-asked, patriotic statues and its this-is-the-truth simplicity. On the far side is the **Museo della Civilta Romana**, a history museum which includes a large-scale model of ancient Rome (L5,000, Tuesday–Saturday 9:00–19:00, Sunday 9:00–13:30, closed Monday, Piazza G. Agnelli, Metro: E.U.R. Fermi, tel. 06/592-6041).

▲▲**Ostia Antica**—Rome's ancient seaport (80,000 people in the time of Christ, later a ghost town, now excavated), less than an hour from downtown, is the next best thing to Pompeii. Start at the 2,000-year-old theater, buy a map, explore the town, and finish with its fine little museum. To get there, take the subway's B Line to the Magliana stop, catch the Lido train to Ostia Antica (twice an hour), walk over the overpass, go straight to the end of that road, and follow the signs to (or ask for) *"scavi* Ostia Antica*"* (L8,000, Tuesday–Sunday 9:00–19:00 or one hour before sunset, closed Monday, museum closes at 14:00, tel. 06/563-58099). Just beyond is Rome's filthy beach (*lido*).

Overrated Sights—The Spanish Steps (with Italy's first, and one of the world's largest, McDonald's—McGrandeur at its greatest—just down the street) and the commercialized Catacombs, which contain no bones, are way out of the city and are not worth the time or trouble. The venerable old Villa d'Este garden of fountains near Hadrian's Villa outside of town at Tivoli is now run-down, overpriced, and disappointing.

Sleeping in Rome
(L1,600 = about $1, tel. code: 06)
Sleep Code: **S**=Single, **D**=Double/Twin, **T**=Triple, **Q**=Quad, **b**=bathroom, **t**=toilet only, **s**=shower only, **CC**=Credit Card (**V**isa, **M**asterCard, **A**mex), **SE**=Speaks English, **NSE**=No English. Breakfast is normally included in the expensive places.

The absolute cheapest doubles in Rome are L70,000, without shower or breakfast. You'll pay L25,000 in a sleazy dorm or hostel. A nicer hotel (L120,000 doubles, L150,000 with bath, L190,000 with air conditioning) provides an oasis and refuge, making it easier to enjoy this intense and grinding city. If you're going door-to-door, prices are soft—so bargain. Hotels list official prices which assume an agency or room-finding service kickback which, if you're coming direct, they avoid. Many hotels have high-season (mid-March–October) and low-season prices. Easter and September are the crowded times. In August, when temperatures climb, prices drop or get very soft. Most of my recommended hotels are small, with huge, murky entrances that make you feel like a Q-Tip in a gas station. Most places speak English, but the amount of English spoken drops with the price. While I've listed mostly places with minimal traffic noise, always ask for a *tranquillo* room. Many prices here are promised only to people who show this book, don't use a credit card, and come direct without using a room-finding service. On Easter, April 25 and May 1 the entire city gets booked up.

Sleeping North of the Train Station

The cheapest hotels in town are north of the station. Avoid places on the seedy south (Colosseum) side of the station. The first four listings are closest in a safe and decent area (which gets a little weird and spooky late at night). With your back to the train tracks, turn right and walk 2 blocks out of the station. A self-serve *lavanderia* (Laundromat) is at 8 Via Milazzo (daily, 8:00–22:00, 6 kilos washed and dried for L12,000, friendly Maria Pia lets you drop off and pick up for no extra charge).

Albergo Sileo is a shiny-chandeliered, ten-room place with an elegant touch that has a contract to house train conductors who work the night shift. With maids doing double-time, they offer rooms from 19:00 to 9:00 only. If you can handle this, it's a great value (D-L65,000, Db-L75,000, Tb-L105,000, elevator; Via Magenta 39, tel. & fax 06/445-0246, Allesandro and Maria Savioli, NSE).

The **Fawlty Towers** is a backpacker-type place well-run by the Aussies from Enjoy Rome. It's young, hip, and English-speaking, with a rooftop terrace, lots of information, and no curfew (shared co-ed, four-bed dorms for L30,000 per bed, S-L50,000, Sb-L65,000, D-L75,000, Db-L90,000, Tb-L100,000, elevator; Via Magenta 39, tel. 06/445-0374, fax 06/445-0734, reservations by credit card but pay in cash).

Hotel Magic is a tiny, just-renovated place run by a mother-daughter team (Carmella and Rosanna). It's clean and high enough off the road to have no traffic problems (ten rooms, Sb-L70,000, Db-L110,000, Tb-L140,000 with this book, tiny breakfast included, thin walls, midnight curfew; Via Milazzo 20, third floor, 00185 Roma, tel. & fax 06/495-9880, little English spoken, unreliable for reservations).

In the same building, also with lots of stairs, **Hotel Fenicia** is eager for your business (Db-L120,000, third person pays L25,000, no breakfast, try café Gima across the street, CC:VM; Via Milazzo 20, tel. & fax 06/490-342, Anna and Georgio).

Sleeping near the Station on/near Via Firenze

The next listings are where I generally stay: tranquil, safe, handy, central, and a short walk from the central station, air-port shuttle, 2 blocks beyond the Piazza Republica and the TI. The first four are family-run. Parking is actually workable on Via Firenze. Double-park below the hotel until a space without yellow lines becomes available and grab it (confirm locally that

Rome's Train Station Neighborhood

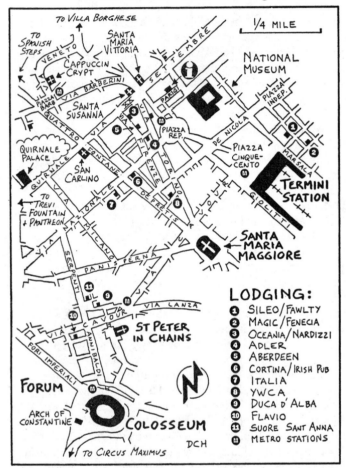

TO VILLA BORGHESE

¼ MILE

TO SPANISH STEPS

SANTA MARIA VITTORIA

NATIONAL MUSEUM

VENETO

CAPPUCCIN CRYPT

VIA BARBERINI

PIAZZA BARB.

SANTA SUSANNA

QUATTRO FONTANE

PIAZZA INDEP.

PIAZZA REP.

DE NICOLA

PIAZZA CINQUE-CENTO

MARSALA

GIOLITTI

TERMINI STATION

QUIRNALE PALACE

SAN CARLINO

QUIRINALE

NAZIONALE

VIA FIRENZE

VIA DE PRETIS

TO TREVI FOUNTAIN + PANTHEON

VIA MILANO

SERPENTI

PANIS PERNA

SANTA MARIA MAGGIORE

VIA

VIA LANZA

VIA CAVOUR

VIA ANNIBALDI

ST PETER IN CHAINS

FORI IMPERIALI

FORUM

ARCH OF CONSTANTINE

COLOSSEUM

N

DCH

TO CIRCUS MAXIMUS

LODGING:
1. SILEO/FAWLTY
2. MAGIC/FENECIA
3. OCEANIA/NARDIZZI
4. ADLER
5. ABERDEEN
6. CORTINA/IRISH PUB
7. ITALIA
8. YWCA
9. DUCA D' ALBA
10. FLAVIO
11. SUORE SANT ANNA
M. METRO STATIONS

it's still legal). The defense ministry is nearby, and you've got heavily armed guards all night. All the orange buses which rumble down Via Nazionale take you to Piazza Venezia. Beyond that, #75 and #170 go to Trastevere (first stop after crossing the river), #64 to the Vatican (last stop—jammed with people and thieves), and #57 to Circus Maximus.

Hotel Nardizzi Americana is the best value in its price range. Traffic noise in the front rooms is a problem in the summer, when you'll want the window open (D-L100,000,

Db-L120,000, T-L140,000, Tb-L160,000, prices promised through 1998 with this book, also four- and five-bed rooms, including breakfast; in summer and winter months they offer four nights for the price of three and discounts for longer stays, CC:VMA; Via Firenze 38, 00184 Roma, elevator, tel. 06/488-0368, fax 06/488-0035, helpful Nik speaks English).

Hotel Oceania (one floor below Nardizzi) is a peaceful slice of air-conditioned heaven. Its nine newly-renovated rooms are spotless, spacious and quiet (Sb-L170,000, Db-L230,000, Tb-L295,000, Qb-L345,000, 10 percent off with this book, includes breakfast, CC:VMA; Via Firenze 38, 00184 Roma, tel. 06/482-4696, fax 06/488-5586, e-mail: hoceania@tin.it, the son Stefano SE).

Residence Adler, with its wide halls, garden patio, and 16 big, quiet, and elegant rooms in a great locale, is a good deal, run by a charming family (D-L125,000, Db-L150,000, T-L145,000, Tb-L200,000, Q-L190,000, Qb-L240,000, including breakfast, CC:VMA, elevator; Via Modena 5, 00184 Roma, tel. 06/484-466, fax 06/488-0940, NSE).

Hotel Aberdeen is my classiest hotel listing and a good value for Rome. It has mini-bars, phones, TVs, and showers in its quiet, modern rooms; offers a first-class breakfast buffet; and is warmly run by Annamaria, with support from her cousins Sabrina and Cinzia, and trusty Reda on the late shift (Sb-L145,000, Db-L210,000, Tb-L250,000, with this book through 1998, L40,000 less per room in August and winter, including fine breakfast, air-con for an extra fee, CC:VMA, garage-L35,000; reach up and swing those knockers at Via Firenze 48, 00184 Roma, tel. 06/482-3920, fax 06/482-1092, SE).

Hotel Cortina, run by the Aberdeen folks, is similarly quiet, classy and comfortable. For the same prices as the Aberdeen, you get less soul but free air-conditioning (15 rooms, Db-L210,000 with breakfast in your room; Via Nazionale 18, 00184 Roma, tel. 06/481-9794, fax 06/481-9220, John Carlo SE).

Hotel Pensione Italia, in a busy, interesting, handy locale, placed safely on a quiet street next to the Ministry of the Interior, is comfortable, airy, bright, clean, and thoughtfully run by English-speaking Andrea and Abdul (23 rooms, Sb-L100,000, Db-L150,000, Tb-L200,000, with breakfast, with cash and this book through 1998, all rooms one-third off in August, elevator; Via Venezia 18, just off Via Nazionale, tel. 06/482-8355, fax 06/474-5550).

The YWCA Casa Per Studentesse accepts women, couples, groups of men, and couples with children but not single men. It's an institutional place, filled with white-uniformed maids, more-colorful Third World travelers, and 75 single beds, closed from midnight to 7:00 a.m. (L35,000 per person in three- and four-bed rooms, S-L50,000, Sb-L70,000, D-L80,000, Db-L100,000, breakfast included; Via C. Balbo 4, 00184 Roma, 5 blocks toward the Colosseum from the station, tel. 06/488-0460, fax 06/487-1028).

Sleeping near the Colosseum (zip code: 00184)

One stop on the subway from the train station (to Metro: Cavour), these places are buried in a very Roman world of exhaust-stained medieval ambience.

Hotel Duca d'Alba is a classy, tight, and modern place just half a block from the metro station (Sb-L180,000, Db-L260,000, with this book through 1998, all air-con and with breakfast, extra bed-L40,000, CC:VMA; Via Leonina 14, 00184 Roma, tel. 06/484471, fax 06/488-4840, SE, e-mail:duca.d'alba@venere.it).

Hotel Flavio is a real hotel with an Old World TV-lounge/lobby, an elevator, and elegant furnishings throughout in a quiet setting. Its weakness is dim lights and lousy tub-showers down the hall for the five cheap doubles (S-L70,000, Sb-L80,000, D-L115,000, Db-L150,000, family rooms available, breakfast extra, CC:VMA; hiding almost torchlit under vines on a tiny street a block toward the Colosseum from Via Cavour at Via Frangipane 34, Metro: Cavour, tel. 06/679-7203, fax 06/679-6246, enough English). They also run the neary Holel Romano (same prices as Falvio, CC:VMA, Largo Corrado Ricci 32, tel. & fax 06/679-5851.

Suore di Sant Anna was built for Ukrainian pilgrims. The sisters are sweet, but the male staff doesn't seem to care. It's clumsy and difficult (23:00 curfew), but once you're in, you've got a comfortable home in a classic Roman village locale (S-L42,000, D-L84,000, including breakfast, consider a monkish dinner for L26,000 more; off the corner of Via dei Serpenti and Via Baccina at Piazza Madonna dei Monti 3, Metro: Cavour, tel. 06/485-778, fax 06/487-1064).

Sleeping near the Campo dei Fiori (zip code: 00186)

Hotel Campo dei Fiori is an ideal location for wealthy bohemians who value centrality, just off the Campo dei Fiori, with comfortable rooms and an unreal rooftop terrace (D-L140,000, Db-L200,000, includes breakfast, CC:VM, lots of stairs and no elevator, Via del Biscione 6, tel. 06/6880-6865, fax 06/687-6003).

The **Albergo del Sole** is filled with German groups but well-located (D-L130,000, small Db-L150,000, Db-L170,000, no breakfast; Via del Biscione 76, tel. 06/688-06873, fax 06/689-3787).

Hotel Navona is a ramshackle 25-room hotel occupying an ancient building in a perfect locale a block off Piazza Navona and run by an Australian named Corry (S-L85,000, Sb-L95,000, D-L125,000, Db-L140,000 with breakfast, family rooms, lots of student groups; Via dei Sediari 8, tel. 06/686-4203, fax 06/688-03802, SE).

Casa di Santa Brigida is also near the characteristic Campo dei Fiori. With soft-spoken sisters gliding down polished hallways, and pearly gates instead of doors, this lavish convent makes the exhaust-stained Roman tourist feel like he's died and gone to heaven. If you're unsure of your destiny, this is worth the splurge (twins with all the comforts-L240,000; Piazza Farnese 96, tel. 06/688-92596, fax 06/688-91573, SE). Some of its 20 rooms overlook the Piazza Farnese.

Sleeping near the Vatican Museum (zip code: 00192)

Pension Alimandi is a good value, run by the friendly and entrepreneurial Alimandi brothers: Paolo, Enrico, Luigi, and Germano (35 rooms, Sb-L130,000, Db-L170,000, Tb-L200,000, 5 percent discount with this book and cash, CC:VMA, elevator, optional grand L15,000 breakfast, great roof garden, self-service washing machines, pool table, L27,000 garage, L70,000 airport pickup; down the stairs directly in front of the Vatican Museum, Via Tunisi 8, near metro: Ottaviano, tel. 06/397-26300, fax 06/397-23943, reserve by phone, no reply to fax means they are full, SE).

Hotel Spring House offers comfortable, clean, quiet rooms with balconies, TVs, refrigerators, and an impersonal staff (Db-L150,000–190,000, fancy Db with air-con L230,000 is best value, with breakfast, CC:VMA; Via Mocenigo 7, a block from Alimandi, tel. 06/397-20948, fax 06/397-21047, e-mail: ~spring~ @flashnet.it).

Hotel Gerber is sleek, modern, air-conditioned, business-like, and set in a quiet residential area (27 rooms, S-L110,000,

Sb-L170,000, Db-L220,000, Tb-L260,000, Qb-L310,000, 10
percent discount with this book, includes breakfast buffet,
CC:VMA; 1 block from Lepanto subway stop, Via degli
Scipioni 24, tel. 06/321-6485, fax 06/321-7048, Peter SE).

Hotel Benjamin is a tiny family affair with seven simple
but decent rooms on the third floor (D-L80,000, Db-L100,000,
T-L90,000, Tb-L100,000 prices promised through 1998 with
this book, no breakfast, no elevator, Metro: Ottaviano, corner of
Via Terenzio at Via Boezio 31, tel. & fax 06/688-02437, Sra
Franca Fondi NSE).

Suore Oblate dell Assunzione, a convent, rents clean,
peaceful and inexpensive rooms. No English is spoken and it's
hard to get in (S-L45,000, D-L90,000, T-L125,000; Via
Andrea Doria 42, 3 blocks from the Vatican Museum entrance,
tel. 06/397-37567, fax 06/397-37020).

Sleeping in Hostels and Dorms

Rome has only one real youth hostel—big, institutional, not
central or worth the trouble. For cheap dorm beds, consider
Fawlty Towers (above) or **Pensione Ottaviano** (25 beds in
two- to six-bed rooms, L25,000 per bed with sheets, no reservations, call from the station). They offer free showers, lockers,
a mini-fridge in each room, a fun, laid-back clubhouse feel, and
a good location (6 blocks from the Ottaviano Metro stop, near
the Vatican, at Via Ottaviano 6, tel. 06/397-37253). The same
slum visionaries run the dumpier **Pensione Sandy** (L25,000
beds, south of station, up a million depressing stairs, Via
Cavour 136, tel. 06/488-4585).

Eating in Rome

The cheapest meals in town are picnics (from *alimentari* shops or
open-air markets), self-serve rotisseries, and stand-up or take-out
meals from a **Pizza Rustica** (pizza slices sold by the weight, 100
grams is a hot cheap snack, 200 grams, or 2 *etti*, make a light
meal). Most alimentari will slice and stuff your sandwich (*panini*)
for you, if you buy the stuff there. For a fast/cheap/healthy
lunch, find a bar with a buffet spread of meat and vegetables and
ask for a mixed plate of vegetables with a hunk of mozzarella.

Eating in Trastevere or on the Campo dei Fiori

Trastevere: My best dinner tip is to go for Rome's Vespa
street ambience and find your own place in Trastevere or on

Campo dei Fiori. Guidebooks list Trastevere's famous places, but I'd wander the fascinating maze of streets near the Piazza Santa Maria in Trastevere and find a mom-and-pop place with barely a menu. Check out the tiny streets north of the church. At Piazza della Scala consider **Taverna della Scala** and the fine little gelateria. For the basic meal with lots of tourists, eat amazingly cheap at **Mario's** (three courses with wine and service for L17,000, near the Sisto bridge at Via del Moro 53, tel. 06/580-3809, closed Sunday).

Campo dei Fiori: For the ultimate romantic square setting, eat at whichever place looks best on Campo dei Fiori. Circle the square, considering each place. **La Carbonara** is the birthplace of pasta carbonara. The **Forno**, next door, is popular for hot greasy snacks. Meals on small nearby streets are a better value but lack that Campo dei Fiori magic. Nearby, on Piazza Farnese, **Da Giovanni Ar Galletto** has an ideal setting, moderate prices, and fine food (Piazza Farnese 102, tel. 06/686-1714, closed Sunday). Piazza Pasquino (a block off Piazza Navona, near Campo dei Fiori) has a couple of interesting eateries (a trendy salad place and **Cul de Sac** for bar munchies). **Trattoria Lilli** is a local favorite (on Via Tor di Nona, between the Tiber and Piazza Navona).

Eating near the Pantheon
Il Delfino is a handy self-service cafeteria on the Largo Argentina square (daily 7:00–21:00, closed Monday, not cheap but fast). Across the street, the **Frullati Bar** sells refreshing fruity frappés. The alimentari on the Pantheon square will make you a sandwich for a temple-porch picnic. **Volpetti** is a lively *tavola calda* (deli) selling hot food by the weight for take-out or to be eaten in their air-con basement dining room (across the street from Alfreddo's, at Via della Scrofa 31, where the famous fettucine was born, tel. 06/686-1940).

Eating near Hotels Nardizzi, Adler, and Aberdeen
Snack Bar Gastronomia is a great local hole-in-the-wall for lunch or dinner (Via Firenze 34, really cheap hot meals dished up from under glass counter, tap water with a smile, open until 20:00, closed Sunday). There's an *alimentari* (grocery store) across the street. **Pasticceria Dagnino**, popular for its top quality Sicilian specialties—especially pastries and ice cream— is where those who work at my recommended hotels eat (in

Galleria Esedra off Via Torino, a block from hotels, daily 7:00–22:00, tel. 06/481-8660). Their *arancino*, a rice, cheese and ham ball, is a greasy Sicilian favorite. Direct the construction of your meal at the bar, pay for your trayful at the cashier, and climb upstairs where you'll find the dancing Sicilian girls (free).

For an air-con, classier, local favorite serving traditional Roman cuisine, run by a group of men who enjoy their work, eat at **Hostaria Romana** (midway between the Trevi fountain and Piazza Barberini, Via del Boccaccio 1, tel. 06/474-5284, closed Sunday). And locals line up for **Ristorante da Giovanni** (L22,000 menu, just off Via XX Septembre at Via Antonio Salandra 1, tel. 06/485-950, closed Sunday). **Lon Fon** serves reasonably priced Chinese food (18:30–23:00, closed Wednesday, Via Firenze 44, tel. 06/482-5261).

The **McDonald's** on Piazza della Republica (free piazza seating outside), Piazza Barberini, and Via Firenze offer air-con interiors and a L7,000 salad bar that no American fast-food joint would recognize. **Greenpizz** is a fun and lively place for good pizza (Via Cernaia 16, tel. 06/474-1322). For pasta with Guinness or a late-night drink with live music, consider the lively **Irish Pub** (2 blocks from recommended hotels at Via Nazionale 18).

Eating near the Vatican Museum and Pension Alimandi

Viale Giulio Cesare is lined with cheap Pizza Rusticas and fun eateries (such as **Cipriani Self-Service Rosticceria** near the Ottaviano subway stop at Via Vespasiano, with pleasant outdoor seating). Turn your nose loose in the wonderful **Via Andrea Doria** open-air market 2 blocks in front of the Vatican Museum (between Via Tunisi and Via Andrea Doria, Monday–Saturday, open late on Tuesday and Friday, otherwise closed by 13:30). Antonio's **Hostaria dei Bastioni** is tasty and friendly with good sit-down meals (L9,000–12,000 pastas, L15,000 *secondi*, no cover charge, at corner of Vatican wall, Via Leone IV 29, tel. 06/397-23034, closed Sunday). **La Rustichella** has a good antipasti buffet (L12,000, enough for a meal) and fine pasta dishes (arrive by 19:30 or wait to get in, closed Monday, opposite church at end of Via Candia, Via Angelo 1, tel. 06/3972-0649).

Transportation Connections—Rome

By train to: Venice (6/day, 5–8 hrs, overnight possible), **Florence** (12/day, 2 hrs), **Pisa** (8/day, 3–4 hrs), **Genova**

(7/day, 6 hrs, overnight possible), **Milan** (12/day, 5 hrs, overnight possible), **Naples** (6/day, 2–3 hrs), **Brindisi** (2/day, 9 hrs), **Amsterdam** (2/day, 20 hrs), **Bern** (5/day, 10 hrs), **Frankfurt** (4/day, 14 hrs), **Munich** (5/day, 12 hrs), **Nice** (2/day, 10 hrs), **Paris** (5/day, 16 hrs), **Vienna** (3/day, 13–15 hrs). **Civita:** Take the Rome–Orvieto train (every 2 hrs, 75 min), catch the bus from Orvieto to Bagnoregio (8/day, 50 min, no service on Sundays), and walk to Civita. Train information: tel. 1478-88088.

Rome's Airport

A slick direct train link connects Rome's Leonardo da Vinci (a.k.a. Fiumicino) airport with the central Termini train station (L15,000 or free with first-class railpass, departures last year at 6:52, 7:22, then hourly at 22 minutes after each hour until 21:22, extra departures at 15:52, 17:52 and 19:52). Your hotel can arrange a taxi to the airport at any hour for about L75,000.

Airport information (tel. 06/65951) can connect you directly to your airline. (British Air tel. 06/6595-4190, Alitalia tel. 06/65642, American tel. 06/4274-1240, Delta tel. 06/1678-64114, KLM tel. 06/652-9286, SAS tel. 06/6501-0771, TWA tel. 06/47211, United tel. 06/1678-25181.)

Driving in Rome

Greater Rome is circled by the Grande Raccordo Anulare. This ring road has spokes that lead you into the center (much like the strings under the skin of a baseball). Entering from the north, leave the autostrada at the Settebagni exit. Following the ancient Via Salaria (and the black-and-white "Centro" signs), work your way doggedly into the Roman thick-of-things. This will take you along the Villa Borghese and dump you right on Via Veneto (where there's an Avis office). Avoid rush hour. Drive defensively: Roman cars stay in their lanes like rocks in an avalanche. Parking in Rome is dangerous. Park near a police station or get advice at your hotel. The garage is L35,000 a day. The Villa Borghese underground garage (Metro: Spagna) is handy.

Consider this: Your car is a worthless headache in Rome. Avoid a pile of stress and save money by parking at the huge, easy, and relatively safe lot behind the Orvieto station (follow "P" signs from autostrada), and catch the train to Rome (every two hours, 75 minutes).

VENICE (VENEZIA)

Soak all day in this puddle of elegant decay. Venice is Europe's best-preserved big city. It's a car-free urban wonderland of 100 islands, laced together by 400 bridges and 2,000 alleys, and doing well on the artificial respirator of tourism.

Born in a lagoon 1,500 years ago as a refuge from barbarians, Venice is overloaded with tourists and slowly sinking (unrelated facts). In the Middle Ages, the Venetians, becoming Europe's clever middleman for east-west trade, created a great trading empire. By smuggling in the bones of St. Mark (San Marco, in about 830), Venice gained religious importance as well. With the discovery of America and new trading routes to the Orient, Venetian power ebbed. But as Venice fell, her appetite for decadence grew. Through the 17th and 18th centuries Venice partied on the wealth accumulated through earlier centuries as a trading power.

Today Venice is home to about 75,000 people in its old city, down from a peak population of around 200,000. While there are about 500,000 in greater Venice (counting the mainland, not counting tourists), the old town has a small-town feel. Locals seem to know everyone. To see small-town Venice through the touristic flak, explore the back streets and try a Stand-Up Progressive Venetian Pub-Crawl Dinner.

Planning Your Time

Venice is worth at least a day on even the speediest tour. Hyper-efficient train travelers take the night train in and/or

Venice

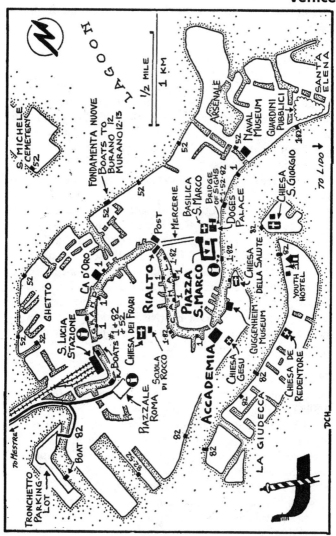

out. Sleep in the old center to experience Venice at its best:
early and late. For a one-day visit: cruise the Grand Canal,
do the major San Marco sights (the square, Doge's Palace,
St. Mark's Basilica), see the Church of the Frari for art, and
wander the back streets on a pub crawl (see Eating, below).

Venice's greatest sight is the city itself. Make time to simply wander. While doable in a day, Venice is worth two. It's a medieval cookie jar, and nobody's looking.

Orientation (tel. code: 041)

The island city of Venice is shaped like a fish. Its major thoroughfares are canals. The Grand Canal winds through the middle of the fish, starting at the mouth where all the people and food enter, passing under the Rialto Bridge, and ending at St. Mark's Square (San Marco). Park your 20th-century perspective at the mouth, and let Venice swallow you whole.

Venice is a car-less kaleidoscope of people, bridges, and odorless canals. The city has no real streets, and addresses are hopelessly confusing. There are six districts: San Marco (most touristy), Castello (behind San Marco), Cannaregio (from the station to the Rialto), San Polo (other side of the Rialto), Santa Croce, and Dorsoduro. Each district has about 6,000 address numbers. Luckily it's easy to find your way, since many street corners have a sign pointing you to the nearest major landmark, such as San Marco, Accademia, Rialto, and Ferrovia (the train station). To find your way, navigate by landmarks, not streets. Obedient visitors stick to the main thoroughfares as directed by these signs and miss the charm of back-street Venice.

Tourist Information

Tourist information offices are at the train station (8:00–19:00, crowded and surly) and near St. Mark's Square (much more helpful, at the vaporetto stop; from the church go to the lagoon, turn right, walk about 150 yards, and you'll run into it, Monday–Saturday 9:00–19:00 in summer, closed Sunday, and early off-season, tel. 041/529-8730). Pick up a free city map, the week's events, the latest museum hours, and confirm your sightseeing plans. The free periodical entertainment guide, *Un Ospite de Venezia* (a monthly listing of events, nightlife, museum hours, train and vaporetto schedules, emergency telephone numbers, and so on) is at the TI or fancy hotel reception desks. The cheap Venice map on sale at postcard racks has much more detail than the TI map. Also consider the little sold-with-the-postcards guidebook, with a city map and explanations of the major sights.

Arrival in Venice

A 2-mile-long causeway (highway and train lines) connects Venice to the mainland. Mestre, the sprawling mainland industrial base of Venice, has fewer crowds, cheaper hotels, plenty of parking lots, but no charm. Don't stop here. Trains regularly connect Mestre with the Santa Lucia station (6/hr, 5 min).

By Train: Venice's Santa Lucia train station plops you right into the old town on the Grand Canal, an easy vaporetto ride or fascinating 40-minute walk from San Marco. Upon arrival, skip the station's TI (San Marco's is better), confirm your departure plan (good train info desk), consider stowing unnecessary heavy bags at *deposito*, then walk straight out of the station to the canal. The dock for vaporettos #1 and #82 is on your left. Buy a L4500 ticket at the window and hop on a boat for downtown (direction Rialto or San Marco).

By Car: At Venice, the freeway ends like Medusa's head. Follow the green lights directing you to a parking lot with space. The standard place is Tronchetto (across the causeway and on the right) with a huge new multi-storied garage (L40,000 per day, half-price with a discount coupon from your hotel). From there you'll find travel agencies masquerading as tourist information offices and vaporetto docks for the boat connection (#82) to the town center. Don't let taxi boatmen con you out of the cheap vaporetto ride. Parking in Mestre is much cheaper (open-air lots L8,000 per day, L10,000-a-day garage across from the Mestre train station).

By Plane: A handy shuttle bus (30 minutes) or the cheaper L1500 bus #5 (60 minutes) connects the airport with the Tronchetto vaporetto stop. Those jetting in can get directly to San Marco by speedboat (L17,000).

Helpful Hints

The Venice fly-trap lures us in and takes our money any way it can. Count your change carefully. Accept the fact that Venice was a tourist town 400 years ago. It was, is, and always will be crowded. While 80 percent of Venice is actually an untouristy place, 80 percent of the tourists never notice. Hit the back streets.

Get Lost: Venice is the ideal town to explore on foot. Walk and walk to the far reaches of the town. Don't worry about getting lost. Get as lost as possible. Keep reminding yourself, "I'm on an island and I can't get off." When it comes time to find your way, just follow the directional arrows on building corners, or simply ask a local, *"Dové San Marco?"* ("Where is St. Mark's?") People in the tourist business (that's most Venetians) speak some English. If they don't, listen politely, watching where their hands point, say *"Grazie"* and head off in that direction.

Rip-offs, Theft, and Help: While petty thieves work the crowded main streets, vaporetto boats, and docks, the dark, late-night streets of Venice are safe. A new service called Venezia No Problem aids tourists who've been mistreated by any Venetian business (tel. 041/167-355920).

Money: Bank rates vary. I like the Banco di Sicilia, a block toward San Marco from Campo San Bartolomeo. American Express, famous for its "no commission," makes up for that with mediocre rates. Non-bank exchange bureaus will cost you $10 more than a bank for a $200 exchange. A 24-hour cash machine near the Rialto vaporetto stop exchanges U.S. dollars and other currencies into lire at fair rates.

The "Rolling Venice" Youth Discount Pass: This L5,000 pass—giving those under 30 discounts on sights, transportation, information on cheap eating and sleeping— is worthwhile for a long stay (Monday–Friday 10:00–13:00, Tuesday and Thursday also open 15:00–18:00, closed Wednesday; behind American Express office, Corte Contarina 1529; tel. 041/274-7637).

Water: Venetians pride themselves on having pure, safe, and tasty tap water piped in from the foothills of the Alps (which you can actually see from Venice bell towers on crisp, clear winter days).

Pigeon Poop: If bombed by a pigeon, resist the initial response to wipe it off immediately—it'll just smear into your hair. Wait until it dries and flake it off cleanly.

Laundry: A handy *lavanderia* (Laundromat) near St. Mark's and near most of my hotel listings is the full-service Laundry Gabriella (Monday–Friday 8:00–19:00, 985 Rio Terra Colonne, one bridge off the Merceria near San Zulian church, down Calle dei Armeni, tel. 041/522-1758). The closest laundromat to the Rialto is Lavanderia S.S. Apostoli (8:30–12:00, 15:00–19:00, closed Sunday, tel. 041/522-6650, on Campo S.S. Apostoli). At either place you can get 9 pounds of laundry washed and dried for L15,000. Drop it by in the morning, pick it up that afternoon. (Call to be sure they're open.)

Etiquette: Walk on the right and don't loiter on bridges. Picnicking is technically forbidden (keep a low profile). Dress modestly. Men should keep their shirts on. When visiting St. Mark's or other major churches, men and women should cover their knees and shoulders.

Getting Around Venice

The public transit system is a fleet of motorized bus-boats called *vaporetti*. They work like city buses except that they never get a flat, the stops are docks, and if you get off between stops, you may drown. For most, only two lines matter: #1 is the slow boat, taking 45 minutes to make every stop along the entire length of the Grand Canal; and #82 is the fast boat which zips down the Grand Canal in 20 minutes, stopping only at Tronchetto (car-park), Piazzale Roma (bus station), Ferrovia (train station), Rialto Bridge, and San Marco. Buy a L4,500 ticket before boarding or (for an extra fee) from a conductor on board. There are 24-hour (L15,000) and 72-hour (L30,000) passes, but I've never ferried enough to merit purchasing one (although it's fun to be able to hop on and off carelessly).

Only three bridges cross the Grand Canal, but *traghetti* (little L700 ferry gondolas, marked on better maps) shuttle locals and in-the-know tourists across the Grand Canal at seven handy locations (see downtown Venice map). Take advantage of these time-savers. They can also save money. For instance, while most tourists take the L4,500 vaporetto to connect St. Mark's with Salute Church, a L700 traghetto also does the job.

Grand Canal Tour of Venice

Grab a front seat on boat #82 (fast, 20 minutes) or #1 (slow, 45 minutes) to cruise the entire Canale Grande from Tronchetto (car-park) or Ferrovia (train station) to San Marco. If you can't snag a front seat, lurk nearby and take one when it becomes available, or find a seat outside at the very back of the boat. While Venice is a barrage on the senses that hardly needs a narration, these notes give the cruise a little meaning and help orient you to this great city. Some city maps (on sale at postcard racks) have a handy Grand Canal map on the back side.

Venice, built in a lagoon, sits on pilings: pine trees driven 15 feet into the mud. More than 100 canals—about 25 miles in length—drain the city, dumping like streams into the Grand Canal.

Downtown Venice

LODGING:

1	GUERATTO	**11**	MASETTO
2	STURION	**12**	MARIN
3	CANADA	**14**	GAMBERO
4	BRUNO	**15**	CAMPIELLO
5	CANEVA	**16**	PAGANELLI
6	RIVA	**17**	ACCADEMIA
7	PIAVA	**18**	GALLERIA
8	TIEPOLO	**19**	ALBORETTI
9	DONI		
10	CORONA		

●1·82 VAPORETTI STOPS
W/ LINE #'s

●••••● TRAGHETTO ROUTES

Venice is a city of palaces. The most lavish were built fronting this canal. This cruise is the only way to really appreciate the front doors of this unique and historic chorus line of mansions from the days when Venice was the world's richest city. Strict laws prohibit any changes in these buildings, so while landowners gnash their teeth, we can enjoy Europe's best-preserved medieval city—slowly rotting. Many of the grand buildings are now vacant. Others harbor chandeliered elegance above mossy ground floors.

Start at Tronchetto (the bus and car-park) or the train station (a good example of Fascist architecture built during Mussolini's time). F.S. stands for "Ferrovie dello Stato," the Italian state railway system. The bridge at the station is one of only three that cross the Canale Grande.

Vaporetto stop #4 (San Marcuola-Ghetto) is near the world's original ghetto, when this area was set aside as the local Jewish quarter in 1516. This urban island developed into one of the most closely knit business and cultural quarters of any Jewish community in Italy.

As you cruise, notice the traffic signs. Venice's main thoroughfare is busy with traffic. You'll see all kinds of boats: taxis, police boats, garbage, even brown-and-white UPS boats. Venice's 500 sleek, black, graceful gondolas are a symbol of the city. They cost up to $35,000 apiece and are built with a slight curve so that one oar propels them in a straight line.

At the Ca d'Oro stop (stop #6), notice the lacy Gothic palace of the same name. Named the "House of Gold," it's considered the most elegant Venetian Gothic palace on the canal. Unfortunately its art gallery interior shows nothing of its palatial origins.

After vaporetto stop #6, on the right, the outdoor produce market bustles with people in the morning, but is quiet with only a few grazing pigeons the rest of the day. Can you see the traghetto gondola ferrying shoppers—standing like Washington crossing the Delaware—back and forth? The huge post office, usually with a postal boat moored at its blue posts, is on the left just before the Rialto Bridge.

A major landmark of Venice, the Rialto Bridge, is lined with shops and tourists. Built in 1592, with a span of 42 meters, it was an impressive engineering feat in its day. Locals call the summit of this bridge the "icebox of Venice" for its cool breeze. But it's also a great place to kiss. "Rialto" means "high river." The restaurants lining the canal beyond the bridge feature high prices and low quality.

The Rialto, a separate town in the early days of Venice, has always been the commercial district, while San Marco was the religious and governmental center. Today a street called the Merceria connects the two, providing travelers with human traffic jams and a gauntlet of shopping temptations.

Take a deep whiff of Venice. What's all this nonsense about stinky canals? All I smell is my shirt. By the way, how's your captain? Smooth dockings? To get to know him, stand up in the bow and block his view.

Notice how the rich marble facades are just a veneer covering no-nonsense brick buildings. And notice the characteristic chimneys.

After the San Silvestro stop you'll see (on the right) a 13th-century admiral's palace. Venetian admirals marked their palaces with twin obelisks.

After the San Tomá stop look down the side canal (on the right) before the bridge to see the fire station and the fireboats ready to go.

The wooden Accademia Bridge crosses the Grand Canal and leads to the Accademia Gallery, filled with the best Venetian paintings. Put up in 1932 as a temporary fix for the original iron one, locals liked it, so it stayed.

Cruising under the bridge, you'll get a classic view of the Salute Church, built as a thanks to God when the devastating plague of 1630 passed. It's claimed that more than a million trees were used for the foundation alone. Much of the surrounding countryside was deforested by Venice. Trees were needed both to fuel the furnaces of its booming glass industry and to prop up this city in the mud.

The low white building on the right (before the church) is the Peggy Guggenheim Gallery. She willed the city a fine collection of modern art.

Just before the Salute stop (on the right), the house with the big view windows and the red and wild Andy Warhol painting on the living room wall was lived in by Mick Jagger. In the 1970s, this was famous as Venice's rock-and-roll-star party house.

The building on the right with the golden ball is the Dogana da Mar, a 16th-century customs house. Its two bronze Atlases hold a statue of Fortune riding the ball.

As you prepare to de-boat at stop #15—San Marco—look from left to right out over the lagoon. A wide harborfront walk leads past the town's most elegant hotels to the green area in the distance. This is the public garden, the only sizable park in town. Farther out is the Lido, Venice's beach. It's tempting with its sand and casinos, but its car traffic breaks into the medieval charm of Venice.

The dreamy church that seems to float is the architect Palladio's San Giorgio. It's just a scenic vaporetto ride away. Find the Tintoretto paintings in the church (such as the *Last Supper*) and take the elevator up the bell tower for a terrific, crowd-free view (L3000, daily 10:00–12:30, 14:30–17:30, tel. 041/522-7827). Beyond San Giorgio (to your right, if you're at San Marco) is a residential chunk of Venice called the Guidecca.

Get out at the San Marco stop. Directly ahead is Harry's Bar. Hemingway drank here when it was a characteristic no-name osteria and the gondoliers' hangout. Today, of course, it's the overpriced hangout of well-dressed Americans who don't mind paying triple for their drinks to make the scene. Piazza San Marco—a much better place to make the scene—is just around the corner.

For more vaporetto fun, ride a boat around the city (ask for the *circulare*, cheer-kew-lah-ray) and out into the lagoon. Plenty of boats leave from San Marco for the beach (Lido), and speedboats offer tours of nearby islands: Burano is a quiet, picturesque fishing and lace town, Murano is the glassblowing island, and Torcello has the oldest churches and mosaics, but is an otherwise dull and desolate island. Boat #12 takes you to these remote points slower and cheaper.

Sights—Venice, on St. Mark's Square

▲▲▲St. Mark's Square (Piazza San Marco)—Surrounded by splashy and historic buildings, Piazza San Marco is filled with music, lovers, pigeons, and tourists by day and is your private rendezvous with the Middle Ages late at night. Europe's greatest dance floor is the romantic place to be. This is the first place to flood, has Venice's best tourist information office (go to lagoon, turn right), and offers fine public restrooms (Albergo Diorno—"day hotel," L500 WC, shower, between Piazza San Marco and American Express office).

With your back to the church, survey one of Europe's great urban spaces and the only square in Venice to merit the title "Piazza." Nearly two football fields long, it's surrounded by the offices of the republic. On the right are the "old offices" (16th-century Renaissance). On the left are the "new offices" (17th-century Baroque). Napoleon enclosed the square with the more simple and austere neoclassical wing across the far end and called this "the most beautiful drawing room in Europe."

The clock tower, a Renaissance tower built in 1496, marks the entry to the Mercerie, the main shopping drag connecting San Marco with the Rialto. From the piazza you can see the bronze men (Moors) swing their huge clappers at the top of each hour. In the 17th century, one of them knocked an unsuspecting worker off the top and to his death—probably the first-ever killing by a robot. Notice the world's first "digital" clock on the tower facing the square (with dramatic flips every five minutes).

For a slow and pricey evening thrill, invest L10,000 (plus L5000 if the orchestra plays) in a beer or coffee in one of the elegant cafés with the dueling orchestras. If you're going to sit awhile and savor the scene, it's worth the splurge. For the most thrills L1500 can get you in Venice, buy a bag of pigeon seed and become popular in a flurry.

▲▲St. Mark's Basilica—Since about 830, it has housed the saint's bones. The mosaic above the door at the far left of the church shows two guys carrying Mark's coffin into the church. Mark looks pretty grumpy after the long voyage from Egypt. The church has 4,000 square meters of Byzantine mosaics. The best and oldest are in the atrium (turn right as you enter and stop under the last dome). Face the piazza, gape up (it's OK, no pigeons), and study the story of Noah, the Ark, and the flood (two by two, the wicked being drowned, Noah sending out the dove, a happy rainbow, and a sacrifice of thanks). Now face the church and read clockwise the story of Adam and Eve that rings the bottom of the dome. Step inside the church (stairs on right lead to bronze horses) and notice the rolling mosaic marble floor. Stop under the central dome and look up for the Ascension. (Modest dress, no shorts or bare shoulders, free, Monday–Saturday 9:45–19:30, Sunday 14:00–17:00, tel. 041/522-5205.) See the schedule board in the atrium listing two free English guided tours of the church each week. The church is particularly beautiful when lit at the 18:45 mass on Saturday, 14:00–17:00 Sunday, and some middays.

In the museum upstairs (L4,000, daily 9:45–17:00), you can see an up-close mosaic exhibition, a fine view of the church interior, a view of the square from the horse balcony, and (inside, in their own room) the newly restored original bronze horses. These well-traveled horses, made during the days of Alexander the Great (fourth century B.C.), were taken to Rome by Nero, to Constantinople/Istanbul by Constantine, to Venice by crusaders, to Paris by Napoleon, back "home" to Venice when Napoleon fell, and finally indoors out of the acidic air.

The treasury and altarpiece of the church (requiring two L3,000 admissions) give you the best chance outside of Istanbul or Ravenna to see the glories of Byzantium. Venetian crusaders looted the Christian city of Constantinople and brought home piles of lavish loot (until the advent of TV evangelism, perhaps the lowest point in Christian history). Much of this plunder is stored in the treasury of San Marco (*tesoro*). As you view these treasures, remember most were made in A.D. 500, while western Europe was still rooting in the mud. Behind the high altar lies the body of St. Mark ("Marxus") and the Pala d'Oro, a golden altarpiece made (A.D. 1000–1300) with 80 Byzantine enamels. Each shows a religious scene set in gold and precious stones. Both of these sights are interesting and historic, but neither is as much fun as two bags of pigeon seed.

▲▲▲**Doge's Palace (Palazzo Ducale)**—The seat of the Venetian government and home of its ruling duke, or *doge*, this was the most powerful half-acre in Europe for 400 years (L14,000 combo-ticket includes Correr museum also, daily 8:30–19:00, last entry at 17:30). While each room has a short English description, the fast-moving 90-minute tape-recorded guided tour wand is wonderfully done and worth the L7,000 if you don't have *Mona Winks* and you're planning to really understand the Palace. (Vagabond lovers, sightseeing cheek to cheek, can crank up the volume and split one wand).

The palace was built to show off the power and wealth of the republic and remind all visitors that Venice was number one. Built in Venetian Gothic style, the bottom has pointy arches and the top has an Eastern or Islamic flavor. Its columns sat on pedestals, but in the thousand years since they were erected, the palace has settled into the mud, and they have vanished.

Enjoy the newly restored facades from the courtyard. Notice a grand staircase (with nearly naked Moses and Paul Newman at the top). Even the most powerful visitors climbed this to meet the doge. This was the beginning of an architectural power trip. The doge, the elected-for-life king of this "dictatorial republic," lived near the halls of power with his family on the first floor. From his lavish quarters, you'll follow the one-way tour through the public rooms of the top floor, finishing with the Bridge of Sighs and the prison. The place is wallpapered with masterpieces by Veronese and Tintoretto. Don't worry much about the great art. Enjoy the building.

In room 12, the Senate Room, the 200 senators met, debated, and passed laws. From the center of the ceiling, Tintoretto's *Triumph of Venice* shows the city in all her glory. Lady Venice, in heaven with the Greek gods, stands high above the lesser nations who swirl respectfully at her feet with gifts.

The Armory shows remnants of the military might the empire employed to keep the east-west trade lines open (and the local economy booming). Squint out the window at the far end for a fine view of Palladio's San Georgio Church and the Lido (cars, casinos, crowded beaches) in the distance.

After the huge brown globes, you'll enter the giant Hall of the Grand Council (180 feet long, capacity 2,000) where the entire nobility met to elect the senate and doge. Ringing the room are portraits of 76 doges (in chronological order). One, a doge who opposed the will of the Grand Council, is blacked out. Behind the doge's throne, you can't miss Tintoretto's monsterpiece, *Paradise*. At 1,700 square feet, this is the world's largest oil painting. Christ and Mary are surrounded by a heavenly host of 500 saints.

Walking over the Bridge of Sighs, you'll enter the prisons. The doges could sentence, torture, and jail their opponents secretly and in the privacy of their own homes. As you walk back over the bridge, wave to the gang of tourists gawking at you.

▲**Museo Civico Correr**—The entire San Marco complex is evolving into one grand sight. The until-lately rarely visited city history museum is now included (whether you like it or not) with the Doge's Palace admission. It offers dusty bits of Venice's glory days (globes, flags, coins, paintings, and so on, all well-explained in English) and fine views of Piazza San Marco. The second floor is a lot of walking and worth a look only if you like musty old oil paintings (Pinacotek–English descriptions) and exhibits on the unification of Italy (Risorgimento–no English). Entry is on the square opposite the church (L14,000 combo ticket with Doge's Palace, daily 9:00–19:00, November–May 9:00–17:00).

▲**Campanile di San Marco**—Ride the elevator 300 feet to the top of the bell tower for the best view in Venice. Photos on the wall inside show how this bell tower crumbled into a pile of bricks in 1902, 1,000 years after it was built. For an ear-shattering experience, be on top when the bells ring

(L6,000, daily 9:00–18:30). The golden angel at its top always faces into the wind.

More Sights—Venice

▲▲**Galleria dell' Accademia**—Venice's top art museum is packed with the painted highlights of the Venetian Renaissance (Bellini, Veronese, Tiepolo, Giorgione, Testosterone, and Canaletto). It's just over the wooden Accademia Bridge (L12,000, Monday–Saturday 9:00–19:00, Sunday 9:00–14:00; expect morning and midday delays, as they allow only 300 visitors at a time, come late to miss crowds, tel. 041/522-2247). There's a fine pizzeria at the bridge (Snack Bar Accademia Foscarini, see Eating, below.)

▲**Peggy Guggenheim Collection**—This popular collection of far-out art, including works by Picasso, Chagall, and Dali, offers one of Europe's best reviews of the art styles of the 20th century (L12,000, Wednesday–Monday 11:00–18:00, closed Tuesday, near the Accademia).

▲▲**Chiesa dei Frari**—This great Gothic Franciscan church, an artistic highlight of Venice featuring three great masters, offers more art per lira than any other Venetian sight. Freeload on English-language tours to get the most out of the Titian *Assumption* above the high altar. Then move one chapel to the right to see Donatello's wood carving of St. John the Baptist almost live. And for the climax, continue right through an arch into the sacristy to sit before Bellini's *Madonna and the Saints*. The genius of Bellini, perhaps the greatest Venetian painter, is obvious in the pristine clarity, believable depth, and reassuring calm of this three-paneled altarpiece. Notice the rich colors of Mary's clothing and how good it is to see a painting in its intended setting. For many, these three pieces of art make a visit to the Accademia Gallery unnecessary (or they may whet your appetite for more). Before leaving, check out the neoclassical pyramid-shaped tomb of Canova and (opposite that) the grandiose tomb of Titian, the Venetian. Compare the carved marble Assumption behind his tombstone portrait with the painted original above the high altar (L2,000, Monday–Saturday 9:00–12:00, 14:30–18:00, free on Sunday 15:00–18:00).

▲**Scuola di San Rocco**—Next to the Frari church, another lavish building bursts with art, including some 50 Tintorettos. The best paintings are upstairs, especially the *Crucifixion* in the smaller room. View the neck-breakingly splendid ceiling paintings with one of the mirrors (*specchio*) available at the entrance (L8,000, daily 9:00–17:30, last entrance 17:00). For *molto* Tiepolo (14 stations of the cross), drop by the nearby Church of San Polo.

Ca' Rezzonico—This 18th-century Grand Canal palazzo is now open as the Museo del '700 Veneziano, offering a good look at the life of Venice's rich and famous in the 1700s, along with frequent temporary exhibits for an additional admission fee (L12,000, Saturday–Thursday 10:00–16:00, closed Friday, at a vaporetto stop of the same name).

▲Gondola Rides—A rip-off for some but a traditional must for romantics; gondoliers charge about L100,000 for a 40-minute ride (less during the day). You can divide the cost—and the romance—by up to six people (some take seven if you beg and they're hungry). Glide through nighttime Venice with your head on someone else's shoulder. Follow the moon as it sails past otherwise unseen buildings. Silhouettes gaze down from bridges, while window glitter spills onto the black water. You're anonymous in the city of masks as the rhythmic thrust of your striped-shirted gondolier turns old crows into songbirds. For cheap gondola thrills, stick to the L700 one-minute ferry ride on a Grand Canal traghetto, or hang out on a bridge along the gondola route and wave at (or drop leftover pigeon seed on) romantics.

▲Glassblowing—Don't go all the way to Murano Island to see glassblowing demonstrations. A demo's a demo. For the handiest show, wait by one of several glassworks near St. Mark's Square and follow any tour group into the furnace room for a fun and free ten-minute show. You'll usually see a vase and a "leetle 'orse" made from molten glass. The commercial that always follows in the showroom is actually entertaining. Prices around St. Mark's have a sizable tour-guide commission built in. Serious glass-shoppers buy at small shops on Murano Island.

Santa Elena—For a pleasant peek into a completely untouristy residential side of Venice, catch the boat from San Marco to the neighborhood of Santa Elena (at the fish's tail). This 100-year-old suburb lives as if there were no tourism. You'll find a kid-friendly park, a few lazy restaurants, and beautiful sunsets over San Marco.

Old-Time Venetian Concerts—Vivaldi is as trendy here as Strauss in Vienna and Mozart in Salzburg. In fact you'll find frilly young Vivaldis all over town hawking concert tickets. The TI has a list of this week's concerts (tickets from L30,000 up). The

Venice Lagoon

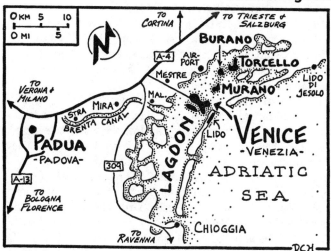

Venice Orchestra plays traditional Vivaldi concerts in 18th-century attire at the Scuola Grande di San Giovanni Evengelista (L30,000–50,000, tel. 041/520-7823).

Sights—Venice Lagoon

Several interesting islands hide out in the Venice Lagoon. **Burano**, famous for its lace-making, is a sleepy island with a sleepy community—village Venice without the glitz. Lace fans enjoy Burano's Scuola di Merletti (L5000, Tuesday–Sunday 10:00–16:00, closed Monday, tel. 041/730-034). **Torcello**, another lagoon island, is dead except for its church, which claims to be the oldest in Venice (L2,000, daily 10:00–12:30, 14:00–17:00, tel. 041/730–084). It's impressive for its mosaics, but not worth a look on a short visit unless you really have your heart set on Ravenna but can't make it there. The island of **Murano**, famous for its glass factories, has the Museo Vetrario, which displays the very best of 700 years of Venetian glassmaking (L8,000, Thursday–Tuesday 10:00–17:00, closed Wednesday, tel. 041/739-586). The islands are reached easily but slowly by vaporetto (from the Fondamente Nuove dock). Four-hour speedboat tours of these three lagoon destinations leave twice a day from the dock near the Doge's Palace.

Sleeping in Venice
(L1,600 = about $1, tel. code: 041)

Sleep Code: **S**=Single, **D**=Double/Twin, **T**=Triple, **Q**=Quad, **b**=bathroom, **t**=toilet only, **s**=shower only, **CC**=Credit Card (Visa, MasterCard, Amex), **SE**=Speaks English, **NSE**=No English. Breakfast is included unless otherwise noted. I never met an elevator in a Venetian hotel.

Reserve a room as soon as you know when you'll be in town. Call first to see what's available. Follow up with a fax unless you're already on the road. Most places will take a credit card for a deposit. If everything's full, don't despair. Call a day or two in advance and fill in a cancellation. While many stay in a nearby less-crowded place and side trip to Venice, I can't imagine not sleeping downtown. If you arrive on an overnight train, your room may not be ready. Drop your bag at the hotel and dive right into Venice.

Don't book (or confirm) through the tourist office (which pockets a L15,000-per-person "deposit"). The prices I've listed here are for those who book direct. Prices may be cheaper (or soft) off-season. If on a budget, ask for a cheaper room or a discount. I've let location and character be my priorities. Rooms are clean, quiet, and generally stark, with high ceilings, slick little modern pre-fab shower/toilet/sink units, bare floors, and rickety freestanding furniture.

Sleeping near St. Mark's Square
(zip code: 30124)

Hotel Caneva is a funky, clean, vinyl-feeling place with plain, big and bright rooms, lots of canal ambience and a wonderful family-run feeling. Seventeen of its 23 rooms overlook a canal (S-L70,000, Sb-L100,000, D-L100,000, Db-L140,000, T-L135,000, Tb-L190,000, CC:VMA; midway between Rialto and San Marco near Chiesa la Fava but very quiet, Ramo Dietro La Fava #5515, 30122 Venezia, tel. 041/522-8118, fax 041/520-8676, Massimo and his family SE).

Hotel Riva, with gleaming marble hallways and bright modern rooms, is romantically situated on a canal along the gondola serenade route. You could actually dunk your breakfast rolls in the canal (but don't). Sandro may hold a corner (*angolo*) room if you ask. Reconfirm reservations you think you've made here. It's behind San Marco where the canals Rio di San Zulian and Rio del Mondo Nouvo hit Rio Canonica o Palazzo (two fourth-floor view D with adjacent showers-L120,000, Db-L150,000, Tb-L220,000; Ponte dell' Angelo, tel. 041/522-7034, fax 041/528-5551, unenthusiastic receptionists don't speak English).

Locanda Piave, with 12 fine rooms above a bright and classy lobby, is newly remodeled and very comfortable (D-L140,000, Db-L200,000, T-180,000, Tb-L260,000, family suites, air-con, CC:VMA; from Campo Santa Maria Formosa, go behind the church, over a bridge and 50 yards to Ruga Giuffa #4838/40, Castello, 30122 Venezia, tel. 041/528-5174, fax 041/523-8512, Mirella and Paolo SE).

Albergo Tiepolo, a simple old seven-room place tucked away down an alley just off Campo SS. Filippo e Giacomo, is pricey but well-located (D-L95,000, Db-L140,000, T-L130,000, Tb-L160,000, Q-160,000, Qb-L200,000; Campo SS. F e G #4510, tel. & fax 041/523-1315).

Albergo Doni is a dark, hardwood, clean, and quiet place with 12 dim-but-classy rooms run by a likable smart-aleck named Gina, who promises my readers one free down-the-hall shower each day (D-L100,000, Db-L140,000, Tb-L190,000, ceiling fans, prices with this book; use credit card to secure telephone reservations but must pay in cash; Riva Schiavoni, San Zaccaria N. #4656 Calle del Vin, tel. & fax 041/522-4267, Nick and Gina SE). From the Bridge of Sighs walk east along Riva Degli Schiavoni, over another bridge, take the first left (Calle del Vin), and follow the signs.

Albergo Corona is a squeaky-clean, confusing Old World place with nine hard-to-get basic rooms (D-L75,000, showers L3,000, lots of stairs; find Campo SS Filippo e Giacomo behind San Marco, go down Calle Sacristia, take first right then go left on Calle Corona to #4464, tel. 041/522-9174, SE).

Alloggi Masetto, well-located with four dirt-cheap rooms, is a homey place filled with birds, goldfish, and stacks of magazines, and run by Irvana Artico, a rude landlady who surprises you with pretty good English (D-L50,000, Db-L60,000, T-L70,000, Tb-75,000, confirm prices carefully two-night minimum, no breakfast, shower rapido or suffer Irvana's wrath; just off San Marco—from American Express head toward San Marco, first left, first left again through "Contarina" tunnel, follow yellow sign to Commmune di Venezia, jog left again and see her sign, Sotoportego Ramo Contarina, Frezzeria, tel. 041/523-0505).

Alloggi Alla Scala, a comfy and tidy seven-room place run by Senora Andreina della Fiorentina, is very central, tucked away on a quiet square with a famous spiral stairway called Corte Contarini del Bovolo (small Db-L100,000, big Db-L120,000, extra bed-L35,000, breakfast extra; near Campo Manin #4306, San Marco, tel. 041/521-0629, fax 041/522-8958).

Locanda Gambero, with 30 rooms, is the biggest one-star hotel in the San Marco area (S-L65,000–70,000, D-L110,000, Ds-L130,000, Db-L150,000, T-L160,000, Ts-L180,000, Tb-L200,000, CC:VM; a straight shot down Calle dei Fabbri from the Rialto vaporetto #1 dock; from Piazza San Marco walk down Calle dei Fabbri, over one bridge to #4685, tel. 041/522-4384, fax 041/520-0431, SE). These prices are as firm as ripe bananas. Gambero runs the pleasant art-deco "La Bistrot," serving old-time Venetian cuisine.

Sleeping near Waterfront and Doge's Palace

These places rub drainpipes with Venice's most palatial five-star hotels, about one canal down from the Bridge of Sighs on or just off the Riva degli Schiavoni waterfront promenade. Each, while pricey for the location and not particularly friendly, is professional and comfortable.

Hotel Campiello is a lacy and bright little 16-room place, ideally located 50 yards off the waterfront (Db-L200,000–250,000, CC:VMA, all air-con; behind Hotel Savoia, Riva Schiavoni, San Zaccaria #4647, tel. 041/520-5764, fax 041/520-5798).

Albergo Paganelli is right on the Riva degli Schiavoni with a few incredible view rooms (D-L150,000, small Db-L190,000, Db-L220,000 or L250,000 with canal view, Tb-L275,000, request *"con vista"* for view, most rooms are air-con, CC:VMA; at the San Zaccaria vaporetto stop, Riva degli Schiavoni #4182, Campo S. Zaccaria 4687, Castello, 30122 Venezia, tel. 041/522-4324, fax 041/523-9267, SE). With spacious rooms, carved and gilded headboards, chandeliers, and hair-dryers, this very hotelesque place is a good value. Seven of their 22 rooms are in a less interesting *dependencia* a block off the canal.

Sleeping near the Rialto Bridge
(zip code: 30125)

Locanda Sturion, with air-con and all the modern comforts, is pricey because it overlooks the Grand Canal (Db-L280,000,

Tb-L360,000, Qb-L380,000, canal view rooms cost extra, CC:VMA, miles of stairs; 100 yards from the Rialto Bridge opposite the vaporetto dock, San Polo, Rialto, Calle Sturion #679, 30125 Venezia, tel. 041/523-6243, fax 041/522-8378, SE, e-mail: sturion@tin.it). They require a bank check for a deposit.

Hotel Canada has 25 small, bright rooms (two D with adjacent bath-L170,000, Db-L200,000, CC:VM; Castello San Lio #5659, 30122 Venezia, tel. 041/522-9912, fax 041/523-5852, SE). A "typical noble Venetian home," it's ideally located on a small, lively square, just off Campo San Lio between the Rialto and San Marco.

Hotel da Bruno, 100 yards from Hotel Canada, has a central location, nice rooms, and all the comforts (Db-L220,000, CC:VMA; Salizzada S. Lio #5726, Castello, 30122 Venezia, tel. 041/523-0452, fax 041/522-1157, SE).

Albergo Guerrato, overlooking a handy and colorful produce market, one minute from the Rialto action, is run by friendly, creative and hard-working Roberto and Piero Caruso. Georgio takes the night shift. Their 800-year-old building is Old World simple, airy, and wonderfully characteristic (D-L105,000, Db-L145,000, T-L140,000, Tb-L190,000, Q-L180,000, Qb-L230,000, including a L4000 city map, prices promised through 1998 with this book, no double beds, CC:VM; walk over the Rialto away from San Marco, go straight about 3 blocks, turn right on Calle drio la Scimia—not Scimia, the block before— and you'll see the hotel sign, Calle drio la Scimia #240a, 30125 San Polo, tel. & fax 041/522-7131 or 528-5927, SE). My tour groups book this place for 50 nights each year. Sorry. If you fax without calling first, no reply within three days means they are booked up. (It's best to call first.)

Sleeping near the Accademia

This quiet area, next to the best painting gallery in town, is a ten-minute walk from any other sightseeing action with three classy hotels and a cheap monastery.

Pension Accademia fills the 17th-century Villa Maravege. While its 27 comfortable and air-con rooms are nothing extraordinary, you'll feel aristocratic gliding through its grand public spaces and lounging in its breezy garden (one S-L85,000, Sb-L160,000, Db-L270,000 or less off-season, family deals, CC:VMA, must send check to reserve; on corner of Rio della

Toletta and Rio di San Trovaso 200 yards from gallery, Dorsoduro #1058, Venezia 30123, tel. 041/523-7846, fax 041/523-9152, SE).

Hotel Galleria is a compact and velvety little 10-room place (S-L80,000, Sb-L115,000, D-L115,000, Db-L140,000-170,000 depending on size and season; overlooking canal next to gallery, Dorsoduro #878a, 20123 Venezia, tel. & fax 041/520-4172).

Hotel Agli Alboretti is a cozy, family-run, 25-room place in a quiet neighborhood a block behind the Accademia Museum (Db-L220,000, air-con, CC:VMA; 100 yards from the Accademia vaporetto stop at #884 Accademia, tel. 041/523-0058, fax 041/521-0158, SE). You'll have breakfast in a shady patio.

Foresteria Domus Cavanis is a simple church-run dorm offering cheap beds (S-L50,000, D-L75,000, breakfast extra; next to Hotel Agli Alboretti at #912 on Rio Antonio Foscarini, tel. & fax 041/528-7374).

Sleeping near the Train Station

Hotel Marin is three minutes from the train station but completely out of the touristic bustle of the Lista di Spagna. Just renovated, cozy, and cheery, it seems like a 19-bedroom home the moment you cross the threshold (S-L75,000, D-L108,000, Db-L135,000, T-L145,000, Tb-L180,000, Q-L185,000, Qb-L215,000, prices good with this book and if you pay cash, CC:VMA; San Croce #670b, tel. & fax 041/718-022 or 041/721-485, e-mail: htl.marin@gpnet.it). It's family-run by helpful, friendly English-speaking Bruno, Nadia, and son Samuel (they have city maps). It's across the canal from the train station behind the green dome (follow Rialto signs for 100 yards, look left).

Dormitory Accommodations

Foresteria della Chiesa Valdese, warmly run by a Protestant church, offers dorm beds at youth-hostel prices in a handy location (halfway between San Marco and Rialto). This rundown but charming old palace has elegant paintings on the ceilings (office open 9:00–13:00, 18:00–20:00, Sunday 9:00–13:00; L28,000 dorm beds or L76,000 doubles with sheets and breakfast, more expensive for one-night stays, with some larger "apartments" for small groups; from

Campo Santa Maria Formosa, walk past the Orologio bar to the end of Calle Lunga and cross the bridge, Castello #5170, tel. 041/528-6797).

The Venice youth hostel, on Giudecca Island, is crowded, cheap, and newly remodeled (office open 7:00–9:30, 13:30–23:00; L24,000 beds with sheets and breakfast in ten- to 16-bed rooms, membership required; tel. 041/523-8211; catch boat #82 from station or San Marco to Zittele). Their budget cafeteria welcomes non-hostelers (nightly 18:00–21:00).

Eating in Venice

Touristy restaurants are the scourge of Venice. I stick to small *cicchetti* bars (see Pub Crawl, below) or simple pizza-like dinners at scenic locations. You'll dine far better for less in other cities in Italy—go for the setting or the pub-crawl experience in Venice. For speed, value, and ambience, you can get a filling plate of local-style tapas at nearly any of the bars described below.

A key to cheap eating in Venice is bar snacks, especially stand-up mini-meals in out-of-the-way bars. Order by pointing. *Panini* (sandwiches) are sold fast and cheap at bars everywhere. Pizzerias are cheap and easy. Those that sell take-out by the slice or gram are cheapest. Fast food and self-serve places are easy to find.

The **produce market** that sprawls for a few blocks just past the Rialto Bridge (best 8:00–13:00, closed Sunday) is a great place to assemble a picnic. The nearby street, Ruga Vecchia, has good bakeries and cheese shops. Side lanes in this area are speckled with fine little hole-in-the-wall munchie bars.

The **Mensa DLF**, the public transportation workers' cafeteria, is cheap and open to the public (11:00–14:30, 18:00–21:30, tel. 041/716-242). Leaving the train station, turn right on the Grand Canal, walk about 150 yards, and you'll run into it.

The Stand-Up Progressive Venetian Pub-Crawl Dinner

A tradition unique to Venice in Italy is a *giro di ombre* (pub crawl)—ideal in a city with no cars. My favorite Venetian dinner is a pub crawl. I've listed plenty in walking order for a quick or extended crawl below. If you've crawled enough, most of the listed bars make a fine one-stop, sit-down dinner.

Venice's residential back streets hide plenty of characteristic bars with countless trays of interesting toothpick-munchie food (*cicchetti*). This is a great way to mingle and have fun with the

Pub Crawl

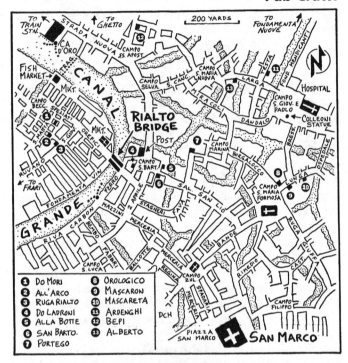

Venetians. Real *cicchetti* pubs are getting rare in these fast-food days, but locals appreciate the ones that survive. As always, the best way to find a landmark is to ask locals, *"Dové . . . ?"* and go where they point. Since Venice is so quiet after dark, you can generally follow the crowds to these places.

Try fried mozzarella cheese, blue cheese, calamari, artichoke hearts, and anything ugly on a toothpick. Ask for a *piatto misto* (mixed plate). Or try *"Un classico piatto di cicchetti misti da cinque mila lire"* (a plate of assorted appetizers for L5,000) or go up to L10,000, depending upon how much food you want. Drink the house wines. A small glass of house red or white wine (*ombre rosso* or *ombre bianco*) or a small beer (*birrino*) costs about L1,000. *Vin bon,* Venetian for fine wine, may run you from L2,000 to L3,000 per little glass. Meat and fish (*pesce:* PAY-shay) munchies are expensive; veggies (*verdura*) are cheap, around L4,000 for a meal-sized plate. Bread sticks (*grissini*) are free for the asking. A good last drink is *fragolino*, the local sweet red wine. A liter of house wine costs around L7,000. Bars don't stay open very late, and the *cicchetti* selection is best early, so start your evening by 18:30. Most bars are closed on Sundays. You can stand around the bar or grab a table in the back for the same price. (I'd appreciate any feedback on this plan.)

Cicchetteria near Rialto Bridge and Campo San Bartolomeo

Start your crawl near the Rialto Bridge. The first places are on the San Polo side. Ai do Ladroni is a block past the bridge towards San Marco. And the last couple are a few blocks beyond the Campo.

Cantina "Do Mori" is famous with locals (since 1462) and savvy travelers (since 1962) as a classy place for fine wine and *frangobollo* (a spicy selection of 20 tiny sandwiches called "stamps"). Choose from the featured wines in the barrel on the bar. From Rialto bridge walk 200 yards down Ruga degli Orefici (opposite San Marco and ask, stand-up only, arrive early before cicchetti are gone, Monday–Saturday 17:00–20:30, closed Sunday, San Polo 429, tel 041/522-5401). The rough-and-tumble **Cantina All' Arco** across the lane is worth a quick *ombra*.

Antica Ostaria Ruga Rialto is less expensive than Do Mori and offers tables, a busier/younger crowd, and a better selection of munchies (near the bright yellow Chinese restaurant sign, just off corner of Ruga Rialto and Ruga degli Orefici, San Polo 692, closed Monday, tel. 041/521-1243). There are several other *cicchetti* bars within a block or two. You could track down: Cantina Do Spade, Vini da Pinto, and Osteria Enoteca Vivaldi (on Campo A. Aponal).

Osteria Ai do Ladroni is a great new place specializing in *"Veneziane piccola cucina"* and popular with locals, half a block off the main Rialto-Campo San Bartolomeo drag (Monday–Saturday 8:00–24:00, closed Sunday, tel. 041/522-7741). They also serve good L10,000 pasta plates.

Osteria "Alla Botte" Cicchetteria is an atmospheric place packed with a young, local, bohemian jazz clientele. It's good for a light meal or a *cicchetti* snack with wine (2 short blocks off Campo San Bartolomeo in the corner behind the statue, tel. 041/520-9775, notice the "day after" photo showing a debris-covered Venice after the notorious 1989 Pink Floyd open-air concert).

If the statue on the Campo San Bartolomeo walked backwards 20 yards, turned left and went under a passageway, he'd hit **Rosticceria San Bartolomeo**. This isn't a pub, but they have a likably surly staff, great fried *mozzarella e prosciutto* (L2,000), and L1,000 glasses of wine. Continue over a bridge to Campo San Lio (a good landmark), go left at the Hotel Canada, and walk straight over another bridge into Osteria Al Portego. This fine local-style bar has plenty of snacks and *cicchetti* (Monday–Saturday 9:00–22:00, closed Sunday, tel. 041/522-9038). From here, ask *"Dové Santa Maria di Formosa?"*

Cicchetteria near Campo Santa Maria di Formosa

Campo Santa Maria di Formosa is just plain atmospheric. For a balmy outdoor sit, you could split a pizza with wine on the square. **Piero's Bar all' Orologio**, opposite the canal, has best setting and friendly service. *Capricciosa* means the house specialty. Or munch a slice of "pizza to go" on the square from **Cip Ciap Pizza Rustica** (over the bridge behind the SMF gelateria on Calle del Mondo Novo, open until 21:00, closed Tuesday). For your salad course, there's a fruit-and-vegetable stand on the square next to the water fountain (open until about 20:00).

From Bar all' Orologio (on Campo S.M. di Formosa), with your back to the church (follow yellow sign to SS Giov e Paolo), head down the street to **Osteria Mascaron** (Gigi's bar, best selection by 19:30, closes at 24:00 and on Sunday).

Gigi also runs **Enoteca Mascareta**, with less food and more wine, 30 yards farther down the street (#5183, tel. 041/523-0744). The piano sounds like they dropped it in the canal, but the wine was saved. If you want more *cicchetti*, check out the two places described below in the Campo Santi Apostoli section. If you're feeling like the painting of Bacchus on the wall looks, it's time for . . .

Gelato: There's a decent gelateria on Campo di Formosa (closes at about 20:00 and on Thursday). There's a top-quality place 2 blocks away on the corner of Calle San Antonio and Calle Paradiso. Or head toward San Marco where the gelaterias stay open later (the best is opposite the Doge's Palace, by the two columns, on the bay). There's also a good late-hours gelateria midway between Campo San Bartolomeo and the Rialto Bridge selling cheap, small cones (on the left).

You're not a tourist, you're a living part of a soft Venetian night . . . an alley cat with money. Streetlamp halos, live music, floodlit history, and a ceiling of stars make St. Mark's magic at midnight. Shine with the old lanterns on the gondola piers where the sloppy Grand Canal splashes at the Doge's Palace . . . reminiscing. Comfort the four frightened tetrarchs (ancient Byzantine emperors) under the moon where the Doge's Palace hits the basilica. Cuddle history.

Eating near Campo San Bartolomeo

The very local, hustling **Rosticceria San Bartolomeo Gislon** is a cheap—if confusing—self-service restaurant on the ground floor (L7,000 pasta, L1000 wine, prices listed at door, no cover or service charge). It's on Calle della Bissa #5424 (starting from the statue in the San Bartolomeo square, it's 20 yards behind the statue to its left, under a passageway; 9:00–21:30, tel. 041/522-3569). While old "example" dishes are left on display, the kitchen whips up fine pastas. Good but pricier meals are served at the full-service restaurant upstairs. Take out or grab a table.

Eating near Campo Santi Apostoli

Trattoria da Bepi caters to a local crowd and specializes in good seafood and Venetian cuisine. Bepi's son, Loris, speaks English and makes a mean *licorice grappa* (midway between the Rialto Bridge and Ca d'Oro, next to the Santi Apostoli church and my recommended laundromat, tel. 041/528-5031, closed Tuesday).

Two colorful osterias are good for *cicchetti*, wine-tasting, or a simple, rustic, sit-down meal surrounded by a boistrous local ambience: **Osteria da Alberto** (18:00–21:30, closed Sunday, midway between Campo Santi Apostoli and Campo S.S. Giovanni e Paolo, next to Ponte de la Panada on Calle larga Giacinto Gallina) and **Osteria Candela** on Calle de l'Oca. You'll find local pubs such as Volante's (near Alberto's) and in the side streets opposite Campo St. Sofia across Strada Nueva.

Antiche Cantine Ardenghi de Lucia e Michael is a leap of local faith. Michael, an effervescent former Murano glass salesman, and his wife Lucia, cook for 20 people a night by reservation only. You must call first. You pay L60,000 and trust them to wine, dine, and serenade you in Venetian class. The evening can be quiet or raucous depending on who and how many are eating. There's no sign and the door's locked. Find #6369 and knock. From Campo S. Giovanni e Paolo, pass the church-looking hospital (notice the illusions painted on its facade), go over the bridge to the left, and take the first right to #6369 (8:30–02:00, closed Sunday, tel. 041/523-7691).

Eating near the Accademia
Snack Bar Accademia Foscarini's staff serves great L8,000 pizzas and L7,000 salads, and offers canal-side or indoor seating, next to the Accademia Bridge and Galleria (Wednesday–Monday 7:00–23:00, closed Tuesday, tel. 041/522-7281).

Transportation Connections—Venice
By train to: Verona (hourly, 1.5 hrs), **Florence** (6/day, 3 hrs), **Dolomites** (8/day to Bolzano, 4 hrs with one transfer; catch bus from Bolzano into mountains), **Milan** (hrly, 3–4 hrs), **Rome** (6/day, 5 hrs, slower overnight), **Naples** (change in Rome), **Brindisi** (3/day, 11 hrs), **Cinque Terre** (two La Spezia trains go directly to Monterosso al Mare daily, 6 hrs, at 9:58 and 14:58), **Bern** (4/day, change in Milan, 8 hrs), **Munich** (5/day, 8 hrs), **Paris** (3/day, 11 hrs), **Vienna** (4/day, 9 hrs). Train and couchette reservations (L24,000) are easily made at the American Express office near San Marco. Venice train info: tel. 1478-88088.

NEAR VENICE: PADUA, VICENZA, VERONA, AND RAVENNA
While the Italian region of Veneto has much more to offer than Venice, few venture off the lagoon. Four important towns and possible side trips, in addition to the lakes and the Dolomites, make zipping directly from Venice to Milan (three-hour trip, hourly departures) a route strewn with temptation.

Planning Your Time
The towns of Padua, Vicenza, Verona, and Ravenna are all, for various reasons, reasonable stops. But none are essential parts of the best three weeks Italy has to offer. Of the towns discussed below, only Ravenna (2.5 hours from Padua or Florence) is not on the main Milan-Venice train line. Each town gives the visitor a low-key slice of Italy that complements the high-powered urbanity of Venice, Florence, and Rome.

High-speed town-hopping between Venice and Bolzano or Milan (with three-hour stops at Padua, Vicenza, and Verona) is a good day. Trains run frequently enough to allow flexibility and little wasted time.

PADUA

Living under Venetian rule for four centuries seemed only to sharpen Padua's independent spirit. Nicknamed "the brain of Veneto," Padua has a prestigious university (founded 1222) and was called home by smart guys like Galileo, Dante, and Petrarch.

The old town is a colonnaded time-tunnel experience, and Padua's museums and churches hold their own in Italy's artistic big league. You'll see Giotto's well-preserved cycle of more than 30 frescoes in the **Chapel of the Scrovegni** (L10,000, daily 9:00–19:00). Don't miss Donatello's *Crucifixion*, with statues of Mary and Padua's six patron saints on the high altar of the Basilica di Sant'Antonio, and his great equestrian statue (the first since ancient Roman times) of the Venetian mercenary General Gattamelata on Piazza del Santo outside the Basilica. For work by Mantegna, see the important (but devastated by WWII bombs) frescoes in the Church of the Hermits (Chiesa degli Eremitani).

The tourist information office is in the train station (tel. 049/875-2077).

Sleeping in Padua: Hotel Piccolo Vienna is small and near the station (D-L52,000, Db-L75,000, Via Beato Pellegrino 133, tel. 049/871-6331). **Hotel Verdi**, in the old center, is friendly and accommodating (S-L40,000; D-L56,000; bus #10 from the station to Teatro Verdi; Via Dondi dell'Orologio 7, tel. 049/875-5744). The well-run **Ostello Citta di Padova** has four-, six-, and 16-bedded rooms (L20,000 per bed with sheets and breakfast; bus #3, #8, #12, or #18 from the station; Via Aleardi 30, tel. 049/875-2219). Many budget travelers enjoy making this hostel a low-stress, low-price home base from which to tour Venice. I'd rather flip-flop it—sleeping in Venice and side-tripping to Padua, 30 minutes away by train.

VICENZA

To many architects, Vicenza is a pilgrimage site. Entire streets look like the back of a nickel. This is the city of Palladio, the 16th-century Renaissance architect who gave us the "Palladian" style so influential in Britain (countless country homes). The U.S.A. Thomas Jefferson's Monticello, a private but sometimes tourable Palladian residence on the edge of Vicenza, was inspired by Palladio's Rotonda. You can rent

Temptations: Venice to Milan

bikes for trips to this and other villas outside the city walls
at Hotel Palladio (L10,000/day, Via Oratorio dei Servi 25,
2 blocks from Piazza Matteoti).

For the casual visitor, a quick stop offers plenty of Palladio.
From the train station, catch bus #1 (L1,400) to Piazza
Matteotti, where you can visit the tourist information office and
pick up a map (Piazza Matteotti 12, tel. 0444/320-854). From
there, see the **Olympic Theater**, Palladio's last work and one of
his greatest (L5,00, open summer 9:00–12:30, 14:15–16:45).
This oldest indoor theater in Europe is still used and is considered one of the world's best.

From the Olympic Theater, begin your stroll down
Vicenza's main drag, a steady string of Renaissance palaces and
Palladian architecture peopled by Vicenzans who keep their
noses above the tourist trade and are considered by their
neighbors to be as uppity as most of their colonnades.

After a few blocks, you'll see the huge basilica standing
over the Piazza dei Signori, which has been the town center
since Roman times. It was young Palladio's proposal to redo
the dilapidated Gothic palace of justice in the neo-Greek style

that established him as Vicenza's favorite architect. The rest of his career was a one-man construction boom. Notice the 13th-century, 280-foot-tall tower and the Loggia del Capitaniato (opposite the basilica), one of Palladio's last works.

If you're staying in Vicenza, **Hotel Vicenza** is a sleepable place in the Palladian center of things (D-L75,000, Db-L90,000, Piazza dei Signori at Stradella dei Nodari, tel. & fax 0444/321-512).

Finish your Corso Palladio stroll by walking to Piazzale Gasperi (where the PAM supermarket is a handy place to grab a picnic for the train ride) and walk five minutes down Viale Roma back to the station. Trains leave about every hour toward Milan/Verona and Venice (less than an hour away).

VERONA

Romeo and Juliet made Verona a household word. But, alas, a visit here has nothing to do with those two star-crossed lovers. You can pay to visit the house falsely claiming to be Juliet's, with an almost believable (but slathered-with-tour-groups) balcony, take part in the tradition of rubbing the breast of Juliet's statue in the courtyard to ensure finding a lover (or picking up the sweat of someone who can't), and even make a pilgrimage to what isn't "La Tomba di Giulietta." Despite the fiction, the town has been an important crossroads for 2,000 years and is therefore packed with genuine history. R and J fans will take some solace in the fact that two real feuding families, the Montecchi and the Capellos, were the models for Shakespeare's Montagues and Capulets. And, if R and J had existed and were alive today, they would recognize much of their "home town."

Verona's main attractions are its wealth of Roman ruins, the remnants of its 13th- and 14th-century political and cultural boom, and its 20th-century, quiet, pedestrian-only ambience. After Venice's festival of tourism, Veneto's second city (in population and in artistic importance) is a cool and welcome sip of pure Italy, where dumpsters are painted by schoolchildren as class projects. If you like Italy but don't need great sights, this town is a joy.

Orientation (tel. code: 045)

The most enjoyable core of Verona is along Via Mazzini between Piazza Brà and Piazza Erbe, Verona's medieval

market square. Head straight for Piazza Brå. Check your bag
at the station (L5,000 for 12 hours). In front of the station
buy a L1,500 ticket (buy from Tobacco shop in station or
from white AMT hut near buses, stamp it on bus, good for
an hour) and ride orange bus #11, #12, #13, or #51 past
Porta Nuova and down boring Corso Porta Nuova, under
the city wall and into Piazza Brå (the big green square with
important-looking buildings). The station-to-Piazza Brå walk
is miserable. Taxis pick up only at taxi stands and cost about
L8,000 to the center or the river. All the sights of importance
are within an easy walk through the old town, which is
defined by a bend in the river. Buses return to the station
from where Corso Porta Nuova hits Piazza Brå (just outside
city wall, under big clock, on right).

   Tourist Information: Verona's TI offices are at the station
(daily 8:00–19:30, closed winter Sundays, tel. 045/800-0861)
and in the center (to the right of the Arena on the side of
the big yellow building with columns at Via Leoncino 61,
Monday–Saturday 8:00–20:00, summer Sundays 8:30–13:30,
tel. 045/592-828). Pick up a free city map (with a list of sights,
hours, and walking tour) and the Verona information booklet.

Sights—Verona

Arena—On Piazza Brå, this elliptical, 140-by-120-meter
amphitheater, the third-largest in the Roman world, is well-
preserved, dates from the first century A.D., and looks great in
its pink marble. Over the centuries, crowds of up to 25,000
spectators have cheered Roman gladiator battles, medieval exe-
cutions, and modern plays (including a popular opera/ballet
festival that takes advantage of the famous acoustics every July
and August). Climb to the top for a fine city view (L6,000,
8:00–19:15, closed Monday).

House of Juliet—This bogus house is a block off Piazza
Erbe (detour right to Via Cappello #23). The tiny, admittedly
romantic courtyard is a spectacle in itself, with Japanese posing
from the balcony, Nebraskans polishing Juliet's bronze breast,
and amorous graffiti everywhere. The info boxes (L500 for
two) offer a good history. ("While no documentation has been
discovered to prove the truth of the legend, no documentation
has disproven it either.") The "museum" is only empty rooms
and certainly not worth the L5,000 entry fee (tour it free via
the security screen at the ticket desk).

▲▲**Evening** *Passeggiata*—For me, the highlight of Verona is the *passeggiata* (stroll)—especially in the evening—from the elegant cafés of Piazza Brà, through the old town on Via Mazzini (one of Europe's many "first pedestrian-only streets") to the bustling and colorful medieval market square, Piazza Erbe. Piazza Erbe is a photographer's delight, with pastel buildings corralling the stalls, fountains, pigeons, and people that have come together here since Roman times.

Walk from Piazza Erbe to the Roman Bridge—From the center of the market square, continue toward the river on Via della Costa into the Piazza dei Signori. Walking under the "arch of the whale's rib," look up and don't worry. The whale's rib has hung there a thousand years. According to legend, it will fall when someone who's never lied walks under it. Enjoy the fine architecture of Piazza dei Signori. The statue of Dante seems to wonder why all the tourists choose Juliet over him. Dante was granted exile in Verona by the Scaligeri family. With the whales rib behind you, you're facing the crenellated 13th-century Scaligeri family residence. Behind Dante is the 15th-century Venetian Renaissance-style Portico of the Counsel. In front of Dante (follow the green "WC" signs) is the 12th-century Romanesque Palazzo della Ragione. From inside its courtyard, a lift takes you to the top of the 13th-century Torre dei Lamberti (L4,000) for a grand view. There's no need to climb any farther than the view level just above the lift. Exit Piazza dei Signori at the end opposite Piazza Erbe, where you'll find the strange and very Gothic tombs of the Scaligeri family, who were to Verona what the Medici family was to Florence.

Walking farther, you'll come to the river. Turn right past two important churches, Sant Anastasia and the Duomo (Verona's historic churches are all open 9:00–18:30 and charge L4,000; there's a L9,000 combo ticket covering all). Next you'll come to the **Ponte Pietra** (a Roman bridge that survived nearly intact until WWII). Just across the river, built into the hill above the Ponte Pietra, is Verona's **Roman Theater**, which stages Shakespeare plays every summer (only a little more difficult to understand in Italian than in Olde English). You can climb the stairs behind the theater for a great town view. From the Duomo, if you hike upstream, you'll pass the well-preserved first-century Roman gateway, the Porta Borsari. Then, just before the castle, is the Roman triumphal arch, the Arco dei Gavi. The medieval castle, the Castelvecchio, is now an art museum with fine 16th- to 18th-century paintings (L5,000, Tuesday–Sunday 8:30–18:30, closed Monday). Finally, a few blocks farther up the river, you'll find the 12th-century **Church of San Zeno Maggiore**. This offers not only a great example of Italian Romanesque, but also Mantegna's San Zeno Triptych and a set of 48 paneled 11th-century bronze doors that are nicknamed "the poor man's Bible." Pretend you're an illiterate medieval peasant and do some reading.

Sleeping and Eating in Verona
(L1,600 = about $1, tel. code 045, zip code: 37100)

Several fine, family-run places are in the quiet streets just off Piazza Brà, within 200 meters of the bus stop, and well-marked with yellow signs. Tiny **Albergo Ristorante Ciopeta**, more *ristorante* than *albergo*, offers five quiet, air-con rooms with the best budget beds I could find (S-L75,000, D-L110,000, T-L140,000, family deals, with breakfast, CC:VMA; Vicolo Teatro Filarmonico 2, tel. 045/800-6843, fax 045/803-3722, Sr. Cristofoli speaks *un poco* English).

Two classier places just off Piazza Brà toward the river are **Hotel Cavour** (16 rooms, Sb-L100,000, Db-L135,000, Tb-L180,000, without breakfast, prices go soft in the off-season, modern showers, air-con for L10,000 more; Vicolo Chiodo 4, tel. 045/590-166, fax 045/590-508, Patricia SE) and, not quite so quiet or atmospheric, **Albergo Al Castello** (nine rooms, S-L55,000, Sb-L70,000, one D-L90,000, Db-L110,000, without breakfast, ceiling fans, CC:VM; Corso Cavour 43, tel. 045/800-4403, Katia SE). For sleek, modern comfort in the same great neighborhood, consider **Hotel Europa** (Db-L205,000 with breakfast, L160,000 in slower times, call a day ahead to check for discounts, air-con, CC:VMA; elevator, Via Roma 8, 37121 Verona, tel. 045/800-2882, fax 045/800-1852, SE). Some of its 46 rooms are smoke-free, a rarity in Italy.

Locanda Catullo is a cheaper, quiet, quirky, and paranoid place deeper in the old town, with good basic rooms up three flights of stairs (21 rooms, S-L55,000, D-L75,000, Db-L95,000; left off Via Mazzini onto Via Catullo, down an alley between 1D and 3A at Via Valerio Catullo 1, tel. 045/800-2786, SE).

The Verona youth hostel is one of Italy's best hostels (eight to ten beds/room, L20,000 beds with breakfast, non-members welcome one night; bus #73 from the station during the day or #90 at night and Sundays; over the river beyond Ponte Nuovo at Salita Fontana del Ferro 15, tel. 045/590-360).

Fast, cheap food on Piazza Brå: For a quick and healthy bite with a great view of Verona's main square, eat at Brek (11:30–15:00, 18:30–22:00, indoor/outdoor seating, cheap salad plates).

Transportation Connections—Verona
By train to: Florence (10/day, 3 hrs), **Milan** (hrly, 90 min), **Rome** (6/day, 6 hrs), **Bolzano** (hrly, 90 min). Town-hopping between **Verona, Padua, Vicenza,** and **Venice** couldn't be easier: all towns are 30 minutes apart on the Venice–Milan line (hrly, 3 hr).

Parking in Verona: Drivers will find lots of free parking at the stadium or cheap long-term parking near the train station. The most central lot is behind the Arena on Piazza Cittadella (guarded, L10,000/day). The town center is closed to regular traffic.

RAVENNA
Ravenna is on the tourist map for one reason: its 1,500-year-old churches decorated with best-in-the-west Byzantine mosaics. Briefly a capital of eastern Rome during its fall, Ravenna was taken by the barbarians. Then in A.D. 539, the Byzantine emperor Justinian turned Ravenna into Byzantium's lieutenant in the west. Ravenna was a light in the Dark Ages. Two hundred years later, the Lombards booted Byzantine out, and Ravenna melted into the backwaters of medieval Italy and stayed out of historical sight for a thousand years. Today the city booms with a big chemical industry, the discovery of offshore gas deposits, and the construction of a new ship canal. It goes busily on its way, while busloads of tourists slip quietly in and out of town for the best look at the glories of Byzantium this side of Istanbul.

While not worth an overnight, it's only a 90-minute detour from the main Venice–Florence train line, and worth the effort for those interested in old mosaics. While all agree that Ravenna has the finest mosaics in the West, many will find their time better spent taking a careful look at the good but not as sublime Byzantine-style mosaics in Venice.

Orientation (tel. code: 0544)

Central Ravenna is quiet, with more bikes than cars, and a
pedestrian-friendly core. On a quick stop, I'd see the basili-
cas, mausoleum, covered market, and Piazza del Popolo.

If you're day-tripping to Ravenna, remember—before
you leave the train station—to jot down when the next
few trains depart for Ferrara (to go to Venice) or Bologna
(to get to Florence).

Tourist Information: The TI is a 25-minute walk
from the train station (daily 9:00–19:00, until 16:00 in winter,
Via Salara 8, tel. 0544/35404). Get a map and ask about a
money-saving pass to the sights. For directions to the TI,
see Orientation Walk, below.

Sights—Ravenna

Orientation Walk—A visit to Ravenna can be as short
as a two-hour loop from the train station. From the station,
walk straight down Viale Farini to Piazza del Popolo. A
right on Via IV Novembre takes you a block to the colorful
covered market (Mercato Coperto, open for picnic fixings
8:00–13:00, closed Sunday). The TI is a block away (on
Via Salaria 8). Ravenna's two most important sights, Basilica
di San Vitale and the Mausoleum of Galla Placidia, are 2
blocks away down Via San Vitale. On the other side of
Piazza del Popolo is the Basilica of St. Apollinare Nuovo,
also worth a look. From there you're about a 15-minute
walk back to the station. (Sights open 9:00–19:00, until
16:30 October–March.)

▲▲**Basilica di San Vitale**—It's impressive enough to see a
1,400-year-old church. But to see one decorated in brilliant
mosaics that still convey the intended feeling that "this peace
and stability was brought to you by your emperor and God"
is rare indeed. Study each of the scenes: the arch of apostles
with a bearded Christ at their head; the lamb on the twinkly
ceiling; the beardless Christ astride a blue earth behind the
altar; and the side panels featuring Emperor Justinian, his
wife Theodora (an aggressive Constantinople showgirl who
used all her charms to gain power with—and even over—her
emperor husband), and their rigid and lavish courts. San
Vitale can be seen as the last of the ancient Roman art and
the first of the Christian era. This church was the prototype
for Constantinople's Hagia Sophia built ten years later, and

it inspired Charlemagne to build the first great church in northern Europe in his capital of Aix-la-Chapelle, now present-day Aachen (L6,000, L10,000 includes entry to adjacent archeological museum and all the churches).

▲▲**Mausoleum of Galla Placidia**—Just across the courtyard is the humble-looking little mausoleum with the oldest—and to many, the best—mosaics in Ravenna. The little light that sneaks through the thin alabaster panels brings a glow and a twinkle to the very early Christian symbolism (Jesus the Good Shepherd, Mark's lion, Luke's ox, John's eagle, the golden cross above everything) that fills the little room. Cover the light of the door with your hand to see the beardless Christ as the Good Shepherd. This was a popular scene with the early church.

▲**Basilica of St. Apollinare Nuovo**—This austere sixth-century church, in the typical early Christian basilica form, has two huge and wonderfully preserved side panels.
One is a procession of haloed virgins, each bringing gifts to the Madonna and the Christ Child. Opposite, Christ is on his throne with four angels, awaiting a solemn procession of 26 martyrs.

Church of Sant' Apollinare in Classe—Featuring great Byzantine art, this church is generally considered a must among mosaic pilgrims (3 miles out of town, easy bus and train connections, closed from 12:00–14:00, tel. 0544/527-004).

Overrated Sights—The nearby beach town of Rimini is an overcrowded and polluted mess.

Sleeping in Ravenna
(L1,600 = about $1, tel. code 0544)
Two cheap hotels near the station are **Al Giaciglio** (D-L55,000, Db-L75,000, Via R. Brancaleone 42, tel. 0544/39403) and **Hotel Ravenna** (D-L70,000, Db-L90,000; Via Varoncelli 12, tel. 0544/212-204, fax 0544/212-077). The **youth hostel** is a ten-minute walk from the station (follow the signs for Ostello Dante, Via Nicolodi 12, tel. 0544/421-164).

Transportation Connections—Ravenna
By train to: Venice (3 hrs with transfer in Ferrara: Ravenna to Ferrara, every 2 hrs, 60 min; Ferrara to Venice, hrly, 1.5 hrs), **Florence** (4 hrs with transfer in Bologna: Ravenna to Bologna, 8/day, 1.5 hrs; Bologna to Florence, hrly, 1.5 hrs). Train information: tel. 1478-88088.

FLORENCE (FIRENZE)

Florence, the home of the Renaissance and birthplace of our modern world, is a "supermarket sweep," and the groceries are the best Renaissance art in Europe.

Get your bearings with a Renaissance walk. Florentine art goes beyond paintings and statues—there's food, fashion, and handicrafts. You can lick Italy's best gelato while enjoying Europe's best people-watching.

Planning Your Time

If you're in Europe for three weeks, Florence deserves a well-organized day. Siena, an easy hour away by bus, has no awesome sights but is a more enjoyable home base. For a day in Florence, see Michelangelo's *David*, tour the Uffizi Gallery (best Italian paintings), tour the underrated Bargello (best statues), and do the Renaissance ramble (explained below). Art lovers will want to chisel another day out of their itinerary for the many other cultural treasures Florence offers. Shoppers and ice-cream lovers may need to do the same. Plan your sightseeing hours carefully. Get an early start. Mondays and afternoons can be sparse. You may very likely lose an hour or two in lines. If the line at *David* depresses you, remind yourself that people think nothing of waiting an hour at Disneyland to see the Tiki Hut.

Orientation (tel. code: 055)

The Florence we're interested in lies mostly on the north bank of the Arno River. Everything is within a 20-minute

Florence Area

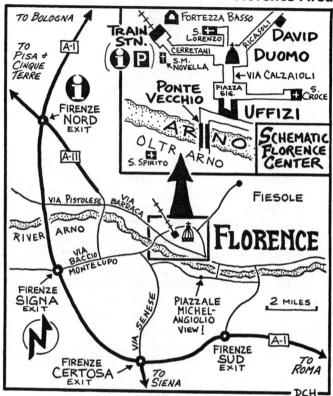

walk of the train station, cathedral, or Ponte Vecchio (Old Bridge). The less impressive but more characteristic Oltrarno (south bank) area is just over the bridge. Orient yourself by the huge red-tiled dome of the cathedral (the Duomo) and its tall bell tower (Giotto's Tower). This is the center of historic Florence.

Tourist Information

Normally overcrowded, under-informed, and understaffed, the train station's tourist information office is not worth a stop if you're a good student of this book. If there's no line, pick up a map (ask for the better "long stay" map), a current museum-hours listing, and the periodical entertainment guide or tourist magazine. The main TI (3 blocks north of Duomo at Via Cavour 1r, Monday–Saturday in summer 8:15–19:15, Sunday 8:15–13:45, tel. 055/290-832 or 055/290-833) is less crowded and more helpful. There's a fine international bookstore (with American guidebooks) across the street at Via Cavour 20r. The free monthly *Florence Concierge Information* magazine lists the latest museum hours, markets, bus and train connections, and events; it's stocked by the expensive hotels (pick one up, as if you're staying there).

Helpful Hints

Museums and Churches: See everyone's essential sight, *David*, right off. In Italy a masterpiece seen and enjoyed is worth two tomorrow; you never know when a place will unexpectedly close for a holiday, strike, or restoration. The Uffizi has one- to two-hour lines on busy days. During lunchtime (before 14:00), lines are shorter. By 17:00, lines are normally gone. Many museums close at 14:00 and stop selling tickets 30 minutes before that. Most close Monday and at 13:00 or 14:00 on Sunday. The *Concierge Information* magazine thoughtfully lists which sights are open afternoons, Sundays, and Mondays (best attractions open Monday: Michelangelo's Casa Buonarroti, Dante's House, Giotto's Belltower, Museo dell' Opera del Duomo, and Palazzo Vecchio). Churches usually close from 12:30 to 15:00 or 16:00. Local guidebooks are cheap and give you a map and a decent commentary on the sights.

Addresses: Street addresses list businesses in red and residences in black or blue (color-coded on the actual street number, and indicated by a letter following the number in printed addresses: n = black, r = red). Pensioni are usually black, but can be either.

Theft Alert: Florence has particularly hardworking thief gangs. They specialize in tourists and hang out where you do, near the train station and major sights. American tourists, especially older ones, are considered the easiest targets.

Medical Help: For a doctor who speaks English call 055/475-411 (reasonable hotel calls, cheaper if you go to the clinic, 24-hour pharmacy at the train station).

American Express is near the Palazzo Vecchio (Monday–Friday 9:00–17:30, Saturdays until 12:30, easy train tickets and reservations, Via Dante 22, tel. 055/50981).

Getting Around Florence

If you organize your sightseeing with some geographic logic, you'll do it all on foot. Taxis takes you from the train station to the Ponte Vecchio for about L8,000. A L1,500 ticket gives you 60 minutes on the buses, L2,500 gives you three hours, and L6,000 gets you 24 hours (tickets not sold on bus, buy in tobacco shop, validate on bus).

A Florentine Renaissance Walk

Even during the Dark Ages, people knew they were in a "middle time." It was especially obvious to the people of Italy—sitting on the rubble of Rome—that there was a brighter age before them. The long-awaited rebirth, or "Renaissance," happened in Florence for good reason. Wealthy because of its cloth industry, trade, and banking; powered by a fierce city-state pride (locals would pee into the Arno with gusto, knowing rival city-state Pisa was downstream); and fertile with more than its share of artistic genius (imagine guys like Michelangelo and Leonardo attending the same high school)—Florence was a natural home for this cultural explosion.

Take a walk through the core of Renaissance Florence by starting at the Accademia (home of Michelangelo's *David*) and cutting through the heart of the city to the Ponte Vecchio on the Arno River. (A ten-page, self-guided tour of this walk is outlined in my museum guidebook, *Mona Winks*. Otherwise, you'll find brief descriptions below.)

At the Accademia you'll look into the eyes of Renaissance man—humanism at its confident peak. Then walk to the cathedral (Duomo) to see the dome that kicked off the architectural Renaissance. Step inside the Baptistery to view a ceiling covered with preachy, flat, 2-D, medieval mosaic art. Then, to learn what happened when art met math, check out the realistic 3-D reliefs on the doors. The painter, Giotto, designed the bell tower—an early example of how a Renaissance genius excelled in many areas. Continue toward the river on Florence's great pedestrian mall, Via de' Calzaioli (or "Via Calz"), which was part of the original grid plan given the city by the ancient Romans. Down a few blocks, compare medieval and Renaissance statues on the exterior of the Orsanmichele Church. Via Calz connects the cathedral with the central square (Piazza della Signoria), the

Florence

LODGING:

❶ CASA RABATTI	❽ ELITE	⓯ BRETAGNA
❷ PEZZATI	❾ SOLE	⓰ AILY HOME
❸ ENZA	❿ CONCORDIA	⓱ SCALETTA
❹ MAGLIANI	⓫ CENTRALE	⓲ SORR. BANDINI
❺ LOGGIATO SERVITI	⓬ BURCHIANTI	⓳ SILLA
❻ DUE FONTANE	⓭ MAXIM	
❼ UNIVERSO	⓮ ABACO	

city palace (Palazzo Vecchio), and the Uffizi Gallery containing the greatest collection of Italian Renaissance paintings in captivity. Finally, walk through the Uffizi courtyard, a statuary think-tank of Renaissance greats, to the Arno River and the Ponte Vecchio.

Sights—Florence

▲▲▲**The Accademia (Galleria dell' Accademia)**—
This museum houses Michelangelo's *David* and powerful
(unfinished) *Prisoners*. Eavesdrop as tour guides explain these
masterpieces. More than any other work of art, when you
look into the eyes of *David*, you're looking into the eyes of
Renaissance man. This was a radical break with the past. Man
was now a confident individual, no longer a plaything of the
supernatural. And life was now more than just a preparation for
what happened after you died.

The Renaissance was the merging of art and science. In a
humanist vein, *David* is looking at the crude giant of medieval
darkness and thinking, "I can take this guy." Back on a religious track (and speaking of veins), notice David's large and
overdeveloped right hand. This is symbolic of the hand of God
that powered David to slay the giant . . . and enabled Florence
to rise above its crude neighboring city-states.

Beyond the magic marble are two floors of interesting
pre-Renaissance and Renaissance paintings, including a
couple of dreamy Botticellis (L12,000, Tuesday–Saturday
8:30–19:00, Sunday 8:30–14:00, closed Monday, Via Ricasoli
60, tel. 055/238-8609).

Behind the Accademia, the Piazza Santissima Annunziata
features lovely Renaissance harmony. Brunelleschi's Hospital
of the Innocents (Spedale degli Innocenti, not worth going
inside), with terra-cotta medallions by della Robbia, was built
in the 1420s and is considered the first Renaissance building.

▲▲**Museum of San Marco**—One block north of the
Accademia on Piazza San Marco, this museum houses the
greatest collection anywhere of medieval frescoes and paintings
by the early Renaissance master Fra Angelico. You'll see why
he thought of painting as a form of prayer and couldn't paint a
crucifix without shedding tears. Each of the monks' cells has a
Fra Angelico fresco. Don't miss the cell of Savonarola, the
charismatic monk who rode in from the Christian right, threw
out the Medici, turned Florence into a theocracy, sponsored
"bonfires of the vanities" (burning books, paintings, and so on),
and was finally burned himself when Florence decided to
change channels (L8,000, daily 8:30–14:00 but closed the
second and fourth Monday of each month).

▲▲**The Duomo**—Florence's mediocre Gothic cathedral has
the third-longest nave in Christendom (free, daily 9:00–18:00,

with an occasional lunch break). The church's noisy neo-Gothic facade from the 1870s is covered with pink, green, and white Tuscan marble. Since nearly all of its great art is stored in the Museo dell' Opera del Duomo, behind the church, the best thing about the inside is the shade. The inside of the dome is decorated by what must be the largest painting of the Renaissance, a huge (and newly restored) *Last Judgment* by Vasari and Zuccari. The cathedral's claim to artistic fame is Brunelleschi's magnificent dome—the first Renaissance dome and the model for domes to follow (ascent L8,000, Monday–Saturday 9:30–18:20). When planning St. Peter's in Rome, Michelangelo said, "I can build a dome bigger, but not more beautiful, than the dome of Florence."

Giotto's Tower—Climbing Giotto's Tower (or Campanile) beats climbing the neighboring Duomo's dome because it's 50 fewer steps, faster, not so crowded, and offers the same view plus the dome (L8,000, daily 8:30–19:00, maybe later in summer).

▲▲**Museo dell' Opera del Duomo**—The underrated cathedral museum, behind the church at #9, is great if you like sculpture. It has masterpieces by Donatello (a gruesome wood carving of Mary Magdalene clothed in her matted hair, and the *cantoria*, a delightful choir loft bursting with happy children) and Luca della Robbia (another choir loft, lined with the dreamy faces of musicians praising the Lord); a late Michelangelo *Pietà* (Nicodemus, on top, is a self-portrait); Brunelleschi's models for his dome; and the original restored panels of Ghiberti's doors to the Baptistery. To get the most out of your sightseeing hours, remember that this is one of the few museums in Florence that stays open late and is open on Monday (L8,000, Monday–Saturday 9:00–18:50, closed Sunday, tel. 055/230-2885).

▲**The Baptistery**—Michelangelo said its bronze doors were fit to be the gates of Paradise. Check out the gleaming copies of Ghiberti's bronze doors facing the Duomo, and the famous competition doors around to the right. Making a breakthrough in perspective, Ghiberti used mathematical laws to create the illusion of 3-D on a 2-D surface. Go inside Florence's oldest building and sit and savor the medieval mosaic ceiling. Compare that to the "new, improved" art of the Renaissance (L3,000 interior open 13:30–18:30, Sunday 9:00–12:30, bronze doors are on the outside so always "open"; original panels are in the Museo dell' Opera del Duomo).

▲**Orsanmichele**—Mirroring Florentine values, this was a combination church-granary. The best L200 deal in Florence is the machine which lights its glorious tabernacle. Notice the grain spouts on the pillars inside. Also study the sculpture on its outside walls. You can see man stepping out of the literal and figurative shadow of the church in the great Renaissance sculptor Donatello's *St. George* (free, daily 9:00–12:00, 16:00–18:00, on Via Calzaioli; if closed, as it often is due to staffing problems, try going through the back door).

▲**Palazzo Vecchio**—This fortified palace, once the home of the Medici family, is a Florentine landmark. But if you're visiting only one palace interior in town, the Pitti Palace is better. The Palazzo Vecchio interior is wallpapered with mediocre magnificence, worthwhile only if you're a real Florentine art and history fan (L10,000, 9:00–19:00, Sunday 8:00–13:00, closed Thursday, handy public WC inside on ground floor). Do step into the free courtyard (behind the fake *David*) just to feel the Medici. Until 1873, Michelangelo's *David* stood at the entrance, where the copy is today. While the huge statues in the square are important only as the whipping boys of art critics and as pigeon roosts, the nearby Loggia dei Lanzi has several important statues. Notice Cellini's bronze statue of Perseus (with the head of Medusa). The plaque on the pavement in front of the fountain marks the spot where Savonarola was burned in LCCCCXCVIII.

▲▲▲**Uffizi Gallery**—The greatest collection of Italian painting anywhere is a must, with plenty of works by Giotto, Leonardo, Raphael, Caravaggio, Rubens, Titian, and Michelangelo, and a roomful of Botticellis, including his *Birth of Venus*. There are no official tours, so buy a book on the street before entering (or follow *Mona Winks*). The long entrance line is a reasonable cost for an interior with no Louvre-style mob scenes. The museum is nowhere near as big as it is great: few tourists spend more than two hours inside. The paintings are displayed (behind obnoxious reflective glass) on one comfortable floor in chronological order from the 13th through 17th centuries.

Essential stops are (in this order): the Gothic altarpieces (narrative, pre-realism, no real concern for believable depth); Giotto's altarpiece in the same room, which progressed beyond "totem-pole angels"; Uccello's *Battle of San Romano*, an early study in perspective (with a few obvious flubs); Fra Lippi's cuddly Madonnas; the Botticelli room, filled with masterpieces including a pantheon of classical fleshiness and the small *La Calumnia*, showing the glasnost of Renaissance free-thinking being clubbed back into the darker age of Savonarola; two minor works by Leonardo; the octagonal classical sculpture room with an early painting of Bob Hope and a copy of Praxiteles' *Venus de Medici*, considered the epitome of beauty in Elizabethan Europe; Michelangelo's only surviving easel painting, the round *Holy Family*; Raphael's noble *Madonna of the Goldfinch*; Titian's voluptuous *Venus of Urbino*; and views from the café terrace at the end (L12,000, Tuesday–Saturday 8:30–19:00, Sunday 8:30–14:00, closed Monday, last ticket sold 45 minutes before closing, go very late to avoid crowds and heat, elevator available; it's now possible to get a reservation by paying in advance in Florence, or you can even order online at www.weekend@firenze.com, tel. 055/234-7941).

Enjoy the Uffizi square, full of artists and souvenir stalls. The surrounding statues honor the earthshaking: artists, plus philosophers (Machiavelli), scientists (Galileo), writers (Dante), explorers (Amerigo Vespucci), and the great patron of so much Renaissance thinking, Lorenzo (the Magnificent) de Medici.

▲▲▲**Bargello (Museo Nazionale)**—This underrated sculpture museum is behind Palazzo Vecchio in a former prison that looks like a mini-Palazzo Vecchio. It has Donatello's *David* (the very influential first male nude to be sculpted in a thousand years), works by Michelangelo, and more (L8,000, daily 8:30–14:00 but closed second and fourth Monday of each month, Via del Proconsolo 4). Dante's house, across the street and around the corner, is interesting only to his Italian-speaking fans.

▲▲**Santa Croce Church**—This 14th-century Franciscan church, decorated by centuries of precious art, holds the tombs of great Florentines (free, Wednesday–Monday 7:15–12:30, 15:00–18:30, closed Tuesday). The loud 19th-century Victorian Gothic facade faces a huge square ringed with tempting touristy shops and littered with tired tourists (and ice-cream cups—Vivoli's is 2 blocks away). Escape into the church.

Working counterclockwise from the entrance you'll find: the tomb of Michelangelo (with the allegorical figures of painting, architecture and sculpture), a memorial to Dante (no body . . . he was banished by his hometown), tomb of Machaivelli, a relief by Donatello of the Annunciation, the tomb of the composer Rossini. To the right of the altar, step into the sacristy where you'll find the bit of St. Francis' cowl (he is supposed to have founded the church around 1290) and old sheets of music with the medieval and mobile C-clef (2 little blocks on either side of the line determined to be middle C). In the bookshop notice the photos high on the wall of the devastating flood of 1966. Beyond that is a touristy—but mildly interesting— "leather school." The chapels lining the front of the church are richly frescoed. The Bardi Chapel (far left of altar) is a master-piece by Giotto featuring scenes from the life of St. Francis. On your way out you'll pass the tomb of Galileo (allowed in by the church long after his death). The neighboring Pazzi Chapel (by Brunelleschi) is considered one of the finest pieces of Florentine Renaissance architecture.

▲**Medici Chapel (Cappelle dei Medici)**—This chapel, containing two Medici tombs, is drenched in incredibly lavish High Renaissance architecture and sculpture by Michelangelo (L10,000, daily 8:30–14:00 but closed the first and third Monday of each month). Behind San Lorenzo on Piazza Madonna, it's surrounded by a lively market scene that I find more interesting. Don't miss a wander through the huge double-decker central market.

Science Museum (Museo di Storia della Scienza)—This is a fascinating collection of Renaissance and later clocks, telescopes, maps, and ingenious gadgets. One of the most talked-about bottles in Florence is the one here containing Galileo's finger. English guidebooklets are available. It's friendly, comfortably cool, never crowded, and just downstream from the Uffizi (L10,000, Monday, Wednesday, and Friday 9:30–13:00, 14:00–17:00, Tuesday and Thursday 9:30–13:00, closed Sunday, Piazza dei Giudici 1).

▲**Michelangelo's Home, Casa Buonarroti**—Fans enjoy Michelangelo's house, which has some of his early, much-less-monumental works (L10,000, Wednesday–Monday 9:30–13:30, closed Tuesday, Via Ghibellina 70).

▲▲**Gelato**—Gelato is an edible art form. Italy's best ice cream is in Florence. Every year I repeat my taste test. And every year Vivoli's wins (on Via Stinche, see map, 8:00–01:00, closed Monday, the last three weeks in August, and winter). Gelateria Carrozze (30 yards from the Ponte Vecchio towards the Uffizi, Via del Pesce 3), Festival del Gelato (Via del Corso) and Perche Non! (Via Tavolini), both just off Via Calzaioli, are also good. That's one souvenir that can't break and won't clut-ter your luggage. Get a free sampleof Vivoli's *riso* (rice, my favorite) before ordering. (The Cinema Astro across the street from Vivoli's plays English/American movies in their original language, closed Mondays.)

Shopping—Florence is a great shopping town. Busy street scenes and markets abound, especially near San Lorenzo, on the Ponte Vecchio, and near Santa Croce. Leather, gold, silver, art prints, and tacky plaster "mini-*Davids*" are most popular.

Scenic City Bus Ride to Fiesole—For a candid peek at a Florentine suburb, ride bus #7 (from Piazza Adua, near the station, extra-urban ticket needed) for about 20 minutes through neighborhood gardens, vineyards, orchards, and large villas to the last stop—Fiesole. Fiesole is a popular excursion from Florence for its small eateries and good views of Florence. (Catch the sunset from the terrace just below the La Reggia restaurant; from the Fiesola bus stop, face the square and take the very steep road on your left to the terrace and good restaurant).

Sights—Florence, South of the Arno River

▲▲**The Pitti Palace**—From the Uffizi, follow the elevated passageway (closed to non-Medicis) across the river to the gargantuan Pitti Palace which has five separate museums. The **Palatine Gallery/Royal Apartments** (First floor, L12,000, Tuesday–Saturday 9:00–19:00, Sunday 9:00–13:00, closed Monday) features palatial room after chandeliered room, its walls sagging with paintings by the great masters. This Raphael collection is the biggest anywhere. The **Modern Art Gallery** (Second floor, L8,000, Tuesday–Sunday 9:00–14:00, closed Monday) features 19th- and 20th-century art (mostly Romanticism, Neo-classicism, Impressionism by Tuscan painters). The **Grand Ducal Treasures** (Il Museo degli Argenti, ground floor, L4,000, Tuesday–Sunday 8:30–14:00, closed Monday) is the Medici treasure chest entertaining fans of applied arts with jeweled crucifixes, exotic porcelain, gilded ostrich eggs, and so on). Behind the palace, the huge semi-landscaped Boboli Gardens offer a cool refuge from the city heat (L4,000, Tuesday–Sunday 9:00–17:30, closed Monday).

▲**Brancacci Chapel**—For the best look at the early Renaissance master Masaccio, see his restored frescoes here (L5,000, 10:00–17:00, Sunday 13:00–17:00, closed Tuesday; across the Ponte Vecchio and turn right a few blocks to Piazza del Carmine). The neighborhoods around here are considered the last surviving bits of old Florence.

▲**Piazzale Michelangelo**—Across the river overlooking the city (look for the huge statue of David), this square is worth the half-hour hike, drive, or bus ride (#13 from the train station) for the view. After dark it's packed with local schoolkids feeding their dates slices of watermelon. Just beyond it is the stark and beautiful, crowd-free, Romanesque San Miniato church.

Evening Side Trip to Siena
Connoisseurs of peace and small towns who aren't into art or shopping (and who won't be seeing Siena otherwise), should consider riding the bus to Siena for the evening (75 min if you take the *"corse rapide"* via the autostrada). Florence has no after-dark magic. Siena *is* after-dark magic. Confirm when the last bus returns.

Sleeping in Florence
(L1,600 = about $1, tel. code: 055)
Sleep Code: **S**=Single, **D**=Double/Twin, **T**=Triple, **Q**=Quad, **b**=bathroom, **s**=shower only, **CC**=Credit Card (Visa, MasterCard, Amex), **SE**=Speaks English, **NSE**=No English. Unless otherwise noted, breakfast is included (but usually optional). English is generally spoken.

The hotel scene in generally crowded and overpriced Florence isn't bad. With good information and a phone call ahead, you can find a stark, clean, and comfortable double with breakfast for L90,000, with a private shower for L120,000. You get roof-garden elegance for L140,000. Most places listed are old and rickety. I can't imagine Florence any other way. Call direct to the hotel. Do not use the tourist office, which costs your host and jacks up the price. Except for Easter, Christmas, May and October, there are plenty of rooms in Florence (dead winter and August are easiest). Budget travelers can call around and find soft prices. If you're staying for three or more nights, ask for a discount. The optional and overpriced breakfast can be a bargaining chip. Call ahead. I repeat, *call ahead.* Places will hold a room until early afternoon. If they say they're full, mention you're using this book.

Sleeping East of the Train Station
East of the station, a handy modern launderette is just off Via Cavour at Via Guelfa 22 red (daily 8:00–22:00, 12 pounds wash and dry for L12,000).

Casa Rabatti is the ultimate if you always wanted to be a part of a Florentine family. It's simple, clean, friendly, and run with motherly warmth by Marcella and her husband Celestino, who speak minimal English (four rooms, D-L70,000, Db-L80,000, L30,000 per bed in shared quad or quint, prices good with this book, no breakfast; 5 blocks from station, Via San Zanobi 48 black, 50129 Florence, tel. 055/212-393).

Soggiorno Pezzati is another quiet little place with six homey rooms (Sb-L55,000, Db-L80,000, no breakfast; Via San Zanobi 22, tel. & fax 055/291-660, Daniela SE).

Hotel Enza has 16 rooms, run by English-speaking Eugenia, who clearly enjoys her work. While Eugenia's chihuahua, Tricky, is tiny, her singles are particularly spacious (S-L65,000, Sb-L70,000, D-L85,000, Db-L120,000, T-L120,000, Tb-L150,000, family loft, discounts for three nights, no breakfast; 6 blocks from station, Via San Zanobi 45 black, 50129 Florence, tel. 055/490-990, fax 055/292-192).

Soggiorno Magliani feels and smells like a great-grandmother's place, central and humble (seven rooms, D-L68,000; at the corner of Via Guelfa and Via Reparata, Via Reparata 1, tel. 055/287-378, run by Vicenza and her English-speaking daughter Christina).

Hotel Loggiato dei Serviti, at the most prestigious address in Florence on the most Renaissance (traffic-free) square in town, gives you Renaissance romance with a place to plug in your hair-dryer (29 rooms, Sb-L200,000, Db-L300,000, family suites, book a month ahead, deals in August, elevator, CC:VMA; Piazza S.S. Annunziata 3, 50122 Florence, tel. 055/289-592, fax 055/289-595). Stone stairways lead you under open-beam ceilings through this 16th-century monastery's elegantly appointed public rooms. The cells, with air conditioning, TVs, mini-bars, and telephones, wouldn't be recognized by their original inhabitants. This place is my kind of classy.

Le Due Fontane Hotel faces the same great square but fills its old building with a modern, business-class ambience. Its air-con rooms are big, modern, and stylish—less memorable and less expensive (57 rooms, Sb-L150,000, Db-L240,000, Tb-L330,000, prices promised by Sr. Borgia through 1998, CC:VMA, elevator; Piazza S.S. Annunziata 14, 50122 Florence, tel. 055/210-185, fax 055/294-461, SE).

Sleeping South of the Station near Piazza Santa Maria Novella
(zip code: 50123)

From the station, follow the underground tunnel to Piazza Santa Maria Novella, a pleasant square by day and a little sleazy after dark. (Theft alert where the tunnel surfaces.) It's handy: 3 blocks from the cathedral, near a good launderette (**La Serena**, Monday–Saturday 8:30–20:00, closed Sunday; Via della Scala 30 red; L20,000 for 11 pounds, tel. 055/218-183), cheap restaurants (on Via Palazzuolo, see below), and the bus and train station. There's a great Massaccio fresco (*The Trinity*) in the church on the square (free).

Hotel Universo, a big, group-friendly hotel with stark concrete hallways but fine rooms, is warmly run by a group of gentle men (D-L100,000, Db-L130,000, Tb-L175,000, Qb-L200,000, to get these discounted prices—promised through 1998—you must show this book, CC:VM, elevator; right on Piazza S. M. Novella at #20, tel. 055/281-951, fax 055/292-335, SE).

Hotel Pensione Elite, with eight comfortable rooms, is a good basic value, run warmly by Maurizio and Nadia (Ss-L85,000, Sb-L100,000, Ds-L100,000, Db-L130,000; at end of square with back to church, go right to Via della Scala 12, second floor, tel. & fax 055/215-395, SE).

The nearby **Albergo Montreal** is cheaper, with clean, airy and comfortable rooms but less character (14 rooms, Db-L90,000 with this book through 1998; Via della Scala 43, tel. 055/238-2331, fax 055/287-491, SE).

Pensione Sole, a clean, cozy, family-run place with seven bright rooms, is well-located just off Santa Maria Novella toward the river (S-L50,000, D-L70,000, Db-L90,000, Tb-L120,000, no breakfast; Via del Sole 8, third floor, lots of stairs, tel. & fax 055/239-6094, Anna NSE).

Albergo Concordia is a modern, well-run, and conveniently located place (16 rooms, one fine Sb-L65,000, Db-L100,000, Tb-L125,000, optional breakfast L15,000 extra, prices promised through 1998, CC:VMA, no elevator, filled with school groups February–April; Via dell'Amorino 14, 50123 Florence, tel. & fax 055/213-233, Fabrizio SE).

Pensione Centrale is very central, Old World-comfortable, and run by Marie Therese Blot and Franco, who make you feel right at home (D-L130,000, Db-L170,000 with an

"American" breakfast, often filled with American students, CC:VMA; elevator near the Duomo at Via dei Conti 3, tel. 055/215-761, fax 055/215-216).

Pensione Burchianti is a spacious old noble house. Each of its 11 rooms has a bit of old Florence surviving on its walls or ceilings (Sb-L70,000, Ds-L110,000, Db-L120,000, extra bed-L30,000–40,000, L5,000 breakfast, prices promised with this book; midway between the station and the Duomo at Via del Giglio 6, tel. & fax 055/212-796). Friendly Gieuseppe SE.

Pensione Maxim is big, ramshackle, and as close to the sights as possible. You'll feel like a rat in a maze navigating its narrow, dingy halls (23 rooms, D-L100,000, Db-L125,000, T-L130,000, Tb-L145,000, Q-L160,000, Qb-L180,000, CC:VMA, in-house laundry service; Via dei Medici 4, elevator at Via dei Calzaiuoli 11, tel. 055/217-474, fax 055/283-729, e-mail: hotmaxim@tin.it).

Soggiorno Abaco is a bohemian, MTV-kind of place listed in most of the student guidebooks and run by friendly, guitar-strumming Bruno (seven rooms, S-L65,000, Sb-L80,000, Ds-L100,000, Db-L120,000, extra roommates-L20,000 each; Via Dei Banchi 1, tel. 055/238-1919, fax 055/282-289, SE).

Sleeping on or near the Arno River and Ponte Vecchio

Pensione Bretagna is a classy, Old World-elegant place with thoughtfully appointed rooms. The hotel is run by the very helpful, English-speaking Antonio, Maura, and Marco. Imagine eating breakfast under a painted, chandeliered ceiling overlooking the Arno River (S-L70,000, Ss-L75,000, Sb-L80,000, D-L105,000, Ds-L120,000, Db-L145,000, Tb-L195,000, including optional L10,000 breakfast, family deals, prices special with this book through 1998, CC:VMA, elevator; just past Ponte San Trinita, at Lungarno Corsini 6, 50123 Firenze, tel. 055/289-618, fax 055/289-619, e-mail: hotelpens.bretagna@agora.stm.it).

Aily Home is a humble, homey, grandmotherly, five-room place tucked away on a peaceful square a block from the Ponte Vecchio (three-night minimum, S-L30,000, D-L60,000, showers-L3,000, elevator; Piazza San Stefano 1, tel. 055/239-6505, Rosaria Franchis NSE).

Sleeping in Oltrarno, South of the River
(zip code: 50125)

Across the river in the Oltrarno area, between the Pitti Palace and the Ponte Vecchio, you'll still find small traditional crafts shops; neighborly piazzas hiding a few offbeat art treasures; family eateries; two distinctive, moderately priced hotels; two student dorms; and a youth hostel. Each of these places is only a few minutes walk from the Ponte Vecchio.

Hotel La Scaletta is elegant, friendly, and clean, with a dark, cool, labyrinthine floor plan and lots of Old World lounges. Owner Barbara, her son Manfredo, and daughters Bianca and Diana run this well-worn place. Your journal becomes poetry when written on the highest terrace of La Scaletta's panoramic roof garden. If Manfredo is cooking dinner, eat here (D-L120,000, Db-L155,000, T-L155,000, Tb-L190,000, Qb-L220,000, CC:VM, from L10,000–20,000 discount if you pay cash; elevator; Via Guicciardini 13 black, 150 yards up the street from the Ponte Vecchio, next to American Express, tel. 055/283-028, fax 055/289-562, web site: www.alba.fi.it, e-mail: LaScaletta.htl@dada.it). Reserve well in advance by phone, then confirm your reservation with a fax and send a check.

Pensione Sorelle Bandini is a ramshackle 500-year-old palace on a perfectly Florentine square, with cavernous rooms, museum warehouse interiors, a musty youthfulness, cats, a balcony lounge-loggia with a view, and an ambience that, for romantic bohemians, can be a highlight of Florence. Mimmo or Sr. Romeo will hold a room until 16:00 with a phone call (D-L140,000, Db-L172,000, T-L210,000, Tb-L242,000, includes breakfast, elevator; Piazza Santo Spirito 9, tel. 055/215-308, fax 055/282-761).

Hotel Silla, a classic three-star hotel with cheery, spacious, pastel and modern rooms, is a fine splurge. It faces the river overlooking a park opposite the Santa Croce church (32 rooms, Db-L220,000, CC:VMA, some rooms with air-con; Via dei Renai 5, 50125 Florence, tel. 055/234-2888, fax 055/234-1437, manager Gabrielle SE).

Institute Gould is a Protestant church-run place with 72 beds in 27 rooms and clean, modern facilities (D-L66,000, Db-L74,000, L37,000 beds in shared doubles, L30,000 in quads; 49 Via dei Serragli, tel. 055/212-576). You must arrive when office is open (Monday–Friday 9:00–13:00, 15:00–19:00, Saturday 9:00–13:00, no check-in on Sunday).

The Catholic-run **Pensionato Pio X-Artigianelli** is more freewheeling and rundown, with 54 beds in 20 rooms, and a midnight curfew (L24,000 beds in three- to five-bed rooms, minimum two nights; Via dei Serragli 106, tel. & fax 055/225-044).

Pension Ungherese, warmly run by Sergio, is good for drivers. It's outside the city center (near Stadio, on route to Fiesole) with easy free street parking and quick bus access into central Florence (Sb-L100,000, Db-L150,000, prices good with this book, extra 7 percent off if you pay cash, CC:VM; Via G. B. Amici 8, tel. & fax 055/573-474, NSE, e-mail: hotel.ungherese @dada.it). It has great singles, a backyard garden terrace, and just-renovated rooms (ask for one on the garden).

Last alternatives: **Ostello Santa Monaca** (L22,000 beds, ten-bed rooms, no breakfast, midnight curfew; very well located a few blocks past Ponte Alla Carraia, Via Santa Monaca 6, tel. 055/268-338, fax 055/280-185), and the classy **Villa Camerata IYHF** hostel (L23,000 per bed and breakfast, four- to ten-bed rooms; ride bus #17A or B then 500-meter walk, tel. 055/601-451) on the outskirts of Florence.

Eating in Florence

Eating in Oltrarno, South of the River

There are several good and colorful restaurants in Oltrarno on or near Piazza Santo Spirito. **Borgo Antico** serves hearty portions to a classy young and local clientele. It's right on a great square with indoor and outdoor seating and worth the extra lire (Piazza Santo Spirito 6 red, tel. 055/210-437). The **Ricchi** bar, #6 on the same square, has fine homemade gelati and outdoor tables shaded by trees (step inside to see the wallful of entries to finish the facade of the Brunelleschi church on the square).

Trattoria Casalinga is an inexpensive and popular standby, famous for its home-cooking (just off Piazza Santo Spirito, near the church at Via dei Michelozzi 9 red, closed Sunday, tel. 055/218-624).

Good food and ambience at reasonable prices are also served at **Trattoria Sabatino** at Borgo S. Frediano 17 blue and **Osteria del Cinghiale Bianco** at Borgo S. Jacopo 43 red (open at 19:00, closed Tuesday and Wednesday, arrive early or call 055/215-706 to reserve).

La Galleria Ristorante is a hard-working family affair with a passion for quality home-cooking in a small modern gallery a block off the Ponte Vecchio (good L20,000 menu, closed Monday, Via Guicciardini 48 red, tel. 055/218-545). Peek into the back to see mama cutting the pasta.

Trattoria Bordino is cozy and friendly, serving fine Florentine cuisine. Its prices aren't cheap, but it's an excellent value (L40,000 dinners, closed Sunday, Via Stracciatella 9 red). Take the second left after crossing Ponte Vecchio and walk under the arch.

Eating near Santa Maria Novella and the Train Station

Two similar chow houses, each offering a L16,000, hearty, family-style, fixed-price menu with a bustling working-class/budget-Yankee-traveler atmosphere, are **Trattoria il Contadino** (Via Palazzuolo 69 red, a few blocks south of the train station, Monday–Saturday 12:00–14:30, 18:15–21:30, closed Sunday, tel. 055/238-2673) and **Trattoria da Giorgio** (across the street at Via Palazzuolo 100 red, Monday–Saturday 12:00–15:00, 18:30–22:00, closed Sunday). Check each before choosing. Get there early or be ready to wait. The touristy **La Grotta di Leo** has a cheap, straightforward menu and edible food (Via della Scala 41 red, closed Wednesday, tel. 055/219-265). And near the recommended Hotel Enza and Via San Zanobi private homes: **Trattoria la Burrasca** is a small inexpensive place serving local-style dishes to Italians in a characteristic setting (12:00–15:00, 19:00–22:00, closed Thursday, near the market at Via Panicale 6r, tel. 055/215-827).

A Quick Lunch near the Sights

I keep lunch in Florence fast and simple, eating in one of countless self-service places, Pizza Rusticas (holes-in-walls selling pizza by weight), or just picnicking (juice, yogurt, cheese, roll: L8,000). For mountains of picnic produce or just a cheap sandwich and piles of people-watching, visit the huge multi-storied **Mercato Centrale** (7:00–14:00, closed Sunday) in the middle of the San Lorenzo street market. Behind the Duomo, **Snack** (15 Pronconsolo) serves decent cheap lunches. For a reasonably priced pizza with a Medici-style view, try one of the pizzerias on Piazza della Signori. A few blocks behind the Palazzo Vecchio, the cozy **Rosticceria Guilano Centro** serves fine food to go or enjoy there (closed Monday, Via Dei Neri

74 red). **Osteria Vini e Vecchi Sapori** is a colorful hole-in-the-wall serving traditional food, including plates of mixed sandwiches, half a block from Palazzo Vecchio (Tuesday–Sunday 9:30–21:30, closed Monday, Via dei Magazzini 3 red). **Cantinetta dei Verrazzano** is a long established bakery/café/winebar which serves elegant sandwich plates and hot focaccia sandwiches in an elegant old-time setting (open until 21:00, closed Sunday, just off Via Calzaiuoli at Via dei Tavolini 18, tel. 055/268-590).

Transportation Connections—Florence
By train to: Assisi (10/day, 2.5 to 3 hrs), **Orvieto** (6/day, 2 hrs), **Pisa** (2/hr, 1 hr), **La Spezia** (for the Cinque Terre, 2/day direct, 2 hrs, or change in Pisa), **Venice** (7/day, 3 hrs), **Milan** (12/day, 3–5 hrs), **Rome** (hourly, 2.5 hrs), **Naples** (2/day, 4 hrs), **Brindisi** (3/day, 11 hrs with change in Bologna), **Frankfurt** (3/day, 12 hrs), **Paris** (1/day, 12 hrs overnight), **Vienna** (4/day, 9–10 hrs). Train info: tel. 1478-88088.

    Buses: The SITA bus station, a block from the Florence train station, offers service to **San Gimignano** (hourly, 1.75 hrs, L8,000) and **Siena** (hourly, 75-min fast buses or 2-hr slow buses, L10,000, faster than the train). Bus info: tel. 055/483-651; some schedules are in Florence's *Concierge* magazine.

Driving Florentine
From the autostrada (north or south) take the Certosa exit (follow signs to Centro, at Porta Romana go under arch and down Via Romana). After driving and trying to park in Florence, you'll understand why Leonardo never invented the car. Cars flatten the charm of Florence. Get near the *centro* and park where you can. Garages charge around L30,000 a day. The big underground lot at the train station charges L2,000 per hour. The cheapest and biggest garage is at Fortezza di Basso (L20,000 per day). Borgo Ognissanti 96, near the Amerigo Vespucci bridge, is reasonable and closer to the center. White lines are free, blue are not. I got towed once in the town of Michelangelo—an expensive lesson.

PISA
Pisa was a regional superpower in her medieval heyday (11th, 12th, and 13th centuries), rivaling Florence and Genoa. Its Mediterranean empire, which included Corsica and Sardinia,

helped make it a wealthy republic. But the Pisa fleet was beaten (1284, by Genoa) and its port silted up, leaving the city high and dry with only its Piazza of Miracles and its university keeping it on the map.

Pisa's three important sights (the cathedral, baptistery, and bell tower) float regally on the best lawn in Italy. Even as the church was being built, the Piazza del Duomo was nicknamed the Campo dei Miracoli, or "Field of Miracles," for the grandness of the undertaking. The style throughout is Pisa's very own "Pisan Romanesque" (surrounded by what may be Italy's tackiest ring of souvenir stands). This spectacle is tourism at its most crass. Wear gloves.

Planning Your Time

Seeing the tower and the square and wandering through the church are 90 percent of the Pisan thrill. Pisa is a touristy quickie. By train it's a joy. By car it's a headache. Train travelers may be changing trains in Pisa anyway. Hop on the bus and see the tower. Since you can't climb the tower, a look doesn't take very long and is worthwhile even after (or before) hours. Sophisticated sightseers stop more for the Pisano carvings in the cathedral and baptistery than for a look at the tipsy tower. There's nothing wrong with Pisa, but I'd stop only to see the "Piazza of Miracles" and get out. By car it's a 45-minute detour from the freeway.

Orientation (tel. code: 050)

Tourist Information: TI offices are at the train station (daily 9:00–19:00, tel. 050/42291) and at the Leaning Tower. The Pisa tourist board has a scheme to get you into its neglected secondary sights. Various sight combination tickets run from L10,000 for any two sights to L15,000 for the works.

Arrival in Pisa

By Train: Train travelers bus easily from the station in the center, over the Arno River, and to the Duomo. Bus #1 (for Duomo) leaves from the bus circle to the right of the station every ten minutes. Buy your L1,300 ticket from the tobacco/magazine kiosk in the station's main hall.

By Car: To get to the Leaning Tower, follow signs to the Duomo or the Piazza dei Miracoli. This is on the north edge of town. Drivers (coming from the Pisa Nord autostrada exit) don't have to mess with the city (although you will have to endure some terrible traffic). There's no option better than the L1,500-per-hour pay lot just outside the town wall near the Duomo.

Sights—Pisa

▲▲**Leaning Tower**—This most famous example of Pisan Romanesque architecture was leaning even before its completion. Notice how the architect, for lack of a better solution, kinked up the top section. The 294 tilted steps to the top are closed while engineers work to keep the bell tower from toppling. The formerly clean and tidy area around the tower is now a construction zone. Steam pipes drying out the subsoil and huge weights are working together to stop the leaning (but not straighten out the tower). For a quick lunch, the pizzeria/trattoria La Buca (near tower at Via S. Maria and Via G. Tassi) is a decent value.

▲▲**Cathedral**—The huge Pisan Romanesque cathedral, with its richly carved pulpit by Giovanni Pisano, is artistically more important than its more famous bell tower (L2,000, daily 8:00–13:00, 15:00–20:00).

Baptistery—The baptistery, the biggest in Italy, with a pulpit by Nicolo Pisano (1260) which inspired Renaissance art to follow, is interesting for its great acoustics (L5,000, daily 9:00–19:30, in front of the cathedral). If you ask nicely and leave a tip, the doorman uses the place's echo power to sing haunting harmonies with himself. Notice that even the baptistery leans about 5 feet. (The Nicolo Pisano pulpit and carvings in Siena were just as impressive to me—in a more enjoyable atmosphere.)

Other Sights—Pisa, of course, is more than the Campo dei Miracoli. Walking from the station to the Duomo shows you a classy Old World town with an Arno-scape much like its rival upstream. But for most, Pisa is just a cliché that needs to be seen and a chance to see the Pisano pulpits. For more Pisan art, see the Museo dell' Opera del Duomo (behind the tower) and the Museo Nazionale di San Matteo (on the river near Piazza Mazzini). The cemetery bordering the cathedral square is not worth the admission, even if its "Holy Land dirt" does turn a body into a skeleton in a day.

Transportation Connections—Pisa

By train to: Florence (hourly, 60 min), **La Spezia** (hourly, 60 min, milk-run from there into coastal villages), **Siena** (change at

Empoli: Pisa–Empoli, hourly, 30 min; Empoli–Siena, hourly, 60 min). Even the fastest trains stop in Pisa, and you'll very likely be changing trains here whether you plan to stop or not. Train info: tel. 1478-88088.

Route Tips for Drivers

To Florence and Siena: The drive from Pisa to Florence is that rare case where the non-autostrada highway (free, more direct, and at least as fast) is a better deal than the autostrada. When departing for Florence, San Gimignano, or Siena, follow the blue "superstrada" signs (green signs are for the autostrada) for the SS road (along the city wall east from the tower—away from the sea) for Florence (and later Siena).

    To the Cinque Terre: From Pisa, catch the Genova-bound autostrada. The white stuff you'll see in the mountains as you approach La Spezia isn't snow—it's Carrara marble, Michelangelo's choice for his great art. From Pisa to La Spezia takes about an hour.

HILL TOWNS OF CENTRAL ITALY

Break out of the Venice-Florence-Rome syndrome. There's more to Italy! Experience the slumber of Umbria, the texture of Tuscany, and the lazy towns of Lazio. For starters, here are a few of my favorites.

Siena seems to be every Italy connoisseur's pet town. In my office whenever Siena is mentioned, someone moans, "Siena? I *luuuv* Siena!" San Gimignano is the quintessential hill town, with Italy's best surviving medieval skyline. Assisi—visited for its hometown boy, St. Francis, who made very good—is best after dark. Orvieto, one of the most famous hill towns, is an ideal springboard for a trip to tiny Civita. Stranded alone on its pinnacle in a vast canyon, Civita's the most lovable.

Planning Your Time

Siena, the must-see town, has the easiest train and bus connections. On a quick trip, consider spending three nights in Siena (with a whole-day side trip into Florence and a day to relax and enjoy Siena). Whatever you do, enjoy a sleepy medieval evening in Siena. After an evening in Siena, its major sights can be seen in half a day. San Gimignano is an overrun, pint-sized Siena. Don't rush Siena for San Gimignano.

Civita di Bagnoregio is the great pinnacle town. A night in Bagnoregio (via Orvieto bus) with time to hike to the town and spend three hours makes the visit worthwhile. Two nights and an entire day is a good way to keep your pain/pleasure ratio in order.

Hill Towns of Central Italy

Assisi is the third most visit-worthy town. It has half a day of sightseeing and another half a day of wonder. While a zoo by day, it's a delight at night.

SIENA

Seven hundred years ago, Siena was a major military power in a class with Florence, Venice, and Genoa. With a population of 60,000, it was even bigger than Paris. The town was weakened by a disastrous plague in 1348. In the 1550s her bitter rival Florence really salted her, making Siena forever a non-threatening backwater. Siena's loss became our sightseeing gain, as its political and economic irrelevance pickled it purely Gothic. Today Siena's population is still 60,000 compared to Florence's 420,000.

Siena's thriving historic center, with traffic-free red-brick lanes cascading every which way, offers Italy's best Gothic city experience. Most people do Siena, just 30 miles south of Florence, as a day trip, but it's best experienced after dark. While Florence has the blockbuster museums, Siena has an easy-to-enjoy soul: courtyards sport flower-decked wells, alleys dead-end at rooftop views, and the sky is a rich blue dome. Right off the bat, Siena becomes an old friend.

For those who dream of a Fiat-free Italy, this is it. Sit at a café on the red-bricked main square. Take time to savor the first European city to eliminate automobile traffic (1966), and then, just to be silly, wonder what would happen if they did it in your city.

Orientation (tel. code: 0577)

Siena lounges atop a hill, stretching its three legs out from Il Campo. This main square is the historic meeting point of Siena's neighborhoods. The old center is nearly pedestrians-only. And most of those pedestrians are students from the local university. Everything I mention is within a 15-minute walk of the square. Navigate by landmarks, following the excellent system of street-corner signs. The typical visitor sticks to the San Domenico-Il Campo axis.

Tourist Information: Pick up the excellent and free topographical town map from the main TI on Il Campo (#56, look for the yellow Change sign, Monday–Saturday 8:30–19:30, Sunday mornings in summer, tel. 0577/280-551).

Arrival in Siena: From Siena's train station, buy a L1,300 bus ticket from the yellow machine near the exit, cross the square, and board any orange city bus heading for Piazza del Sale. Your hotel is probably within a ten-minute walk.

From the autostrada, drivers take the Porta San Marco exit and follow the Centro, then "Stadio" signs (stadium, soccer ball). The soccer-ball signs take you to the stadium lot (L1,300/hour, L15,000/day) at the huge bare-brick San Domenico church. You can drive into the pedestrian zone (a pretty ballsy thing to do) only to drop bags at your hotel. You can park free in the lot below the Albergo Lea, white-striped spots behind Hotel Villa Liberty, and behind the fortezza. (Note the L200,000 tow fee incentive to learn the days of the week in Italian).

Sights—Siena

Siena is one big sight. Its essential individual sights come in two little clusters: the square (city hall, museum, tower) and the cathedral (baptistery, cathedral museum with its surprise viewpoint). Check these sights off, and you're free to wander.

Siena

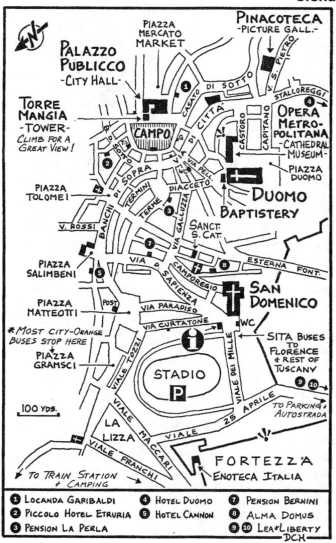

❶ Locanda Garibaldi	❹ Hotel Duomo	❼ Pension Bernini
❷ Piccolo Hotel Etruria	❺ Hotel Cannon	❽ Alma Domus
❸ Pension La Perla		❾ ❿ Lea+Liberty

▲▲▲**Il Campo**—Siena's great central piazza is urban harmony at its best. Like a people-friendly stage set, its gently tilted floor fans out from the tower and city hall backdrop. It's the perfect invitation to loiter. Think of it as a trip to the beach without sand or water. Il Campo was located at the historic junction of Siena's various competing districts, or *contrada*, on the old marketplace. The brick surface is divided into nine sections, representing the council of nine merchants and city bigwigs who ruled medieval Siena. Don't miss the Fountain of Joy at the square's high point, with its pigeons politely waiting their turn to gingerly tightrope down slippery snouts to slurp a drink, and with the two naked guys about to be tossed in. At the base of the tower, the Piazza's chapel was built in 1348 as a thanks to God for ending the Black Plague (after it killed more than a third of the population). The market area behind the city hall, a wide-open expanse since the Middle Ages, originated as a farming area within the city walls to feed the city in times of seige.

▲**Museo Civico**—The Palazzo Pubblico (City Hall), at the base of the tower, has a fine and manageable museum housing a good sample of Sienese art. You'll see, in the following order, the Sala Risorgimento with dramatic scenes of Victor Emanuel's unification of Italy (surrounded by statues that don't seem to care); the chapel with impressive inlaid wood chairs in the choir; and the Sala del Mappamondo, with Simone Martini's *Maesta* (Enthroned Virgin) facing the faded *Guidoriccio da Fogliano* (a mercenary providing a more concrete form of protection). Next is the Sala della Pace, which has two interesting frescoes showing "The Effects of Good and Bad Government." Notice the whistle-while-you-work happiness of the utopian community ruled by the utopian government (in the best-preserved fresco) and the fate of a community ruled by politicians with more typical values (in a terrible state of repair). The message: without justice there can be no prosperity. Later you'll see a particularly gruesome *Slaughter of the Innocents*. The big stairs lead to a loggia with a nothing-special view (L6,000, Monday–Saturday 9:00–19:00, Sunday and daily off-season 9:00–13:30, tel. 0577/292-111).

▲**City Tower (Torre del Mangia)**—Siena gathers around its city hall, not its church. It was a proud republic and its "declaration of independence" is the tallest secular medieval tower in Italy, the 100-yard-tall Torre del Mangia (named after a hedonistic watchman who consumed his earnings like a glutton consumes food; his statue is in the courtyard, to the left as you enter). Its 300 steps get pretty skinny at the top, but the reward is one of Italy's best views (L5,000, daily

10:00–18:00 or 19:00, limit of 30 towerists at a time, avoid the midday crowd).

The Palio—The feisty spirit of each of Siena's 17 *contrada* lives on. These neighborhoods celebrate, worship, and compete together. Each even has its own historical museum. Contrada pride is evident any time of year in the colorful neighborhood banners and parades. (If you hear distant drumming, run to it for the medieval action). But *contrada* pride is most visible twice a year (July 2 and August 16), when they have their world-famous Palio di Siena. Ten of the 17 neighborhoods compete (chosen by lot), hurling themselves with medieval abandon into several days of trial races and traditional revelry. On the big day, Il Campo is stuffed to the brim with locals and tourists, as the horses charge wildly around the square in this literally no-holds-barred race. Of course, the winning neighborhood is the scene of grand celebrations afterward. The grand prize: simply proving your *contrada* is *numero uno*. All over town, sketches and posters depict the Palio. The TI has a free scrapbook-quality Palio brochure with English explanations. While the actual Palio really packs the city, you could side trip in from Florence to see horse-race trials each of the three days before the big day (usually at 9:00 and 19:45).

▲▲▲**The Duomo**—Siena's cathedral is as Baroque as Gothic gets. The striped facade is piled with statues and ornamentation; the interior is decorated from top to bottom. The heads of 172 popes peer down from the ceiling over the fine inlaid art on the floor. This is one busy interior.

To orient yourself in this *panforte* of Italian churches, stand under the dome and think of the church floor as a big clock: you're the middle, the altar is high noon: you'll find the *Slaughter of the Innocents* roped off on the floor at 10:00, Pisano's pulpit between two pillars at 11:00, Bernini's chapel at 3:00, two Michelangelo statues (next to snacks, shop, and WC) at 7:00, the library at 8:00, and a Donatello statue at 9:00. Take some time with the floor mosaics in the front. Nicolo Pisano's wonderful pulpit is crowded but delicate Gothic story-telling from 1268. To understand why Bernini is considered the greatest Baroque sculptor, step into his sumptuous *Cappella della Madonna del Voto*. This last work in the cathedral, from 1659, is enough to make a Lutheran light a candle. Move up to the altar and look back at the two Bernini statues: St. Jerome playing the crucifix like a violinist lost in beautiful music, and Mary Magdalene in a similar state of spiritual ecstasy. The Piccolomini altar is most interesting for its two Michelangelo statues (the lower big ones). Paul, on the left, may be a self-portrait. Peter, on the right, resembles Michelangelo's more famous statue of Moses. Originally contracted to do 15 statues, Michelangelo left the project early (1504) to do his great *David* in Florence. The Piccolomini Library (worth the L2,000 entry), brilliantly frescoed with scenes glorifying the works of a pope from 500 years ago, contains intricately decorated, or "illuminated," music scores and a Roman copy of three Greek graces. Donatello's statue of St. John the Baptist is being restored (church open 7:30–19:30, less in off-season, modest dress required).

Santa Maria della Scala—This newly opened and renovated old hospital (opposite the Duomo entrance) displays a rich treasury and a lavishly frescoed hall. The frescoes show medieval Siena's innovative healthcare and social welfare system in action. Unfortunately the high-tech gadgetry and signs are entirely in Italian (L5,000, daily 10:30–15:30).

▲**Baptistery**—Siena is so hilly that there wasn't enough flat ground to build a big church on. What to do? Build a big church and prop up the overhanging edge with the baptistery. This dark and quietly tucked-away cave of art is worth a look (and L3,000) for its cool tranquility and the bronze carvings of Donatello (the six women, or angels) and Ghiberti on the baptismal font (open same hours as the Duomo).

▲▲**Cathedral Museum (Opera Metropolitana)**—Siena's most enjoyable museum, on the Campo side of the church (look for the yellow signs), was built to house the cathedral's art. The ground floor is filled with the cathedral's original Gothic sculpture by Pisano (who spent ten years here carving and orchestrating the decoration of the cathedral in the late 1300s) and a fine Donatello *Madonna and Child*. Upstairs to the left awaits a private audience with Duccio's *Maesta* (Enthroned Virgin). Pull up a chair and study one of the great pieces of medieval art. What was the flip side of the *Maesta* (displayed on the opposite wall), with 26 panels—the medieval equivalent of pages—shows scenes from the passion of Christ. At the end of the top floor, a little sign directs you to the "panorama." Climb to the first landing, then take the skinnier second spiral for Siena's surprise view. Look back over the Duomo, then consider this: when rival republic Florence began its grand cathedral, proud Siena decided to build the biggest church in all Christendom. The existing cathedral would be used as a transept. You're atop what would have been the entry. The wall below you, connecting the Duomo with the museum of the cathedral, was as far as Siena got before a plague killed the city's ability to finish the project. Were it completed, you'd be looking straight down the nave (L6,000, daily 9:00–19:15, closing at 18:30 in spring and fall, 13:30 off-season, tel. 0577/283-048).

Church of San Domenico—This huge brick church is worth a quick look. The simple, bland interior fits the austere philosophy of the Dominicans. Walk up the steps in the rear of the church for a look at various paintings from the life of Saint Catherine, patron saint of Siena and, since 1939, of all Italy. Halfway up the church on the right, you'll find her head (free, daily 7:00–13:00, 15:00–17:30, less in winter).

Sanctuary of Saint Catherine—A few downhill blocks toward the center from San Domenico (follow signs to the Santuario di Santa Caterina), step into Catherine's cool and peaceful home. Siena remembers its favorite hometown girl, a simple, unschooled, but almost mystically devout girl who, in the mid-1300s, helped get the pope to return from France to Rome. Pilgrims have come here since 1464. Wander around to enjoy art depicting scenes from her life. Her room is downstairs (free, daily 9:00–12:30, 15:30–18:00, via Tiratoio).

▲The Pinacoteca (National Picture Gallery)—Siena was a power in Gothic art. But the average tourist, wrapped up in a love affair with the Renaissance, hardly notices. This museum takes you on a walk through Siena's art, chronologically from the 12th through 15th centuries. For the casual sightseer, the Sienese art in the city hall and cathedral museums is adequate. But art fans enjoy this opportunity to trace the evolution of Siena's delicate and elegant art (L8,000, Monday 8:30–13:30, Tuesday–Saturday 9:00–19:00, Sunday 8:00–13:00, tel. 0577/281-161). From the Campo, walk out Via di Citta to Piazza di Posdierla and go left on San Pietro.

Tours by Roberto—Roberto Bechi is a hardworking Sienese tour guide who runs a tour business on the internet. Roberto, who ran a restaurant in the U.S.A. for years and is married to an American, communicates well with Americans. His passions are Sienese culture and local cuisine. He tailors half-day ($40 per person) and full-day ($80 per person, less for groups) tours of Siena and the region by mini-bus. For info and to book a tour, contact him at tel. 0577/704-789, fax 0577/48627, web site: www.zaslon.si/roberto, e-mail: tourrob@box.tin.it.

Sleeping in Siena
(L1,600 = about $1, tel. code: 0577, zip code: 53100)
Sleep Code: **S**=Single, **D**=Double/Twin, **T**=Triple, **Q**=Quad,
b=bathroom, **t**=toilet only, **s**=shower only, **CC**=Credit Card
(Visa, MasterCard, Amex), **SE**=Speaks English, **NSE**=No
English. Breakfast is generally not included. Have breakfast
on Il Campo or in a nearby bar.

Finding a room is tough during Easter or for the Palio
in early July and mid-August. Call ahead, as Siena's few budget places are listed in all the budget guidebooks. While day-
tripping tour groups turn the town into a Gothic amusement
park in midsummer, Siena is basically yours in the evenings
and off-season. Nearly all listed hotels lie between Il Campo
and the church of San Domenico.

Lavarapido Wash and Dry is a modern coin-op self-
service laundromat (L12,000 per 8 kilo load in an hour, daily
8:00–22:00, near the Campo at Via di Pantaneto 38).

Sleeping near Il Campo
Each of these first listings is forgettable but inexpensive and
just a horse-wreck away from one of Italy's most wonderful
civic spaces.

Piccolo Hotel Etruria, a good bet for a real hotel with
all the comforts but not much soul, is just off the square
(S-L53,000, Sb-L63,000, Db-L100,000, Tb-L135,000,
Qb-L170,000, breakfast-L6,000, CC:VMA; with back to
the tower, leave Il Campo to the right, Via Donzelle 1-3,
tel. 0577/288-088, fax 0577/288-461).

Albergo Tre Donzelle is a plain, institutional, but
decent place next door that makes sense only if you think
of Il Campo as your terrace (S-L40,000, D-L66,000,
Db-L86,000; Via Donzelle 5, tel. 0577/280-358, fax
0577/223-933, Senora Iannini SE).

Pension La Perla is a funky, jumbled, 13-room place with
a narrow maze of hallways, basic rooms, and a laissez-faire environment (Sb-L60,000, Db-L90,000, Tb-L125,000, rooms have
tiny box showers; a block off the square on Piazza Independenza
at Via della Terme 25, tel. 0577/47144). Attilio and his
American wife, Deborah, take reservations only a day or two
ahead. Ideally, call the morning you'll arrive.

Hotel Duomo is the best in-the-old-town splurge, a
classy place with spacious, elegant rooms (Sb-L130,000,

Db-L200,000, Tb-L270,000, includes breakfast, CC:VMA, elevator; follow Via di Citta, which becomes Via Stalloreggi, to Via Stalloreggi 38; tel. 0577/289-088, fax 0577/43043, SE).

Hotel Cannon d'Oro, a few blocks up Via Banchi di Sopra, is spacious and group-friendly (30 rooms, Sb-L90,000, Db-L110,000, prices promised through 1998 with this book, family deals, CC:VMA; Via Montanini 28, tel. 0577/44321, fax 0577/280-868, SE).

Locanda Garibaldi is a modest, very Sienese restaurant-albergo. Gentle Marcello wears two hats, running a busy restaurant with seven neglected doubles upstairs. This is a fine place for dinner but a bit noisy and dirty for some to sleep in (D-L75,000, T-L100,000, no credit cards, takes reservations only a few days in advance; half a block downhill off the square at Via Giovanni Dupre 18, tel. 0577/284-204, NSE).

Sleeping Closer to San Domenico Church

These hotels are listed in order of closeness to Il Campo—max ten minutes walk. The first two enjoy views of the old town and cathedral (which sits floodlit before me as I type). The first three are the best values in town.

Albergo Bernini makes you part of a Sienese family in a modest, clean home with nine newly renovated rooms. Friendly Nadia and Mauro, who welcome you to picnic on their spectacular view terrace for breakfast or dinner, get the "we try hardest in Siena" award. The mynah bird (Romeo) actually says *"ciao"* as you come and go from the terrace (Sb-L95,000, D-L100,000, Db-L120,000, family deals, prices drop off season and for drop-ins; midnight curfew; on main San Domenico-Il Campo drag at Via Sapienza 15, tel. & fax 0577/289-047, NSE but has fun trying).

Alma Domus is ideal—unless nuns make you nervous, you need a double bed, or you plan on staying out past the 23:30 curfew. This quasi-hotel (not a convent) is run with firm but angelic smiles by sisters who offer clean, quiet, rooms for a steal and save the best views for foreigners. Bright lamps, quaint balconies, fine views, grand public rooms, top security, and a friendly atmosphere make this a great value. The checkout time is strictly 10:00, but they have a *deposito* for luggage (Db-L90,000, Tb-L110,000, Qb-L130,000; from San Domenico, walk downhill with church on your right toward the view, turn left down Via

Camporegio, make a U-turn at the little chapel down the brick steps to Via Camporegio 37, tel. 0577/44177 and 0577/44487, fax 0577/47601, NSE).

Hotel Chiusarelli, a proper hotel in a fine location, is another wonderful value (50 rooms, S-L60,000, Sb-L90,000, Db-L130,000, CC:VMA, pleasant garden terrace, tiny free parking lot; just outside the old town, across from San Domenico and overlooking the stadium at Viale Curtone 15, tel. 0577/280-562, fax 0577/271-177, SE).

For a reasonable place in a classy residential neighborhood a few blocks away from the center (past San Domenico), with easy parking on the street, consider **Albergo Lea** (S-L70,000, Db-L115,000, Tb-L150,000, Qb-L175,000, with breakfast, CC:VMA, Hertz desk in their lobby; Viale XXIV Maggio 10, tel. & fax 0577/283-207, SE). If you're traveling with rich relatives who want sterility near the action, the **Hotel Villa Liberty** has big bright and comfortable rooms (Db-L180,000 with breakfast, CC:VMA, elevator, air-con, TVs, mini-bars, etc.; facing the fortress at Viale V. Veneto 11, tel. 0577/44966, fax 0577/44770, SE).

The tourist office lists private homes that rent rooms for around L25,000 per person. Many require a stay of several days, but some are central and a fine value. Siena's **Guidoriccio Youth Hostel** has 120 cheap beds, but given the hassle of the bus ride and the charm of downtown Siena at night, I'd skip it (office open 7:00–9:00, 15:00–23:30; L21,000 beds in doubles, triples, and dorms with sheets and breakfast, cheap meals; bus #10 from Piazza Gramsci or the train station to Via Fiorentina 89 in the Stellino neighborhood, tel. 0577/52212, SE).

Eating in Siena

Restaurants are reasonable by Florentine and Venetian stan-dards. Even with higher prices and lower quality food, consider eating on Il Campo. Eating in Il Campo ambience is a classic European experience. **Pizzeria Spadaforte** has a great setting, mediocre pizza, and tables steeper than its prices (daily 12:00–15:00, 19:00–22:00, tel. 0577/281-123).

Ristorante Gallo Nero is a friendly but uneven "grotto" for authentic Tuscan cuisine. This "black rooster" serves a mean *ribollita* (hearty Tuscan bean soup), offers a "medieval menu," and has cheap Chianti (3 blocks down Via del Porrione from the Campo at #65, tel. 0577/284-356).

Just around the corner, **Il Verrochio** serves a decent L22,000 menu (Logge del Papa 1). For authentic Sienese dining at a fair price, eat at the **Locanda Garibaldi**, down Via Giovanni Dupre a few steps from the square (L25,000 menu, open at 19:00, arrive early to get a table, closed Saturday). Marcello does a nice little L5,000 *piatto misto dolce*, featuring several local sweets with sweet wine. For a peasant's dessert, take your last glass of Chianti (borrow the *bicchiere* for *dieci minuti*) with a chunk of bread to the square, lean against a pillar, and sip Siena Classico. Picnics are royal on the Campo.

At **Antica Osteria Da Divo** the ambience is slippery as you climb deep into an Etruscan cellar to find your table. You'll pay a little extra here but the cuisine is local and good (daily 19:00–22:00, near Baptistry and Duomo, Via Franciosa 29, tel. 0577/284-381).

Osteria la Chiacchera is a wonderfully medieval, tasty, and affordable hole-in-the-brick-wall (12:00–15:00, 19:00–24:00, closed Tuesday, below Pension Bernini at Costa di San Antonio 4, tel. 0577/280-631). **Pizza Rustica** places, scattered throughout Siena, serve up cheap pizza-to-go, sold by the gram (100 grams for a snack, 200 grams for a filling meal). The **Enoteca Italia** is a good wine bar in the Fortezza.

For a chance to enjoy a treat on a balcony overlooking the Campo, stop by **Gelateria Artigiana La Costarella** (ice cream), **Bar Paninoteca** (sandwiches), **Bar Barbero d'Oro** (*panforte*—L3,500/100 grams—and cappuccino, best balcony open in summer), each on Via di Citta.

Siena's claim to caloric fame is its *panforte*, a rich, chewy concoction of nuts, honey, and candied fruits that impresses even fruitcake-haters (although locals I met prefer a white macaroon and lemon cookie called *ricciarelli*, and they were right). All over town Prodotti Tipici shops sell Sienese specialties.

Sala di Te, a local late night game and tea room with a curiously welcoming atmosphere, is popular with visiting American students (50 yards past recommended Gallo Nero restaurant, turn right off Via del Porrione down the Vicolo del Vannello, no sign, get close and ask).

Don't miss the evening *passeggiata* (peak strolling time is 19:00) along Via Banchi di Sopra with gelato in hand. **Nannini's** at Piazza Salimbeni has fine gelato (daily 10:30–24:00).

Transportation Connections—Siena

To: Rome (by bus, 1/day, 3 hrs, L20,000; by train, 8/day, 3.5 hrs, including a 20-minute connection in Chiusi), **Viterbo** (for Civita, 1/day).

To Florence: Take the *rapide* SITA bus from Siena's train station to downtown Florence (8/day, 70 min, L10,000, buy ticket before boarding at the *biglietteria* (tel. 0577/204-111 or 0577/204-245). Don't confuse the blue (intercity) and orange (city) buses. Fast buses are marked *"corse rapide."* Don't panic if there are too many people. They generally add buses when necessary. The milk-run bus is much slower but more scenic, offering an interesting glimpse of small-town and rural Tuscany. Trains, which take longer than SITA buses, require a change in Empoli. Shuttle buses connect the train station with the old town center.

SAN GIMIGNANO

The epitome of a Tuscan hill town with 14 medieval towers still standing (out of an original 72!), San Gimignano is a perfectly preserved tourist trap so easy to visit and visually pleasing that it's a good stop. In the 13th century, back in the days of Romeo and Juliet, towns were run by feuding noble families. And they'd periodically battle things out from the protective bases of their respective family towers. Pointy skylines were the norm in medieval Tuscany. But in San Gimignano, fabric was big business and many of its towers were built simply to hang dyed fabric out for drying.

While the basic three-star sight here is the town of San Gimignano itself, there are a few worthwhile stops. From the town gate, shop straight up the traffic-free town's cobbled main drag to the Piazza del Cisterna (with its 13th-century well). The town sights cluster around the adjoining Piazza del Duomo.

Tourist Information is in the old center on Piazza Duomo (daily 9:00–13:00, 15:00–19:00, tel. 0577/940-008).

Sights—San Gimignano

The **Collegiata,** with the round windows and wide steps, is a Romanesque church filled with fine Renaissance frescoes (free entry). In Palazzo del Popolo (facing the same piazza), you'll find the city museum and San Gimignano's tallest tower. The **Museo Civico** has a classy little painting collection with a 1422 altarpiece by Taddeo di Bartolo honoring Saint

Gimignano. You can see him with the town in his hands surrounded by events from his life (L12,000 including the tower, Tuesday–Sunday 9:30–19:30, closed Monday). You can climb the 180-foot-tall **Torre Grossa** (9:30–19:30) but the free **Rocco** (castle), a short climb behind the church, offers a better view and a great picnic perch, especially at sunset. Thursday is market day (8:00–13:00), but for local merchants, every day is a sales frenzy.

Transportation Connections—San Gimignano

To: Florence (regular departures, 75 min, change in Poggibonsi; or catch the frequent 20-min shuttle bus to Poggibonsi, and train to Florence), **Siena** (16/day, 1.5 hr, change in Poggibonsi), **Volterra** (6/day, 2 hrs). Bus tickets are sold at the bar just inside the town gate. San Gimignano has no baggage-check service.

Drivers: You can't drive within the walled town of San Gimignano, but a car-park awaits just a few steps outside.

ASSISI

Around the year 1200, a simple monk from Assisi challenged the decadence of church government and society in general with a powerful message of nonmaterialism, simplicity, and a "slow down and smell God's roses" lifestyle. Like Jesus, Francis taught by example. A huge monastic order grew out of his teachings, which were gradually embraced (some would say co-opted) by the church. Clare, St. Francis' partner in poverty, founded the Order of the Poor Clares. Catholicism's purest example of simplicity is now glorified in beautiful churches. In 1939, Italy made Francis and Clare its patron saints.

Any pilgrimage site will be commercialized, and the legacy of St. Francis is Assisi's basic industry. In summer the town bursts with splash-in-the-pan Francis fans and Franciscan knickknacks. Those able to see past the tacky monk mementos can actually have a "travel on purpose" experience. Francis' message of love and simplicity and sensitivity to the environment has a broad appeal.

Orientation (tel. code: 075)

Assisi, crowned by a ruined castle, is beautifully preserved and has a basilica nearly wallpapered by Giotto. Most visitors are day-trippers. Assisi after dark is closer to a place Francis could call home.

Tourist Information: The TI is on Piazza del Comune (Monday–Saturday 9:00–13:00, 15:30–18:30, Sunday 9:00–13:00, tel. 075/812-534).

Arrival in Assisi: Buses connecting Assisi's train station (near Santa Maria degli Angeli) with the old town center (L1,200, 2/hr, 5 km) stop at Piazza Unita d'Italia (Basilica di San Francisco), Largo Properzio (Santa Chiara), and Piazza Matteotti (top of old town).

Excursions: If you want to visit the sights near Assisi, Gino's car and van taxi service can help: one hour is L12,000 per person (four minimum), two hours about L20,000 per person (tel. 033/764-7780).

Sights—Assisi

▲▲▲**The Basilica of St. Francis**—In 1230, at his request, St. Francis was buried outside of his town with the sinners on the "hill of the damned." Now called the "Hill of Paradise," this is one of the artistic highlights of medieval Europe. It's frescoed from top to bottom by Cimabue, Giotto, Simone Martini, and the leading artists of the day.

Note: The basilica, which suffered fresco damage during the earthquakes of Oct. '97, may be closed or scaffolded at least part of '98. Call the TI to confirm status.

The three-part basilica (upper and lower churches built over the saint's tomb) is a theological work of genius—but difficult for the 20th-century tourist/pilgrim to appreciate. Since the basilica is the reason most visit Assisi and the message of St. Francis has even the least devout blessing the town Vespas, I've designed a *Mona Winks*-type tour with the stress on the place's theology rather than art history. It's adapted from the excellent little *The Basilica of Saint Francis—A Spiritual Pilgrimage* by Goulet, McInally, and Wood (L4,000 in the bookshop).

Enter the church from the parking lot at the lower level. At the doorway look up and see St. Francis who (sounding a bit like John Wayne) greets you with the Latin inscription saying the equivalent of "Slow down and be joyful, pilgrim. You've reached the Hill of Paradise and this church will knock your spiritual socks off." Start with the tomb (turn left into the nave and go down the "Tomba" stairs). Grab a pew right in front of his tomb.

The message: Francis' message caused a stir. He traded a life of power and riches for one of obedience, poverty, and

Assisi

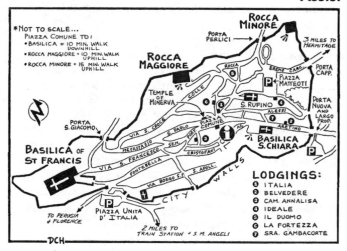

Not to scale...
PIAZZA COMUNE TO:
• BASILICA = 10 MIN. WALK DOWNHILL
• ROCCA MAGGIORE = 10 MIN. WALK UPHILL
• ROCCA MINORE = 15 MIN. WALK UPHILL

ROCCA MINORE
PORTA PERLICI
3 MILES TO HERMITAGE
ROCCA MAGGIORE
ROCCA
EREMO CARC.
PORTA CAPP.
PIAZZA MATTEOTI
TEMPLE OF MINERVA
COLLE
S. RUFINO
ALESSI
PORTA NUOVA AND LARGO PROP.
PORTA S. GIACOMO
VIA S. CROCE
S. PAOLO
PIAZZA COMUNE
ARETINO
METASTASIO
SEM.
BASILICA OF ST FRANCIS
VIA S. FRANCESCO
FONTEBELLA
CRISTOFANI
BASILICA S. CHIARA
PORTA
VIA BORGO S.P.
S. APOLL.
CITY WALLS
TO PERUSIA & FLORENCE
PIAZZA UNITA D' ITALIA
2 MILES TO TRAIN STATION & S.M. ANGELI

LODGINGS:
❶ ITALIA
❷ BELVEDERE
❸ CAM. ANNALISA
❹ IDEALE
❺ IL DUOMO
❻ LA FORTEZZA
❼ SRA. GAMBACORTE

—DCH—

chastity. The Franciscan existence (Brother Sun, Sister Moon, and so on) is a space where God, man, and the natural world frolic harmoniously. Franciscan friars, known as the "Jugglers of God," were a joyful part of the community. In an Italy torn by fighting between towns and families, Francis promoted peace and the restoration of order. (He set an example by reconstructing a crumbled chapel.) While the Church was waging bloody Crusades, Francis pushed ecumenism and understanding. Even today, the leaders of the world's great religions meet here for summits.

This rich building seems to contradict the teachings of the poor monk it honors. But it was built as an act of religious and civic pride to remember the hometown saint. It was also designed and still functions as a pilgrimage center and a splendid classroom.

The tomb: Holy relics were the "ruby slippers" of medieval Europe. They gave you power—got your prayers answered and helped you win wars—and ultimately helped you get back to your eternal Kansas. For obvious reasons of security, you didn't flaunt your relics. In fact, Francis' tomb was hidden until 1818, when this crypt was opened to the public. The saint's remains are above the altar in the stone box with the iron ties. His four best friends are buried in the corners of the room. Opposite the altar, up four steps in between the entrance and exit, notice the remains of Francis' rich Roman patron, Jacopa dei Settesoli, in an urn behind the black metal grill.

The lower basilica is appropriately Franciscan, subdued and Romanesque. The nave was frescoed with parallel scenes from the lives of Christ and Francis—connected by a ceiling of stars. Unfortunately, after the church was built and decorated, the popularity of the Franciscans meant side chapels needed to be built. Huge arches were cut out of the scenes, but some scenes survive. The first panels show Jesus being stripped of his clothing, across the nave from the famous scene of Francis stripping off his clothes in front of his father. In the second arch fresco on the right wall, Christ is being taken down from the cross (just half his body can be seen) and it looks like the story is over. Defeat. But in the opposite fresco we see Francis preaching to the birds, reminding the faithful that through baptism, the message of the Gospel survives.

These stories directed the attention of the medieval pilgrim to the altar where, through the sacraments, he met God. The church was thought of as a community of believers sailing toward God. The prayers coming out of the nave (*navis*, or ship) fill the triangular sections of the ceiling—called *vele*, or sails—with spiritual wind. With a priest for a navigator and the altar for a helm, faith propelled the ship.

Stand behind the altar (toes to the bottom step) and look up. The three scenes in front of you are, to the right, "Obedience" (Francis wearing a yoke); to the left, "Chastity" (in a tower of purity held up by two angels); and straight ahead, "Poverty." Here, Jesus blesses the marriage as Francis slips a ring on Lady Poverty. In the foreground, two "self-sufficient" merchants (the new rich of a thriving North Italy) are throwing sticks and stones at the bride. But Poverty, in her patched wedding dress, is fertile and strong, and even those brambles blossom into a rosebush crown.

Putting your heels to the altar and bending back like a drum major, look up at Francis, who traded a life of earthly simplicity for glory in heaven. Turn to the right and march . . .

St. Francis' patched robe is on display down the steps under the right transept. Back upstairs, look around at the painted scenes in this transept. In 1300, this was radical art—believable homespun scenes, landscapes, trees, real people. Check out the crucifix (by Giotto) with the eight sparrow-like angels. For the first time, holy people are expressing emotion—one angel turns her head sadly at the sight of Jesus; another scratches her hands down her cheeks, drawing blood. The up-until-now-in-control Mary has fainted in despair. The Franciscans, with their goal of bringing God to the people, found a natural partner in Europe's first modern painter, Giotto.

Francis' friend, "Sister Death," was really not all that terrible. In fact, Francis would like to introduce you to her now (to the right of the door leading into the bright court-yard). Go ahead, block the light and meet her. I'll wait for you in the courtyard.

From the courtyard you can enter the bookshop and the skipable Museum-Treasury (Gothic fine arts and paintings, no English explanations, L3,000). Monks in robes are not my idea of easy-to-approach people, but the Franciscans are still God's Jugglers (and most of them speak English). Climb the stairs to the upper basilica.

The upper basilica, built later than the lower, is brighter and Gothic. It's a gallery of frescoes by Giotto and his assistants showing 28 scenes from the life of St. Francis. Follow the great events of Francis' life, starting at the altar and working clockwise.

Immediately to the right of the altar, the first panel shows God looking over 20-year-old Francis, a dandy imprisoned in his selfishness. A medieval pilgrim, fluent in symbolism, would understand this because the Temple of Minerva (which you'll see today on Assisi's Piazza del Comune) was a prison at that time. The rose window never existed but symbolizes the eye of God. A common man, recognizing Francis as one who will do great things, spreads his cape before Francis as a sign of honor. In the next panel, after Francis was captured in battle, held as a prisoner of war, and then released, he offers his cape to a needy stranger. Next, he's visited by the Lord in a dream and told to leave the army and go home. Two scenes later is the sad scene of Francis giving his dad his clothes, his credit cards, and even his time-share condo on Capri. Naked Francis is covered by the bishop, symbolizing his transition from a man of the world to a man of the church. Next is a vision the pope had of a simple man propping up his teetering church. This led to the papal acceptance of the Franciscan reforms.

Skip to the other side (fourth panel from the door). Here, Christ appears to Francis being carried by a seraph (six-winged angel). For the strength of his faith, Francis is given the marks of his master, the "battle scars of love" . . . the stigmata. Throughout his life, Francis was interested in chivalry; now he's joined the spiritual knighthood. The weeds in the foreground were an herb which, in olden days, "drove away sadness and made men merry and joyful." Pilgrims smiled.

Turning to leave, notice the scene to the right of the door. Here Francis (sans seraph) is preaching to the birds. Francis was more than a nature lover. Notice that the birds are of different species. They represent the diverse flock of humanity and nature—all created and loved by God and worthy of each other's love.

This is the message that the basilica hopes the pilgrim will take home. Stepping out the door you see the Latin *Pax* (peace) and the Franciscan *Tau* cross in the grass. Tau, the last letter in the Hebrew alphabet, is symbolic of faithfulness to the end. Francis signed his name with this simple character. Tau and Pax. (For more pax, take the high lane back to town, up to the castle or into the countryside.) The church is free (daily 7:00–19:00, sometimes closed for lunch or mass, tel. 075/812-238). (Tours are limited to 9:00–12:00 and 14:00–17:00—times you may want to avoid.) The modest dress code is strictly enforced.

▲**Basilica di Santa Chiara (Saint Clare)**—Dedicated to the founder of the order of the Poor Clares, this Umbrian Gothic church (1265, with the huge buttresses added in the next century) is simple, in keeping with the Poor Clares' dedication to a life of contemplation. The interior's fine frescoes were white-washed in the Baroque days. The Chapel of St. George on the right (actually an earlier church incorporated into this one) has the crucifix which supposedly spoke to St. Francis, leading to his conversion in 1206. In the back of that chapel are some important Franciscan relics, including Clare's robe. Stairs lead from the nave down to the tomb of Saint Clare. The attached cloistered community of the Poor Clares has flourished for 700 years (church open 6:30–12:00, 14:00–19:00, Sunday till 18:00; 18:30 mass in English Saturday and Sunday, May–October, in the upper church). For a change of pace, cross the street behind the church at the arch and dip into the goofy mechanical and water-powered Biblical world of Silvano Gianbolina.

Piazza del Comune—This square (straight up Via San Francesco from the basilica) is the center of town. You'll find the Roman temple of Minerva, a Romanesque tower, banks, the post office, the Pinacoteca (pathetic art gallery, not worth the admission), and the tourist information office. For a look at Assisi's Roman roots, tour the **Roman Forum** (Foro Romano, L4,000, 10:00–13:00, 15:00–19:00) which is actually under the Piazza del Comune. The floor plan is sparse, and the odd bits and pieces obscure, but it's well explained in English, and it is ancient.

▲**Rocca Maggiore**—The "big castle" offers a good look at a 14th-century fortification and a fine view of Assisi and the Umbrian countryside (L5,000, daily 10:00–19:00). If you're counting lire, the view is just as good from outside the castle and the interior is pretty bare—except for a model of a guillotine with an interesting history in English. Inside, for an extra fee, there is a Torture Museum with four rooms filled with gruesome examples of medieval creativity—explained almost joyously in English. For a picnic with the same birds and views that inspired St. Francis, leave all the tourists and hike to the Rocca Minore (small castle) above Piazza Matteotti.

▲▲**Santa Maria degli Angeli**—This huge Baroque church, towering above the buildings below Assisi, was built around the tiny but historic Porziuncola chapel. St. Francis took Jesus literally when he told him to "go and restore my house." Twenty-four-year-old Francis put the ruined and abandoned chapel back together. It was in this chapel that Francis heard the command to organize his following into an order. As you enter St. Mary of the Angels, notice the sketch on the door showing the original little chapel with the monks' huts around it, and Assisi before it had its huge basilica. Francis lived here after he founded the Franciscan Order in 1208, and this was where he consecrated St. Clare as the Bride of Christ. The other "sights" in the church (a chapel on the spot where Francis died, the rose garden, a museum which has a few monastic cells upstairs) are not very interesting (daily 9:00–12:00 and 14:00–18:30).

Sleeping in Assisi
(L1,600 = about $1, tel. code: 075, zip code: 06081)
The town accommodates large numbers of pilgrims on religious holidays. Finding a room any other time should be easy.

Albergo Italia is clean and simple with great beds and delightful owners. Some of its 13 rooms overlook the town square (Ss-L37,000, D-L50,000, Db-L70,000, T-L63,000, Tb-L90,000, Qb-L100,000, CC:VM; just off the Piazza del Comune's fountain at Vicolo della Fortezza, tel. 075/812-625, fax 075/804-3749, SE).

Hotel Belvedere offers comfortable rooms and good views, and is run by friendly Enrico and his American wife, Mary (D-L70,000, Db-L100,000, breakfast-L10,000; 2 blocks past St. Clare's church at Via Borgo Aretino 13, tel. 075/812-460, fax 075/816-812, SE). Their attached restaurant is also good.

Camere Annalisa Martini is a cheery home swimming in vines, roses, and bricks in the town's medieval core. Annalisa speaks English and enthusiastically accommodates her guests with a picnic garden, washing machine, refrigerator, and homey, lived-in-feeling rooms (S-L38,000, Sb-L40,000, D-L58,000, Db-L60,000, T-L80,000, Q-L100,000, five rooms sharing three bathrooms; breakfast not included; 1 block below the Piazza del Comune, then left on Via S. Gregorio to #6, tel. 075/813-536).

Hotel Ideale is on the far edge of town, overlooking the valley, with a peaceful garden, free parking, view balconies, all the modern comforts, and an English-speaking welcome (Sb-L60,000–75,000, Db-L100,000–120,000 depending on season, breakfast buffet-L10,000, CC:VMA; Piazza Matteotti 1, tel. 075/813-570, fax 075/813-020, Lara SE).

Albergo Il Duomo is tidy and quiet on a stairstep lane **1** block up from San Ruffino (nine rooms, Sb-L45,000–55,000, D-L52,000–65,000, Db-L67,000–80,000 depending on season, L7,000 breakfast, CC:VM; Vicolo S. Lorenzo 2, tel. 075/812-742, fax 075/812-284, Carlo SE).

Hotel La Fortezza is small, very clean, tranquil, modern, and quite comfortable (Db-L90,000, Qb-L140,000, CC:VMA; just up the lane from the Piazza del Comune at Vicolo della Fortezza 19b, tel. 075/812-993, fax 075/812-418, SE).

La Pallotta has clean, bright rooms above its busy restaurant (see Eating, below). Ask for rooms #12 or #18 to get a great view (Db-L85,000 including breakfast, CC:V; Via San Ruffino 4, tel. & fax 075/812-307, SE).

Senora Gambacorte rents several decent rooms on a quiet lane just above St. Clare's with a roof terrace, and no sign. Ask for assistance at the shop across the street if there's no answer at the door (L35,000 per person; 9 via Sermei, tel. 075/815-206 or 075/812-454, fax 075/813-186, NSE,

www.umbrars.com/gambacorta, e-mail: geo@krenet.it). She
also has an apartment for stays of one week or more.

Francis probably would have bunked with the peasants in
Assisi's **Ostello della Pace** (L20,000 beds with breakfast, in
four- to six-bed rooms; a 15-minute walk below town at Via di
Valethye, at the San Pietro stop on the station-town bus, tel.
& fax 075/816-767, SE).

Eating in Assisi

For the best Assisian perch and fine regional cooking, relax on
a terrace overlooking the Piazza del Commune at the **Taverna
dei Consoli** (L24,000 menu, two steps straight across from the
Albergo Italia, laid-back owner Moreno SE, tel. 075/812-516).

La Pallotta, run by a friendly hardworking family, is
locally popular and offers excellent regional specialties such as
piccione (pigeon), *coniglio* (rabbit), and much more. (L26,000
menu, just 1 block up from the Piazza del Commune, Via San
Ruffino 4, tel. 075/812-649, closed Tuesday).

The **Pozzo della Mensa** has a good L23,000 menu with
simple, hearty cooking (1 block from Santa Chiara, hidden
down a quiet alley at Via della Menza 11, tel. 075/816-247).

Transportation Connections—Assisi

By train to: Rome (9/day, 2.5 hrs with a change in Foligno),
Florence (10/day, 2.5 hrs, sometimes changing at Terontola-
Cortona), **Siena** (5/day, 4 hrs), **Orvieto** (4/day, 2–3 hrs). Train
info: tel. 1478-88088. There are one or two buses a day to
Rome and Florence.

ORVIETO

Umbria's grand hill town, while no secret, is still worth a
quick look. Just off the freeway, with three popular gimmicks
(its ceramics, cathedral, and Classico wine), it's loaded with
tourists by day—quiet by night.

Ride the back streets of Orvieto into the Middle Ages.
The town sits majestically on tufa rock. Streets lined with
buildings made from the exhaust-stained volcanic stuff seem
to grumble Dark Ages.

Piazza Cahen is only a transportation hub at the entry to
the hilltop town. It has a ruined fortress with a garden, a
commanding view, and a popular well which is an impressive
(although overpriced) double helix carved into tufa rock.

Orvieto

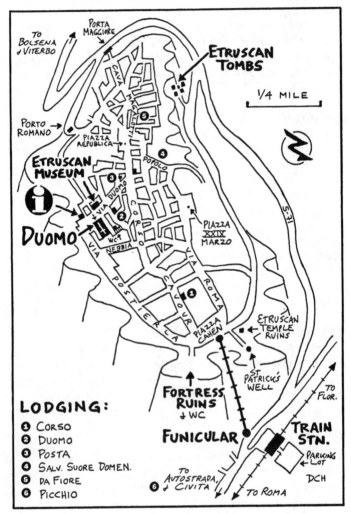

LODGING:
1. CORSO
2. DUOMO
3. POSTA
4. SALV. SUORE DOMEN.
5. DA FIORE
6. PICCHIO

Tourist Information: The TI is at #24 Piazza Duomo on the cathedral square (weekdays 8:00–13:45, 16:00–18:45, weekends from 10:00, tel. 0763/341-772).

Arrival in Orvieto: A handy funicular/bus shuttle takes visitors quickly from the train station and car-park to the top of the town (4/hr, L1,400 ticket includes Piazza Cahen-Piazza Duomo minibus transfer, where you'll find everything that matters).

First buy your ticket at the train station tobacco shop, then cross the street to the funicular. At the top of the funicular, walk right onto the waiting orange bus. The shuttle bus drops you at the tourist office (last stop, in front of the Duomo). Drivers park at the base of the hill at the huge, free lot behind the Orvieto train station (follow the "P" and *funicolare* signs).

Sights—Orvieto

▲▲**Duomo**—Orvieto's cathedral has Italy's most striking facade (from 1330). Grab a gelato (to the left of the church) and study this fascinating mass of mosaics and sculpture (daily 7:30–12:45, 14:30–19:15, November–March closing at 17:15). Inside the cathedral notice how the downward-sloping floor diminishes the perspective, giving it an illusion of being shorter than it is. Notice also the alabaster windows.

To the right of the altar, the **Chapel of St. Brizio** features Signorelli's brilliantly lit and restored frescoes of the Apocalypse. Step into the chapel and you're surrounded by vivid scenes showing the Preaching of the Antichrist, the End of the World, the Resurrection of the Bodies, the Last Judgment, and a gripping pietà. For a bonus, check out Fra Angelico's painting of Jesus, the angels, and the prophets on the ceiling. This room is Orvieto's artistic must-see (get L3,000 ticket at the TI across the square, see TI hours above).

Near the striped cathedral are a fine **Etruscan Museum/ Archeological Museum** (L4,000, Monday–Saturday 9:00– 13:30, 14:30–19:00, Sunday 9:00–13:00) and unusually clean public toilets (down the stairs from the left transept). Drinking a shot of wine in a ceramic cup as you gaze up at the cathedral lets you experience all of Orvieto's claims to fame at once.

Underground Orvieto Tours—Guides weave a good archeo- logical history into an hour-long look at about 100 meters of caves (L10,000, tours twice daily at 11:00 and 16:00 from the TI, tel. 0763/375-084 or the TI). Orvieto is honeycombed with Etruscan and medieval caves. You'll see only the remains of an old olive press, two impressive 40-meter-deep Etruscan well shafts, and the remains of a primitive cement quarry, but if you want underground Orvieto, this is the place to get it.

Wine Tasting—Orvieto Classico wine is justly famous. For a peek into a local winery, visit **Tenuta Le Velette**, where English-speaking Corrado and Cecilia Bottai welcome those who call ahead to set up an appointment for a look at their

winery (L15,000 for tour and tasting, Monday–Friday
8:30–12:00, 14:00–17:00, Saturday 8:30–12:00, closed Sunday,
tel. 0763/29090, fax 0763/29114). At their sign (five minutes
past Orvieto at top of switchbacks just before Canale, on
Bagnoregio road) cruise down long tree-lined drive, park at
striped gate (call ahead; no drop-ins).

Sleeping in Orvieto
(L1,600 = about $1, tel. code: 0763, zip code: 05018)
Here are six places in the old town, one in a more modern
neighborhood near the station, and one on a local farm.

Hotel Virgilio is a decent hotel with bright modern—if
overpriced—rooms shoe-horned into an old building ideally
located on the main square facing the cathedral (Db-
L150,000–165,000 including breakfast, CC:VM, elevator;
Piazza Duomo 5, tel. 0763/341-882, fax 0763/343-797, SE).
They also have a "dependence" with Db-L100,000 rooms.

Hotel Corso is small, clean, and friendly, with comfy
modern rooms (Db-L135,000, CC:VM; on the main street
up from the funicular toward the Duomo at Via Cavour 339,
tel. & fax 0763/342-020).

Hotel Duomo is a funky, brightly colored, Old World
place with not-quite-clean rooms and a great location (17
rooms, S-L40,000, D-L60,000, Db-L85,000; a block from
the Duomo, behind the gelateria at Via di Maurizio 7, tel.
0763/341-887, fax 0763/341-105).

Albergo Posta is a five-minute walk from the cathedral
into the medieval core. It's a big, old, formerly elegant, but
well-cared-for-in-its-decline building with a breezy garden, a
grand old lobby, and spacious, clean, plain rooms with vintage
rickety furniture and springy beds (20 rooms, D-L68,000,
Db-L88,000; Via Luca Signorelli 18, tel. 0763/341-909).

The sisters of the **Instituto Salvatore Suore Domenicane**
rent 15 spotless twin rooms in their heavenly convent
(Db-L80,000, loosely enforced two-night minimum; just off
Piazza del Populo at Via del Populo 1, tel. & fax 0763/342-910).

Hotel Picchio is a concrete-and-marble place, more comfortable but with less character, and family-run by Marco and
Picchio. It's in the lower, plain part of town, 300 yards from
the train station (D-L50,000, Db-L70,000, Tb-L90,000; Via
G. Salvatori 17, 05019 Orvieto Scalo, tel. 0763/301-144 or
0763/90246). A trail leads from here up to the old town.

For a long list of rural B&Bs, farms, and apartments in Canale, Bagnoregio, and Lubriano, contact Cecilia Bottai at the winery (Db-L80,000, tel. 0763/29090, fax 0763/29114, SE).

Agriturismo Pomonte is a great farm-and-family experience (Db-L80,000, Canino N. 1, Corbara, Orvieto, house on a hilltop at curve in road 3 km before Corbara, tel. 0763/304-080, Cesari family).

Transportation Connections—Orvieto

By train to: Rome (14/day, 60 min, consider leaving your car at the large car-park behind the Orvieto station), **Florence** (14/day, 1.5 hrs), **Siena** (10/day, 2–3 hrs, change in Chiusi).

By bus to Bagnoregio: It's a 50-minute L3,000 bus ride (6:25, 7:20, 9:10, 12:40, 13:55, 15:45, 17:35, and 18:35 from Orvieto's Piazza Cahen and from its train station daily except Sunday, buy tickets from the "cafe snack bar" at the station, confirm return times from the conductor, tel. 0763/792-237). If the bus is empty, develop a relationship with your driver. He may let you jump out in Lubriano for a great photo of distant Civita. Note: While there is no bus service on Sunday the boys at Al Boschetto may be able to shuttle you to Orvieto.

CIVITA DI BAGNOREGIO

Perched on a pinnacle in a grand canyon, the traffic-free village of Civita is Italy's ultimate hill town. Curl your toes around its Etruscan roots.

Civita is terminally ill. Only 15 residents remain as, bit by bit, it's being purchased by rich big-city Italians who escape here. Apart from its permanent (and aging) residents and those who have weekend homes here, there is a group of Americans, introduced to the town through a small University of Washington architecture program, who have bought into the rare magic of Civita. When the program is in session, 15 students live with residents and study Italian culture and architecture.

Civita is connected to the world and the town of Bagnoregio by a long pedestrian bridge. While Bagnoregio lacks the pinnacle-town romance of Civita, it is a pure and lively bit of small-town Italy. It's actually a healthy, vibrant community (unlike Civita, the suburb it calls "the dead city"). Get a haircut, sip a coffee on the square, walk down to the old laundry (ask, *"Dové la lavanderia vecchia?"*). A lively market fills the parking lot each Monday.

Civita

From Bagnoregio, yellow signs direct you along its long, skinny spine to its older neighbor, Civita. Enjoy the view as you head up the bridge to Civita. A shuttle bus runs from the base of the Civita bridge to Bagnoregio and maybe to Al Boschetto (see Sleeping, below) about hourly in season (L1,000). Be prepared for the little old ladies of Civita who have become aggressive at getting lire out of visitors. Off season Civita, Bagnoregio, and Al Boschetto are all deadly quiet—and cold. I'd side trip in quickly from Orvieto or skip the area altogether.

Civita Orientation Walk

Civita was once connected to Bagnoregio. The saddle between the separate towns eroded away. Photographs around town show the old donkey path, the original bridge. It was bombed in WWII, and replaced in 1965 with the new bridge you'll climb today. The town's hearty old folks hang on the bridge's hand railing when fierce winter weather rolls through.

Entering the town you'll pass through a cut in the rock (made by Etruscans 2,500 years ago) and under a 12th-century Romanesque arch. This was the main Etruscan road leading to the Tiber Valley and Rome.

Inside the town gate, on the left, notice the old Laundromat (in front of the WC). On the right, a fancy door and windows lead to thin air. This was the facade of a Renaissance palace—one of five which once graced Civita. It fell into the valley riding a chunk of the ever-eroding rock pinnacle. Today the door leads to a remaining chunk of the palace—complete with Civita's first hot tub—owned by the "Marchesa," a countess who married into Italy's biggest industrialist family.

Poke through the museum next door and check out the viewpoint around the corner near the long-gone home of Civita's one famous son, Saint Bonaventura.

Now wander to the town square in front of the church where you'll find Civita's only public phone, bar, restaurant— and a wild donkey race each August 15. The church marks the spot where an Etruscan temple, and then a Roman temple, once stood. The pillars which stand like giants' barstools are ancient—Roman or Etruscan.

Go into the church and find Anna. She'll give you a tour, proudly pointing out frescos and statues from "the school of Giotto" and "the school of Donatello," a portrait of the patron saint of your teeth (notice the scary-looking pincers), and an altar dedicated to Marlon Brando (or St. Ildebrando). Tip her and buy your postcards from her.

The basic grid street plan of the ancient town survives. Just around the corner from the church, on the main street, is Rossana and Antonio's cool and friendly wine cellar. Pull up a stump and let them or their children, Arianna and Antonella, serve you *panini* (sandwiches), *bruschetta* (garlic toast with tomato), wine, and a local cake called *ciambella*. Climb down into the cellar and note the traditional wine-making gear and the provisions for rolling huge kegs up the stairs. Tap on the kegs in the cool bottom level to see which are full.

The ground below Civita is honeycombed with ancient cellars (for keeping wine at the same temperature all year) and cisterns (for collecting rainwater, since there was no well in town). Many of these date from Etruscan times.

Explore farther down the street but remember, nothing is abandoned. Everything is still privately owned. After passing an ancient Roman tombstone on your left, you'll come to Victoria's **Antico Mulino**, an atmospheric collection of old olive-presses (give a donation of about L1,500). Her grandchildren, running the local equivalent of a lemonade stand, toast delicious *bruschetta* on weekends and holidays. For about L5,000 you get a fun light lunch featuring a *piatto misto* of bruschetta, local cheese, and salami with wine.

Farther down the way, Maria (for a donation of about L1,500) will show you through her garden with a grand view (Maria's Giardino) and historical misinformation (she says Civita and Lubriano were once connected).

At the end of town the main drag peters out and a trail leads you down and around to the right to a tunnel that has cut through the hill under the town since Etruscan times. It was widened in the 1930s so farmers could get between their scattered fields easier.

Evenings on the town square are a bite of Italy. The same people sit on the same church steps under the same moon, night after night, year after year. I love my cool late evenings in Civita. If you visit in the cool of the early morning, have cappuccino and rolls at the small café on the town square.

Whenever you visit, stop halfway up the donkey path and listen to the sounds of rural Italy. Reach out and touch one of the monopoly houses. If you know how to turn the volume up on the crickets, do so.

Sleeping and Eating near Civita
(L1,600 = about $1, tel. code: 0761, zip code: 01022)
When you leave the tourist crush, life as a traveler in Italy becomes easy and prices tumble. Room-finding is easy in small-town Italy. Just outside Bagnoregio is **Al Boschetto**. The Catarcia family speaks no English. Have an English-speaking Italian call for you (D-L85,000–90,000, Db-L90,000–95,000, breakfast L6,000, CC:V; Strada Monterado, Bagnoregio/ Viterbo, Italy, tel. 0761/792-369, walking and driving instructions below). Most rooms, while very basic, have private showers (no curtains, slippery floors—be careful not to flood the place; sing in search of your shower's resonant frequency).

The Catarcia family (Angelino, his wife Perina, sons Gianfranco and Domenico, daughter-in-law Giuseppina, and the grandchildren) offer an honest look at rural Italian life. Giuseppina serves uninspired meals. If the boys invite you down deep into the gooey, fragrant bowels of the cantina, be warned: the theme song is "Trinka Trinka Trinka," and there are no rules unless the female participants set them.

The Orvieto bus drops you at the town gate. (Remember, no bus service at all on Sunday.) Al Boschetto is a 15-minute walk out of town past the old arch (follow Viterbo signs), turn left at the pyramid monument, and right at the first fork (follow Montefiascone sign). Civita is a pleasant 45-minute walk (back through Bagnoregio) from Al Boschetto.

Hotel Fidanza, in Bagnoregio near the bus stop—tired, with incredibly low blood pressure—is the only other hotel in town. Rooms 206 and 207 have views of Civita (Db-L90,000, breakfast-L20,000; Via Fidanza 25, Bagnoregio/Viterbo, tel. 0761/793-444).

For information about a two-bedroom, fully furnished/ equipped Civita apartment with terrace and cliffside garden, rentable May through October ($700/week, $2,200/month, one week minimum), call Carol Watts in Kansas (tel 785/539-0815, evenings or e-mail: cmwatts@ksu.edu).

The nearest cheap beds are back in Orvieto at Camere Da Fiora (near the station, see Orvieto section).

Casa San Martino, in the village of Lisciano Niccone (near Carona and Perugia), is a 250-year-old farmhouse run as a B&B by American Italophile Lois Martin. Using this comfortable hilltop countryside homebase, those with a car can tour Assisi, Orvieto, and Civita. While Lois reserves the summer for one week stays, she'll take guests staying a minimum of two nights for the rest of the year ($40 per person, Casa San Martino 19, Lisciano Niccone, tel. 075/844288, reserve in the U.S.A. via Tennessee tel. 423/928-8119, fax 423/928-8496).

Your best bets for dinner: Hearty country cooking at **Al Boschetto** (see above) or lighter more creative cuisine at the **Hostaria del Ponte** (at the car park at the base of the bridge to Civita, great view terrace, good food and prices, tel. 0761/793-565, closed Monday). For a simple meal in Civita, try **Trattoria al Forno** (serves a decent pasta-and-wine lunch or dinner, open daily for lunch at 12:30 and dinner at 19:30, June–September, sometimes October, tel. 0761/793-651). Or, for the best cooking in Bagnoregio, check out **Restorante Nello il Fumatore** (Piazza Fidanza, closed Friday).

Transportation Connections—Bagnoregio

To Civita: It's a 30-minute walk. Taking the shuttle bus (nearly hrly, 10 min; service halts during the 13:00–15:00 siesta) still involves a walk (15 min up the donkey path from the bus stop).

To Orvieto: Public buses (8/day, 50 min) connect Bagnoregio to the rest of the world via Orvieto (1997 departures from Bagnoregio: 6:50, 10:05, 13:00, 14:25, 17:20, see Connections—Orvieto, above). While there's no official baggage-check service in Bagnoregio, I've arranged with Laurenti Mauro, who runs the Bar Enoteca just outside the Bagnoregio old town gate (near the bus station), to let you leave your bags there (open 6:00–24:00 with a short lunch break, closed Thursday). Pay him L2,000 per bag or buy breakfast there (better than Al Boschetto's).

Driving from Orvieto to Bagnoregio: Orvieto overlooks the autostrada (and has its own exit). The shortest way to Civita from the freeway exit is to turn left (below Orvieto) and follow signs to Lubriano and Bagnoregio. The more winding and scenic route takes 20 minutes longer: From the freeway, pass under hillcapping Orvieto (on your right, signs to Lago di Bolsena, on Viale I Maggio), take the first left (direction: Bagnoregio), winding up past great Orvieto views, the Orvieto Classico vineyard (see above), through Canale, and through farms and fields of giant shredded wheat to Bagnoregio, where the locals (or rusty old signs) will direct you to Al Boschetto, just outside town. Either way, just before Bagnoregio, follow the signs left to Lubriano and pull into the first little square by the church on your right for a breathtaking view of Civita. Then return to the Bagnoregio road. Drive through Bagnoregio (following yellow "Civita" signs) and park at the base of the steep donkey path up to the traffic-free, 2,500-year-old, canyon-swamped pinnacle town of Civita di Bagnoregio.

Sights—Near Orvieto, Bagnoregio, and Civita

▲**Etruscan Tomb**—Driving from Bagnoregio toward Orvieto, stop just past Porano to tour an Etruscan tomb. Follow the yellow road signs, reading "Tomba Etrusca", to Giuseppe's farm. Walk behind the farm and down into the lantern-lit, 2,500-year-old Hescanos family tomb discovered 100 years ago by Giuseppe's grandfather. New excavations on the site may turn it into the usual turnstile-type visit (daily 9:00–12:00, 14:00–17:00, tel. 0761/65242).

Monsters—South of Orvieto, off the autostrada to Rome, Bomarzo has a gimmicky monster park (Parco di Mostri), filled with stone giants and dragons. Built about two centuries ago, it proves that Italy has a long and distinguished tradition of tacky.

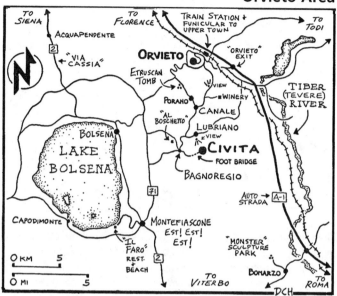

Orvieto Area

More Hill Towns

Italy is spiked with hill towns. **Perugia** is big and reeks with history. **Cortona** is smaller with a fine youth hostel (tel. 0575/601-765). **Todi** is nearly untouristed. **Pienza** (a Renaissance-planned town) and **Montepulciano** (with its dramatic setting) are also worth the hill-town lover's energy and time. **Sorano** and **Pitigliano** have almost no tourism. **Bevagna** (near Assisi) is as dazed as its town fool who stands between the twin dark Romanesque churches on its main square. Paranoid **Orte** filled its tufa perch so completely that there's no room for charm, and traffic circulates on a single skinny one-way lane. You'll see Orvieto's poor cousin—which must be the densest town in Italy—from the freeway, 30 minutes north of Rome. Train travelers often use the town of Chiusi as a home base for the hill towns. The region's trains (to Siena, Orvieto, Assisi) go through or change at this hub, and there are several reasonable hotels near the station.

THE CINQUE TERRE

The Cinque Terre (CHINK-wuh TAY-ruh), a remote chunk of the Italian Riviera, is the traffic-free, low-brow, under-appreciated alternative to the French Riviera. There's not a museum in sight. Just sun, sea, sand (well, pebbles), wine, and pure unadulterated Italy. Enjoy the villages, swimming, hiking, and evening romance of one of God's great gifts to tourism. For a home base, choose among five villages, each of which fills a ravine with a lazy hive of human activity. Vernazza is my favorite.

The area was first described in medieval times as "the five castles." Tiny communities grew up in the protective shadows of the castles ready to run inside at the first hint of a Turkish "Saracen" pirate raid. Many locals were kidnapped and ransomed or sold into slavery somewhere far to the east. As the threat of pirates faded, the villages grew with economies based on fish and grapes. Until the advent of tourism in this generation, they were very remote. Even today, traditions survive and each of the five villages comes with a distinct dialect and proud heritage.

Planning Your Time

The ideal minimum stay is two nights and a completely uninterrupted day. The Cinque Terre is served by the milk-run train from Genoa and La Spezia. Speed demons arrive in the morning, check their bag in La Spezia, take the five-hour hike through all five towns, laze away the afternoon on the beach or rock of their choice, and zoom away on the overnight train to somewhere back in the real world. Each town has its own

Cinque Terre

character, and all are a few minutes apart by an hourly train. There's no checklist of sights or experiences, just the hike, the towns, and your fondest vacation desires.

For a good Cinque Terre day consider this: Pack your beach and swimming gear, wear your walking shoes, and catch the train to town #1: Riomaggiore. (Since I still get the names mixed up, I think of the five Cinque Terre towns by number.) Walk the cliff-hanging Via dell' Amore to Manarola (#2) and buy food for a picnic, then hike to Corniglia (#3) for a rocky but pleasant beach. Swim here or in the more resorty Monterosso (#5, a ten-minute train ride away). From #5, hike or catch the boat home to Vernazza (#4).

If you're into *il dolce far niente* (the sweetness of doing *nada*) and don't want to hike, you could enjoy the blast of cool train-tunnel air that announces the arrival of every Cinque Terre train and go directly to Monterosso al Mare, where a sandy "front door"-style beach awaits. The Cinque Terre has a strange way of messing up momentum.

Getting Around the Cinque Terre

The city of La Spezia is the gateway to the Cinque Terre. In La Spezia's train station, the milk-run Cinque Terre train schedule is posted at the information window. Take the L2,000 half-hour train ride into the Cinque Terre town of your choice.

Cinque Terre Train Schedule: Since the train is the Cinque Terre lifeline, any shop or restaurant posts the current schedule (La Spezia train info: tel. 0187/714-960, Monterosso train info tel. 0187/817-458).

Trains leave La Spezia for the Cinque Terre villages (last year's schedule) at 6:12, 7:17, 8:15, 10:06, 11:23, 12:30, 13:20, 14:24, 15:00, 16:30, 17:02, 17:48, 18:25, 19:06, 19:36, 21:19, 22:36.

Trains leave Monterosso al Mare for La Spezia (departing Vernazza about three minutes later, last year's schedule) at 5:16, 6:33, 7:05, 8:44, 10:15, 11:02, 12:19, 13:31, 14:18, 15:01, 15:54, 17:05, 18:08, 19:09, 19:57, 20:07, 22:06, 23:14.

To orient yourself, remember that directions are *"per* (to) *Genoa"* or *"per La Spezia,"* and any train that stops at any of the villages other than Monterosso, will stop at all five. (Note that many trains leaving La Spezia skip them all or stop only in Monterosso.) The five towns are just minutes apart by train. Know your stop. After leaving the town before your destination, go to the door to slip out before mobs pack in. Since the stations are small and the trains are long, you might need to get off the train deep in a tunnel, and you might need to open the door yourself.

If the train station is not staffed, buy your ticket from the tobacco shop (in Vernazza, near the harbor) or on board from the conductor. If you buy from the conductor, explain, *"La stazione era chiusa"* (the station was closed); otherwise you'll pay a bit more.

Since a one-town hop costs the same as a five-town hop (L1,500), and every ticket is good all day with stopovers, save money and explore the region in one direction on one ticket. Stamp the ticket at the station machine before you board. Stations sell a L5,000 all day 5-Terre pass. Don't spend a railpass flexi-day on the Cinque Terre.

VERNAZZA

With the closest thing to a natural harbor, overseen by a ruined castle and an old church, and only the occasional noisy

Vernazza

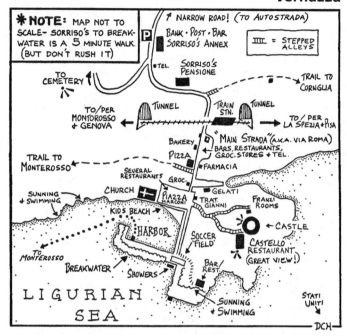

slurping up of the train by the mountain to remind you these are the 1990s, Vernazza is my Cinque Terre home base.

The action is at the harbor, where you'll find a kids' beach, plenty of sunning rocks, outdoor restaurants, a bar hanging on the edge of the castle (great for evening drinks), the tiny town soccer field, and a tailgate-party street market each Tuesday morning.

The town's 500 residents, proud of their Vernazzan heritage, brag that "Vernazza is locally owned. Portofino has sold out." Fearing the change it would bring, they stopped the construction of a major road into the town and region. Families are tight and go back centuries; several generations stay together. Leisure time is spent wandering lazily together up and down the main street. Sit on a bench and study Vernazza's *passeggiata*. Then explore the characteristic alleys called *carugi*. In October the cantinas are draped with drying grapes. In the winter the population shrinks, as many people move to more comfortable big-city apartments.

An hourly boat service connects Vernazza and Monterosso (departures last year: 10:00, 11:00, 12:00, 14:30, 15:30, 16:30, 17:30, and 18:30, daily April–October, L4,000 one way, L6,000 round-trip, canceled when windy). A five-minute steep hike in either direction from Vernazza gives you a classic village photo op. Franco's Bar, with a panoramic terrace, is at the tower on the trail toward Corniglia.

The banks at the top of the town have decent rates. The nearest laundromat is a self-serve in La Spezia near its market square and full-service places in Monterosso.

Sights—Vernazza

▲▲Vernazza Town Top Down Orientation Walk—Walk uphill until you hit the parking lot, two banks, and post office. The tidy new square is called "Fontana Vecchia" after a long-gone fountain. Older locals remember the river filled with townswomen doing their washing. Begin your saunter downhill to the harbor.

Just before the "Pension Sorriso" sign you'll see the ambulance barn on the right. A group of volunteers are always on call for a dash to the hospital, 30 minutes away in La Spezia. Opposite that is a big empty lot behind Pension Sorriso. Like many landowners, Sr. Sorriso had plans to expand but the government said no. The old character of these towns is carefully protected.

Across from the "Pension Sorriso" sign is the honorary clubhouse for the ANPI (members of the local WWII resistance). Only five ANPI old-timers survive. Cynics consider them less than heroes. After 1943 Hitler called up any boy over 15. Like any reasonably smart person, they escaped to the hills rather than fight for Hitler on the front. Only to remain free did they become "resistance fighters."

A few steps farther you'll see a monument to those killed in WWII. Not a family was spared. The tiny monorail "*trenino*" is parked quietly here except in September and October when it's busy helping locals bring down the grapes. From here the path leads to Corniglia. The school bus picks up children from the many tiny neighboring villages. Today only about 25 children attend the Vernazza elementary school. At this point, Vernazza's tiny river goes underground.

Under tracks you'll find posters for various volunteer organizations. The second track was recently renovated to lessen the disruptive noise.

Until the 1950s, Vernazza's river ran open through the center of town from here to the gelateria. You can see where it once flowed.

Wandering through the main business center you'll pass many locals doing their *vasca* (laps) past the tiny Chapel of Santa Marta where mass is celebrated only on Palm Sunday, the Blue Marlin bar (a good breakfast place and the only night spot in town), the bakery, grocery, and pharmacy. Tiny lanes lead up in both directions (the best *carugi* are on the right).

To the left of the gelateria an arch leads to what was a beach and where the river used to flow out of town. Continue on down to the harbor square and breakwater or follow the trail (second path above the church toward Monterosso) to the classic view of Vernazza (best photos just before sunset).

▲▲▲**The Burned-Out Sightseer's Visual Tour of Vernazza**—Sit on the harbor breakwater (perhaps with a glass of local white wine from the Cantina del Molo, last door on left), face the town and see . . .

The harbor: In a moderate storm you'd be soaked as waves routinely crash over the *molo* (breakwater, built in 1972). The train line, built 130 years ago to tie a newly united Italy together, linked Turin and Genoa with Rome. A second line (hidden in a tunnel at this point) was built in the 1960s. The yellow building was Vernazza's first train station. You can see the four bricked-up waiting alcoves. Vernazza's fishing fleet is down to three small fishing boats (with the net spools)—the town's restaurants buy up everything they catch. Vernazzans are more likely to own a boat than a car. In the '70s tiny Vernazza had one of the top water polo teams in Italy and the harbor was their "pool." Later, when a real pool was required, Vernazza dropped out of the league.

The castle: On the far right, the castle (now a pleasant park, open daily 9:00 or 10:00–19:00, L2000) still guards the town. The Belforte Bar (the fort was named *"bea forte"* or "loud screams," for the warnings it made back in pirating days) is a great and grassy perch. The lowest deck (follow the rope) is great for a glass of wine. (Inside the submarine-strength door, a photo of a major storm shows the entire tower under a wave.) The highest umbrellas mark the recommended Castello restaurant (see Eating, below).

The town: From the lower castle, the houses were interconnected with an interior arcade—ideal for fleeing attacks.

The pastel colors are regulated by a commissioner of good taste in the community government. The square before you is locally famous for some of the region's finest restaurants. The big red central house, the 12th-century site where Genoan ships were built, used to be a kind of guardhouse.

Above the town: The ivy-covered tower, another part of the city fortifications, reminds us of Vernazza's importance in the Middle Ages, when it was an important ally of Genoa (whose arch enemies were the other maritime republics of Pisa, Amalfi, and Venice). Franco's Bar (closed Tuesday), just behind the tower, welcomes hikers finishing (starting, or simply contemplating) the Corniglia–Vernazza hike with great town views. Vineyards fill the mountainside beyond the town. Wine production is down nowadays, as the younger residents choose less physical work. But locals still work their plots and proudly serve their family wine. A single steel train line winds up the gully behind the tower. This is for the vintner's *trenino*, the tiny service train.

The church and city hall: Vernazza's Ligurian Gothic church dates from 1318. The grey and red house above and to the left of the spire is the school. The red building to the right is the former monastery and present city hall. Vernazza and Corniglia function as one community. In 1995, they elected their popular mayor, a Communist, to his second five-year term. The party's banner (now the PDS or "people's democratic party of the left") decorates town walls. High school is in the "big city," La Spezia. Finally, on the top of the hill, with the best view of all, is the town cemetery where most locals plan to end up (*tutto completo* . . . but a new wing is under construction).

Sleeping in Vernazza
(L1,600 = about $1, tel. code: 0187, zip code: 19018)
Sleep Code: **S**=Single, **D**=Double/Twin, **T**=Triple, **Q**=Quad, **b**=bathroom, **t**=toilet only, **s**=shower only, **CC**=Credit Card (Visa, MasterCard, Amex), **SE**=Speaks English, **NSE**=No English. Breakfast is included only in real hotels.

While the Cinque Terre is too rugged for the mobs that ravage the Spanish and French coasts, it's popular with Italians, Germans, and Americans in the know. Room-finding is difficult only on Easter, in August, and on summer Fridays and Saturdays. August weekends are worst. Important: Any other time, for the best value, arrive by midday, ask around, visit three private rooms and snare the best. Going direct cuts out a middleman and softens prices. Off-season, empty rooms abound. Private rooms are generally bigger and more comfortable than those offered by the pensions.

Vernazza, the essence of the Cinque Terre, is my favorite town. There is just one real pension, but two restaurants have about a dozen simple rooms each, and most locals rent extra rooms. Anywhere you stay here will require some climbing. Night noises can be a problem if you're near the station or the church bell tower. Address letters to 19018 Vernazza, Cinque Terre, La Spezia.

Trattoria Gianni rents 21 small rooms just under the castle. The funky ones are artfully decorated à la shipwreck, up lots of tight, winding, spiral stairs mostly with tiny balconies and grand views. The new more comfy rooms lack views but have modern bathrooms and a super-scenic, cliff-hanger private garden. The Franzi family splits the work: Gianni maintains the restaurant's good reputation, and stoic Marisa (who doles out smiles like a rich gambler on a losing streak) runs the rooms (they require a two-night minimum, S-L50,000, D-L85,000, Db-L100,000, Tb-L135,000, CC:VMA; Piazza Marconi 5, closed January–February, tel. & fax 0187/812-228, tel. 0187/821-003). Pick up your keys at the restaurant/reception on the harbor square and hike up the stairs to #41 (funky) or #47 (new) at the top. The nephew Alberto speaks English but communication can be difficult. No reply to your fax means they don't want to make a reservation (they get piles of requests and my tour company books this place out 50 nights of the season). Ideally, telephone three days in advance and leave your first name and time of arrival.

Pension Sorriso knows it's the only real pension in town. Don't expect an exuberant welcome (D-L75,000 per person with obligatory uninspired dinner and breakfast, Db-L90,000 per person with dinner and breakfast, cash only; 50 yards up from station; closed November–February; tel. 0187/812-224, fax 0187/821-198, no answer to your fax means Sorriso is full, some English spoken). While train sounds rumble through the front rooms of the main building, the annex up the street is quieter.

Locanda Barbara, on the harbor square, is run spittoon-style by Giacomo at the Taverna del Capitano (ten rooms with three public showers and WCs, S-L60,000, tiny loft D-L70,000, bigger D-L80,000, family deals; Piazza Marconi 21,

tel. 0187/812-201, closed December–January, charming
Valerio speaks English and loves the girls). The big doubles
come with grand harbor views and are the best value (top two
floors of the big red vacant-looking building facing the harbor). Guests get a free bottle of wine with dinner per couple
at Trattoria del Capitano.

Affitta Camere: Vernazza is honeycombed year-round with
pleasant, rentable private rooms and apartments (cheap for families, with kitchens). They are reluctant to reserve rooms ahead.
To minimize frustration, call a day or two in advance, or simply
show up by midday and look around. All are comfortable and
inexpensive (L30,000–40,000 per person depending on the view).
Some are lavish with killer views, and cost the same as a small
dark place on a back lane over the train tracks. Little or no
English is spoken at these places. Any main street business has a
line on rooms for rent.

Affitta Camere da Filippo is a good network of 15 rooms
and apartments run by Antonio and his mother Rita (D-L70,000,
Db-L80,000, apartments-L100,000; Via A. Del Santo 62 or ask
at the Blue Marlin bar, tel. 0187/812-244). For rooms with some
of the best harbor views in town, see the harborfront Gambero
Rosso restaurant (closed Monday, tel. 0187/812-265). Trattoria
Il Baretto also rents rooms (ask Francesca, tel. 0187/812-381).
Affitta Camere da Nicolina has great views over the harbor,
but is close to the noisy church bell tower (ask at the harborside
Vulnetia restaurant/pizzeria, tel. 0187/821-193). Or try Affitta
Camere da Anna-Maria (Db-L80,000 with view or terrace;
turn left at pharmacy, climb via Carattino to #64, tel. 0187/821-
082). Her German-speaking husband, Franco, runs the "Bar la
Torre" and rents noisy rooms at the top of the town. The lady at
the grocery store across from the gelateria has a line on rooms
(Giuseppina's villa is a modern, deluxe apartment without view,
Db-L80,000, Qb-L140,000; Via S. Giovanni Battista 5, tel.
0187/812-026). Trattoria Sandro also has rooms (Louisa's has
great sea views).

Eating in Vernazza

If you're into Italian cuisine, Vernazza's restaurants are worth
the splurge. All seem good and have similar prices. At about
20:00 wander around and compare the ambience. The Castello,
run by gracious and English-speaking Monica and her family,
serves good food just under the castle (12:00–22:00, closed

Wednesday and November–April, also rents rooms, tel. 0187/812-296). On the harborfront, **Trattoria Franzi** and **Trattoria del Capitano** are more atmospheric and famous. **Gambero Rosso**, considered Vernazza's best restaurant, feels classy and costs only a few thousand lira more than the others. **Trattoria da Sandro** and the more off-beat and intimate **Trattoria Piva** (closed Monday) may come with late-night guitar-strumming.

You can get good pizza by the slice on the main street. Grocery stores (open 7:30–13:00, 17:00–19:30) make inexpensive sandwiches to order. The town's only gelateria is good, and most harborside bars will let you take your glass on a breakwater stroll.

Locals take breakfast about as seriously as flossing. A cappuccino and a pastry or a piece of focaccia bread does it. The two harborfront bars offer the most ambience. The bakery is open early and makes ham and cheese toast. The **Blue Marlin** bar, just below the station, offers the best selection and toasted cheese and ham sandwiches.

Cinque Terre Experiences

▲▲▲**Hiking**—All five towns are connected by good trails. Experience the area's best by hiking from one end to the other. The entire hike can be done in about four hours, but allow five for dawdling. While you can detour to hilltop sanctuaries, I'd keep it simple by following the easy red-and-white-marked low trails between the villages. A good L5,000 hiking map (sold in all the towns, not necessary for this described walk) covers the expanded version of this hike from Porto Venere through all the five Cinque Terre towns to Levanto.

Riomaggiore–Manarola (20 min): From the train station in Riomaggiore (town #1), the Via del' Amore affords a film-gobbling promenade (wide enough for baby strollers) down the coast to Manarola. While there's no beach here, stairs lead down to sunbathing rocks.

Manarola–Corniglia (45 min): From the Manarola (#2) waterfront, it's easiest to take the high trail out of town. The broad and scenic low trail ends with steep stairs leading to the high road. The walk from #2 to #3 is a little longer, and a little more rugged, than from #1 to #2. The high alternative via the hamlet of Volastra takes two hours and offers sweeping views and a closer look at the vineyards. Ask locally about the more difficult 6-mile inland hike to Volastra. This tiny village, perched between Manarola and Corniglia, offers great views and the 5-Terre wine co-op; stop by the Cantina Sociale.

Corniglia–Vernazza (90 min): The hike from Corniglia (#3) to Vernazza (#4)—the wildest and greenest of the coast—is most rewarding. From the Corniglia station and beach, zigzag up to the town. Ten minutes past Corniglia toward Vernazza, you'll see the well-hung Guvano beach far below (see below). The trail leads past a bar and picnic tables, through lots of fragrant and flowery vegetation, and scenically into Vernazza.

Vernazza–Monterosso (90 min): The trail from Vernazza to Monterosso (#5) is a scenic, up-and-down-a-lot trek. Trails are rough (and some readers report "very dangerous") but easy to follow. Camping at the picnic tables midway is frowned upon. The views just out of Vernazza are spectacular.

▲**Swimming**—Wear your walking shoes and pack your swim gear. Each beach has showers that may work better than your hotel's. (Bring soap and shampoo.) Monterosso's beaches, immediately in front of the train station, are easily the best (and most crowded). It's a sandy resort with everything rentable . . . lounge chairs, umbrellas, paddle boats, and usually even beach access (L2,000). Vernazza has a sandy children's cove, sunning rocks, and showers by the breakwater. The tiny "Acque Pendente" (waterfall) cove that locals call their *laguna blu* between Vernazza and Monterosso is accessible only by small hired boat. Forget Manarola or Riomaggiore for beaches. I do my Cinque Terre swimming on the pathetic but peaceful manmade beach below the Corniglia station. Unfortunately, much of it has washed away, and it's almost nonexistent when the surf's up. What's left is clean and less crowded than the Monterosso beach, and the beach bar has showers, drinks, and snacks.

The nude Guvano (GOO-vah-noh) beach (between Corniglia and Vernazza) made headlines in Italy in the 1970s, as clothed locals in a makeshift armada of dinghies and fishing boats retook their town beach. But big-city nudists still work on all-around tans in this remote setting. From the Corniglia train station (follow the road north, zigzag below the tracks, follow signs to tunnel) travelers buzz the intercom and the hydraulic "Get Smart"-type door is opened from the other end. After a 15-minute hike through a cool, moist, and dimly-lit unused old train tunnel, you'll emerge at the Guvano beach—and be charged L5,000 (L4,000 with this guidebook,

water, no WC). A steep (free) trail also leads from
up to the Corniglia–Vernazza trail.

The crowd is Italian counterculture: pierced r
tooed punks, hippie drummers in dreads, and nud
men. The ratio of men to women is about three t
half the people on the pebbly beach keep their sv

▲▲Pesto—This is the birthplace of pesto. Tr
trofie, or *trenette*. Basil, which loves the tempe
climate, is mixed with cheese (half *parmigian*
half *pecorino* sheep cheese), garlic, olive oil, a
then poured over pasta. If you become addi
of it are sold in the local grocery stores.

▲▲Wine—The Vino delle Cinque Terre,
Italy, flows cheap and easy throughout the
sweet, sherry-like wine, the local Sciacche
splurge (L5,000 per glass, often served wi
10 kilos of grapes yield 7 liters of local wi
made from near-raisins, and 10 kilos of gi
1.5 liters of Sciachetra. If your room is up
warned: Sciachetra is 18 percent alcohol,
only 11 percent. In the cool, calm evenin
breakwater with a glass of wine and watch
the waves. While red wine is sold as Cinque Terre wine,
fantasy designed to please the tourists.

Cinque Terre Towns

(Note: Readers of this book fill Vernazza. For this reason, you
might prefer to stay in another town with fewer Americans.
See Sleeping, below.)

▲▲Riomaggiore (town #1)—The most substantial non-resort
town of the group, Riomaggiore is a disappointment from the
train station. But walk through the tunnel next to the train tracks
(or take the scenic high road, straight up and to the right), and
you land in a fascinating tangle of pastel homes leaning on each
other as if someone stole their crutches. There's homemade
gelato at the Bar Central and if Ivo is there, you'll feel right at
home. A cliff-hanging trail leads out of town to a botanical garden and old WWII bunkers. Another climbs scenically to the
Madonna di Montenero sanctuary high above the town.

▲Manarola (town #2)—Like town #1, #2 is attached to
its station by a 200-yard-long tunnel. Manarola is tiny and
rugged, a tumble of buildings bunny-hopping down its ravine

to the tiny harbor. Buy a picnic (stores close from 13:00–17:00) before walking to the beaches of Corniglia.

▲▲**Corniglia (town #3)**—From the station, a footpath zigzags up 370 stairs to the only town of the five not on the water. Originally settled by a Roman farmer who named it for his mother, Cornelia, its ancient residents produced a wine so famous that vases found at Pompei touted its virtues. Today its wine is still its lifeblood. Follow the pungent smell of ripe grapes into an alley cellar and get a local to let you dip a straw into her keg. Remote and less visited, Corniglia has cooler temperatures, a windy belvedere, a few restaurants, and more than enough private rooms for rent. Past the train station is the Corniglia beach and Albergo Europa, a bungalow village filled with Italians doing the Cinque Terre in 14 days.

▲▲**Monterosso al Mare (town #5)**—This is a resort with cars, hotels, rentable beach umbrellas, and crowds. Walk east of the station through the tunnel for the Old World charm (and the nearly hourly boat to Vernazza, 1997 departures: 10:15, 11:15, 12:15, 14:15, 15:45, 16:45, 17:45, 18:45). If you want a sandy beach, this is it. Adventurers may want to rent a rowboat or paddleboat and find their own private cove. The TI is open 10:00–12:00, 15:30–19:30, and closed Sunday afternoon (tel. 0187/817-506).

Sleeping Elsewhere on the Cinque Terre
(L1,600 = about $1, tel. code: 0187)
If you're trying to avoid my readers, stay away from Vernazza and Mama Rosa's. Rich, sun-worshipping softies like Monterosso. Winos and mountain goats prefer Corniglia. Students sleep cheap in Riomaggiore. Sophisticated Italians and Germans take stuffy Manarola. (See "Sleeping in Vernazza," above, for room-finding tips.)

Sleeping in Riomaggiore
(tel. code: 0187, zip code: 19017)
Riomaggiore is bursting with private rooms. It's a very competitive scene. **Mar Mar Rooms** is a well-organized network of private rooms run by English-speaking Mario Franceschetti (Db-L70,000, bunky family deals, you can request kitchen, balcony, open year-round; Via Don Minzoni 6, tel. 0187/920-932, fax 0187/920-932, when full they will not return your fax).

Michielini Anna rents good rooms (five D-L70,000 with kitchens; across from the Central Bar at Via Colombo 143, tel. 0187/920-950 for English-speaking Daniela). **Luciano and Roberto Fazioli** have five apartments, nine rooms, and a slummy seven-bed mini-hostel. Prices range from L25,000 to L50,000 per person (Via Colombo 94, tel. 0187/920-587 or 0187/920-904). **Edi** has a similar network of rooms (Via Colombo 111, tel. & fax 0187/920-325, cellular: 033-8619-0434). If friendly Ivo is on duty at the **Bar Central**, he'll help you find a room (tel. 0187/920-208). Ivo lived in San Francisco and speaks great English. His Bar Central is a good stop for breakfast and prize-winning gelato, and it's the only lively late-night place in town.

Youth Hostel Mama Rosa is run with a splash of love and craziness by Rosa Ricci (an agressively friendly character who snares backpackers at the train station), her husband, Carmine (a.k.a. "Papa Rosa"), and their English-speaking son, Silvio. This unique comedy of errors creates a special bond among the young, rugged, and poor who sleep here. Many consider it a slum. It's a chaotic but manageable jumble with the ambience of a YMCA locker room filled with bunk beds (L25,000 beds—price promised through 1998; 20 yards directly in front of the station; no curfew; just show up without a reservation—the earlier the better, no telephone). The nine coed rooms, with four to ten beds each, are plain, basic, and poorly ventilated. But a family atmosphere rages with hand-wash laundry facilities, trickle-down showers (best in afternoon), and Silvio's five cats. This is one of those rare places where perfect strangers become good friends with the slurp of spaghetti, and wine supersedes the concept of ownership. For sanity, sleep at the new Manarola hostel. For value, spend a few extra lire and find a private room. For new friends, the aroma of cat pee, and memories you'll be unable to forget, it's Mama Rosa's.

Eat well at **La Lampara** (check out their *frutti di mare* pizza, *trenete al pesto*, and the rice with seafood, closed Tuesday) on Via Colombo. The Pizzeria at Via Colombo 26 serves thick pizza by the delicious slice.

Sleeping and Eating in Manarola
(tel. code: 0187, zip code: 19010)
Marina Piccola has ten bright, modern rooms on the water, so I guess they figure a warm welcome is unnecessary (Db-L120,000,

requires dinner in July and August, CC:VMA, tel. 0187/920-103, fax 0187/920-966).

Up the hill, the utterly normal **Albergo ca' d'Andrean** is quiet, comfortable, modern, and very hotelesque, with ten big sunny rooms and a cool garden complete with orange trees. One-night drop-ins are OK, but not one-night reservations (Db-L105,000, closed November; Via A. Discovolo 101, tel. 0187/920-040, fax 0187/920-452, Simone SE).

Farther up the street, **Casa Capellini** rents four rooms (D-L70,000, the *alta camera* on the top with a kitchen, private terrace, and knockout view-L80,000; take a hard right on the church square, then two doors down the hill on your right, Via Antonio Discovolo 6 or Via Ettore Cozzani 12, tel. 0187/920-823, run by a quiet older man and his daughter, who speak no English).

Manarola Ostello, Manarola's new youth hostel, is at the top of the town overlooking the church (beds-L25,000, 48 beds total; Via Riccobaldi 21, tel. 0187/920-113 fax 0187/920-866). While this is great news for travelers, the conservative people of Manarola are worried that the hostel crowd will disrupt the town's decency and tranquility. Please be sensitive to their concerns.

Sleeping in Corniglia
(tel. code: 0187, zip code: 19010)
At the town-end promontory, **Maria Guelfi** (tel. 0187/812-178) and **Senora Silvana** (tel. 0187/513-830) offer rooms. **Affittasi Vista Mare** has rooms scattered all over town (tel. 0187/812-293). **Pellegrini** has three rooms (D-L60,000, Via Solferino 34, tel. 0187/812-184) or try **Villa Sandra** (Via Fieschi 100, tel. 0187/812-384). The **Bar-Ristorante Dan Tinola** offers good meals and cheap rooms as does **Villa Cecio** (on main road 100 yards toward Vernazza, views, 0187/812-043). There is a good chance someone will be waiting for stray travelers at the station with a car to run you up to their place in the town.

Sleeping in Monterosso
(tel. code: 0187, zip code: 19016)
Monterosso al Mare, the most beach-resorty of the five Cinque Terre towns, offers maximum comfort and ease. There are plenty of hotels, rentable beach umbrellas, shops, and cars. The TI (Pro Loco) can find you a L40,000-per-person room in a private home (below station, open 10:00–12:00 and 15:30–19:30, closed Sunday afternoon, tel. 0187/817-506). If driving

to Monterosso, leave the freeway at Carrodano exit (30 minutes from there to Monterosso) and park (L10,000/day) in the huge beachfront guarded lot.

The following hotel listings are listed in the order you'll see them as you head either right or left out of the station.

Turn right leaving the station to the **Hotel Baia**. Facing the beach, over half of the Baia's 30 comfortable rooms come with great beachfront balconies (Db-L150,000–180,000 including breakfast, CC:VM; Via Fegina 88, tel. 0187/817-512, fax 0187/818-322). Farther on, **Hotel Cinque Terre** is a slick new building with 54 similar rooms on the big road into (not out of) town near the beach (Db-L180,000, Db-L200,000, breakfast included, dinner is required in July and August, open April–October, CC:VMA, reconfirm reservations, signs say "Hotel 5 Terre," easy parking; Via IV Novembre 21, tel. 0187/817-543, fax 0187/818-380).

Turn left out of the station to the bright, airy **Pension Agavi** (eight rooms, some with balcony, Db-L110,000, tel. 0187/817-171, fax 0187/818-264, Claudia SE). The tunnel then leads to the old town and three unexceptional places that require dinner mid-June through mid-September: the neglected but cheap **Albergo Marina** (D-L95,000, Db-L110,000, open March–October; Via Buranco 40, tel. & fax 0187/817-242 or 0187/817-613); the fancy and more expensive **Albergo degli Amici** (no views; next door at Via Buranco 36, tel. 0187/817-544, fax 0187/817-424); and **Ristorante/ Pensione al Carugio** (D-L80,000, Db-L90,000, modern, blocky, no-view apartment at top of town; 15 Via S. Pietro, tel. 0187/817-453).

Farther on, the lovingly managed **Hotel Villa Steno** features great view balconies, private gardens off some rooms, TVs, telephones, all the comforts, and the friendly help of English-speaking Matteo. Of his 16 rooms, 12 have view balconies (Sb-L100,000, Db-L160,000, Tb-L190,000, Qb-L220,000, with hearty buffet breakfast, L10,000 discount per room per night if you pay with cash and show this book; ten-minute hike from the station at the top of the old town at Via Roma 109, tel. 0187/817-028 or 0187/818-336, fax 0187/817-056, web site: www.pasini.com, e-mail: steno@pasini.com). Readers get a free glass of the local sweet wine, Sciacchetrà, when they check in— ask. The Steno has a tiny parking lot (free, but call to reserve a spot). The same family runs the **Albergo Pasquale**, a place with more stars but less soul on the beach (and train tracks). While Villa Steno is quieter, it's a climb from the beach and station. If Steno is full, they'll honor Steno prices at Pasquale (first place after tunnel; air-con, Via Fegina 4, tel. 0187/817-550 or 0187/817-477, fax 0187/817-056, Felicita SE).

Sleeping near the Cinque Terre

La Spezia: When all else fails, you can stay in a noisy, bigger town like La Spezia. Each of the following places is within a block of the train station. The elegant, old, newly restored **Hotel Firenze e Continentale** has all the classy comforts but no parking (Db-L190,000, maybe L160,000 in slow time, includes buffet breakfast, good group rates, CC:VMA, air-con, elevator; Via Paleocapa 7, 19122 La Spezia, tel. 0187/713-200, fax 0187/714-930, Maria Gabriella Liconti SE). **Albergo Parma,** bright and bleachy clean with TVs and folding metal furniture in the rooms, is located just below the station, down the stairs (D-L70,000, Db-L85,000, less for two nights, CC:VM; Via Fiume 143, 19100 La Spezia, tel. 0187/743-010, fax 0187/743-240). **Hotel Terminus** has filthy rooms with worn-out carpets, yellow walls, and old plumbing (D-L60,000, Db-L75,000; Via Paleocapa 21, just down from the station, tel. 0187/703-436). There's an automatic laundromat nearby. Friday morning a huge open-air market sprawls for about a mile from the station.

Santa Margherita Ligure: If you need the movie-star's Riviera, park your yacht at Portofino. Or you can settle down in nearby more personable Santa Margherita Ligure (20 minutes by bus from Portofino and an hour train-ride north of the Cinque Terre). While Portofino's velour allure is tarnished by snobby residents and a nonstop traffic jam in peak season, Santa Margherita tumbles easily downhill from its huggable train station. The town has a fun resort character with a breezy promenade (TI: 0185/287-485). Buses go from the station and the harborfront to Portofino (3/hr, L2,000), but the boat does it with more class and without the traffic jams. Hikers count the SM–PF hike as one of the best on the Riviera. The friendly Sabini family offers 12 nonsmoking rooms in the stately old **Hotel Nuova Riviera** (D-L100,000, Db-L150,000, T-L140,000, Tb-L160,000, with a big breakfast, CC:V, easy parking, peaceful garden; ten-minute walk from the station; walking or driving, follow signs to hospital, on Piazza Mazzini see hotel signs, Via Belvedere 10-2, 16038 S. Margherita Ligure, tel. & fax 0185/287-403, son John

Carlo SE). Mama Sabini cooks a great dinner (L30,000) and Papa makes sure you enjoy the family wine. **Hotel Terminus,** right at the station, also works hard to keep its travelers happy (D-L100,000, Db-L140,000 with huge breakfast, CC:VMA, good meals, tel. 0185/286-121, fax 0185/282-546, the son, Angelo SE).

Transportation Connections—Cinque Terre
The five towns of the Cinque Terre are on a milk-run train line described earlier in this chapter. Hourly trains connect each town with the others, La Spezia, and Genoa. While a few of the milk-run trains go to more distant points (Milan or Pisa), it's faster to change in La Spezia to a bigger train.

From La Spezia by train to: **Rome** (10/day, 4 hrs), **Pisa** (hrly, 60 min), **Florence** (hrly, 2.5 hrs, change at Pisa), **Milan** (hrly, 3 hrs, change in Genoa), **Venice** (2 direct 6-hr trains/ day—also from Monterosso).

Killing time in La Spezia's station? The station bar is OK, but 2 blocks down the street, **C'est Bon Casa del Cioccolato** serves crepes, gelati, and designer chocolates in turn-of-the-century splendor (15:00–23:00, closed Tuesday, Piazza Saint Bon 1, tel. 0185/705-850).

Driving in the Cinque Terre
Milan to the Cinque Terre (130 miles): Drivers speed south by autostrada from Milan, skirt Genoa, and drive along some of Italy's most scenic and impressive freeways toward the port of La Spezia. The road via Parma is faster but less scenic.

It's possible to snake your car down the treacherous little road into the Cinque Terre and park above the town, but this is risky in August and on Saturday or Sunday, when Italian day-trippers clog the region. Throughout the tourist season you may have to park far above the town. Monterosso has a huge beach-front parking lot which rarely fills up (L10,000/day). Vernazza has several small lots above, and Riomaggiore has a huge but expensive garage. To drive to Monterosso or Vernazza, leave the autostrada at Uscita Carrodano just west of La Spezia. To drive to Riomaggiore, leave the freeway at La Spezia.

You can also park your car near the train station in La Spezia. Spots on Via Paleocapa below the station are free for long stays. Confirm that parking is OK and leave nothing inside to steal. The "Autorimessa Stationi" garage immediately below the station can store your car for about L20,000 per day.

MILAN (MILANO)

They say that for every church in Rome, there's a bank in Milan. Italy's second city and the capital of Lombardy, Milan is a hardworking, fashion-conscious, time-is-money city of 2 million. Milan is a melting pot of people and history. Its industriousness may come from the Teutonic blood of its original inhabitants, the Lombards, or from the region's Austrian heritage. Milan is Italy's industrial, banking, TV, publishing, and convention capital. The economic success of modern Italy can be blamed on this city of publicists and pasta power-lunches.

As if to make up for its shaggy parks, blocky Fascist architecture and recently-bombed-out feeling (WWII), its people are works of art. Milan is an international fashion capital with a refined taste. Window displays are gorgeous. Even the cheese comes gift-wrapped.

Three hundred years before Christ, the Romans called this place Mediolanum or "the central place." By the fourth century A.D., it was the capital of the western half of the Roman Empire. It was from here that Emperor Constantine issued the Edict of Milan, legalizing Christianity. After some barbarian darkness, medieval Milan rose to regional prominence under the Visconti and Sforza families. By the time of the Renaissance, it was called "the New Athens" and was enough of a cultural center for Leonardo to call home. Then came 400 years of foreign domination (Spain, Austria, France, more Austria). Milan was a center of the 1848 revolution against Austria and helped lead Italy to unification in 1870.

Mussolini left a heavy Fascist touch on the city's architecture (such as the central train station). His excesses also led to the WWII bombing of Milan. But Milan rose again. The 1959 Pirelli Tower (the skinny skyscraper in front of the station) was a trendsetter in its day. Today Milan is pedestrian-friendly with a great transit system. There are banks everywhere and reassuringly, enough police.

Many tourists come to Italy for the past. But Milan is today's Italy, and no Italian trip is complete without seeing it. While it's not big on the tourist circuit, Milan has plenty to see. It's no more expensive than other Italian cities, and it's well-organized and completely manageable.

Planning Your Time

OK, it's a big city, so you probably won't linger. But with two nights and a full day, you can gain an appreciation for the town and see the major sights. With 36 hours, I'd sleep in and focus on the center. Tour the Duomo and the La Scala museum, hit what art you like (Brera Gallery, Michelangelo's *Pietà*, Leonardo's *Last Supper*), browse through the elegant shopping area and the Gallery, and try to see an opera. Technology buffs like the Science and Technology Museum, while medieval art buffs dig the city's very old churches. People-watchers and pigeon-feeders could spend an entire vacation never leaving sight of the Duomo.

Since Milan is a cold Italian plunge and most flights to the U.S.A. leave Milan early in the morning, you may want to start your Italian trip softly by going directly from Milan to Lake Como (one-hour trip to Varenna) or the Cinque Terre (four hours to Vernazza) and spending a night or two in Milan at the end of your trip before flying home.

Three-hour tour: If you're just changing trains in Milan (as sooner or later you will), consider this blitz tour: Check your bag at the station, pick up a city map at the station TI, ride the subway to the Duomo (in front of train station, follow line 3 direction "per San Donato" four stops to "Duomo"), peruse the square, explore the cathedral's rooftop and interior, have a scenic coffee in the Galleria, give the Taurus a spin, see the opera museum at La Scala, do the "Quadrilateral" high-fashion window-shopping stroll to Metro: Montenapoleone, and return by subway to the station (line 3, direction "Zara"). Art fans might make time for the Leonardo or the Michelangelo.

Orientation (tel. code: 02)

Tourist Information: Milan has two TIs. One is in the central train station (Monday–Saturday 8:00–18:00, less on Sunday, top level, with back to tracks, on the left next to a telephone center and the APT public transit info office) and the other is on Piazza Duomo (less crowded, to the right as you face the church, Monday–Saturday 8:30–20:00, Sunday 9:00–17:00, tel. 02/725-24300). Confirm your sightseeing plans and pick up the Milan is Milan map (free, with lots of extra info, a handy close-up of center), the classy *Museums in Milan* booklet (with latest hours of all sights), and the *Milano Mese* monthly (if you're interested in entertainment or special events). The free *Dove Come Quando* ("Where, How and When" if available in English) booklet lists shopping, restaurants, nightlife, and sports.

Arrival in Milan

By Train: The huge, sternly decorated, Fascist-built train station is a city and a sight in itself. Orient from the top level with your back to the tracks. On the right: train information (tel. 02/1478-88088, validate railpasses here at refund window) and baggage check (L5,000/12 hours). On the left: 24-hour drug store, TI, city transit information. Out the side exit on left: airport shuttle-buses and Via Scarlatti (leading to recommended hotels). Downstairs straight ahead: train tickets, a great and huge supermarket/cafeteria (open daily 7:00–24:00), metro station, and Hertz/Avis/Europcar offices.

For most quick visits, the giant city is one simple axis from the train station to Duomo. To get downtown, go straight into the Metro (look for red M), buy a L1,500 ticket (bills or coins), follow signs for line 3 (yellow), direction S. Donato. To return to the station, take the yellow line 3, direction "Zara." After one trip on the Metro, you'll dream up other excuses to use it.

You can buy train tickets and reserve couchettes for the station price without the station lines near the Duomo at CIT (in Galleria Vittorio Emanuele, Monday–Saturday 9:00–19:00, closed Sunday, tel. 02/8637-0228) or American Express (up Via Verdi from La Scala, Via Brera 3, tel. 02/7200-3694).

By Plane: Catch a frequent shuttle-bus from either of Milan's airports to the central train station. For details, see Transportation Connections, below.

Helpful Hints

Theft Alert: Be on guard. Milan's thieves (many, these days, from the former Yugoslavia) target tourists. At the station and around the Duomo, thieves dressed as beggars roam, usually in gangs of three too-young-to-arrest children.

    Scheduling: Monday is a terrible sightseeing day since most museums are closed. August is rudely hot and muggy. Locals who can, vacate, leaving the city just about dead. Those visiting in August find many shops closed, nightlife pretty quiet, hotels empty and discounted. I've listed which recommended hotels offer air-conditioning.

Getting Around Milan

Use Milan's great subway system. The clean, spacious, fast, and easy three-line Metro zips you anywhere you may want to go. Transit tickets (L1,500 at newsstands, normally in the subway station) are good for one subway ride followed by 75 minutes of bus or tram travel. The L5,000 24-hour pass is a handy option (sold at major stations and some newsstands, 48 hours for L9,000). I've keyed sightseeing to the subway system. While most sights are within a few blocks of each other, Milan is an exhausting city for walking. You'll rarely wait more than two minutes for a subway train and the well-marked buses can be useful. Small groups go cheap and fast by taxi (metered, drop charge L6,000 and L1,300 per km, often easiest to walk to a taxi stand rather than try to hail a taxi).

Sights—Milan

Compared to Rome and Florence, Milan's art is mediocre, but the city does have unique and noteworthy sights. To maximize your time, use the Metro and note which places stay open through the siesta. I've listed sights in a logical geographical order.

    While I've listed enough to keep you hectic for two days, there's much more to see in Milan than I've listed. Its many thousand-year-old churches make it clear that Milan was an important beacon in the Dark Ages. Local guidebooks and the tourist information office can point you in the right direction if you have more time.

▲▲**Duomo**—Milan's cathedral, the city's centerpiece, is the third-largest church in Europe (after the Vatican's and Sevilla's). At 480 feet long and 280 feet wide, with 52 150-foot-tall sequoia pillars inside and more than 2,000 statues,

Milan Metro

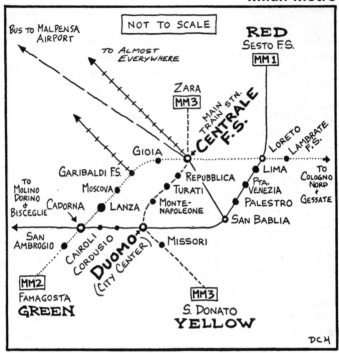

NOT TO SCALE

BUS TO MALPENSA AIRPORT

TO ALMOST EVERYWHERE

RED
SESTO F.S.
MM1

ZARA
MM3

MAIN STN.
TRAIN STN.
CENTRALE F.S.

GIOIA

LORETO
LAMBRATE F.S.

GARIBALDI F.S.

TO MOLINO DORINO & BISCEGLIE

MOSCOVA
CADORNA
LANZA

REPUBBLICA
TURATI
MONTE-NAPOLEONE

LIMA
PTA. VENEZIA
PALESTRO

TO COLOGNO NORD & GESSATE

SAN AMBROGIO
CAIROLI
CORDUSIO

SAN BABLIA

DUOMO
(CITY CENTER)

MISSORI

MM2
FAMAGOSTA
GREEN

MM3
S. DONATO
YELLOW

DCH

the place seats 12,000 worshipers. If you do two laps, you've done your daily walk. Built from 1386 until 1810, this construction project originated the Italian phrase meaning "never-ending": "like building a cathedral." It started Gothic (best seen in the apse behind the altar) and was finished under Napoleon. It's an example of the flamboyant, or "flamelike," overripe final stage of Gothic, but architectural harmony is not its forte. Make a circuit simply to enjoy the giant stained-glass windows trying to light the cavernous interior (church free, daily 7:00–19:00; enforced dress code: no shorts or bare shoulders; Metro: Duomo). For most, the Tesoro (treasury) isn't worth the time or L2,000.

The rooftop is a fancy forest of spires with great views of the city, the square, and—on clear days—even the Swiss Alps. Overlooking everything is the 13-foot-tall gilt Virgin Mary, 300 feet above the ground (climb the stairs for L6,000 or ride the elevator for L8,000, daily 9:00–17:30; enter out-

Milan

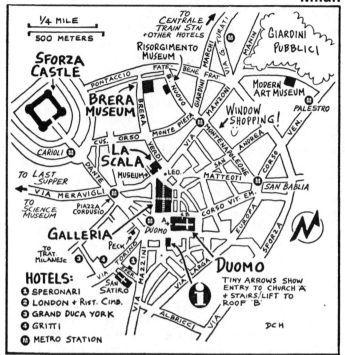

side from near the west end; clue: in Europe old churches face roughly east).

Museo del Duomo—The cathedral's museum is a scrapbook of 600 years of cathedral history, offering a close look at the stained glass, statues, and gargoyles (L8,000, L12,000 for combo ticket with rooftop, Tuesday–Sunday 9:30–12:30, 15:00–18:00, closed Monday, 14 Piazza Duomo, Metro: Duomo).

▲**Piazza Duomo and nearby**—Piazza Duomo is a classic European scene. Professionals scurry, label-conscious kids loiter, young thieves peruse. For that creepy-crawly pigeons-all-over-you experience, buy a bag of seed. Is the fountain the Duomo facade in motion, or am I all wet? Behind the Duomo is a pedestrian shopping zone. Within a block of the piazza are a few interesting glimpses of old Milan. The center of medieval Milan was Piazza Mercanti, a small square just opposite the Duomo. It's a strangely peaceful place today with a fine smattering of old time Milano architecture and pigeon sprinkle.

The church of **Santa Maria presso San Satiro** (just off Via Torino, a few yards past Via Speronari) was the scene of a temper tantrum in 1242, when a losing gambler vented his anger by hitting the baby Jesus in the Madonna-and-Child altarpiece. Blood "miraculously" spurted out, and the beautiful little church has been on the pilgrimage trail ever since. It's worth a visit to see the illusion of depth (trompe l'oeil), designed by Bramante, behind the basically flat altar. The **Duomo Center** is a modern mall with a mega music store, book shop with maps and English travel guides, one-hour photo service, decent pizzeria, and the recommended Ciao cafeteria (with easy access WCs) upstairs. For a fine view of the Duomo, climb the steps to the balcony above the TI.

▲▲**Galleria Vittorio Emanuele**—Milan is symbolized by its great four-story, glass-domed arcade. Here you can turn an expensive cup of coffee into a good value with Europe's best people-watching (or enjoy the same view for peanuts from the strategically placed McDonald's). Stand under the central dome and enjoy the art above. For good luck, locals step on the testicles of the mosaic Taurus on the floor's zodiac design. Two local girls explained that it works better if you spin.

Under the Galleria dome is the CIT travel agency and an SIP cluster of public phone booths. The "Comune di Milan" office at the La Scala end has tourist information (Metro: Duomo).

▲▲**La Scala Opera House and Museum**—From the Galleria, you'll see a statue of Leonardo. He's looking at a plain but famous neoclassical building, possibly the world's most prestigious opera house, Milan's Teatrale alla Scala. La Scala opened in 1778 with an opera by Antonio Salieri (of *Amadeus* fame). While tickets are as hard to get as they are expensive, anyone can have a peek into the grand theater from a box connected to the museum. Opera buffs will love the museum's extensive collection of things that would mean absolutely nothing to the MTV crowd: Verdi's top hat, Rossini's eyeglasses, Toscanini's baton, Fettucini's pesto, and original scores, busts, portraits, and death masks of great composers and musicians (L5,000, Monday–Saturday 9:30–12:30, 14:00–17:30 and summer Sundays, Metro: Duomo, tel. 02/805-3418).

The opera season is December to July; September to November for ballet and classical concerts. La Scala is closed in August. Decent (and very expensive) seats generally sell out long in advance. Sky-high but affordable gallery seats are often available two hours before the performance. Or drop by a half-hour before curtain time for one of 200 L10,000 standing room spots (*posto in piedi*). These are usually easy to get. While ushers will invite you to a no-view seat, the best view is from standing in the center rear (tel. 02/720-03744 or 02/861-772, showtime usually 18:30 or 20:00, standing spots sold at museum entry). La Scala has a fine web site: http:// lascala.milano.it.

▲**World-Class Window-Shopping**—The "Quadrilateral," the elegant, high-fashion shopping area around Via Montenapoleone, is worth a wander. In this land where cigarettes are still chic, the people-watching is as fun as the window-shopping. Via Montenapoleone and Via Spiga are the best streets. From La Scala, walk up Via Manzoni to the Metro stop: Montenapoleone, browse down Montenapoleone to Piazza San Babila and then down the pedestrians-only Corso Vittorio Emanuele II to the Duomo.

Museums of Milan and of Contemporary History—These museums (both at Via Sant'Andrea 6) are free and offer a quick walk through wall-sized pages of Milan's past, including the especially interesting 1914 to 1945 period (free, Tuesday–Sunday 9:30–17:30, often with a lunch break, closed Monday; Metro: Montenapoleone).

▲**The Brera Art Gallery**—Milan's top collection of paintings (Italian, 14th–20th centuries) is world-class, but it can't top Rome or Florence. Established in 1809 to house Napoleon's looted art, it fills the first floor above an art college. On the ground level wander past the nude *Napoleon* (by Canova) in the courtyard and straight through the art school to a great L600 cappuccino machine. Back in the courtyard climb the stairway following signs to "Pinacoteca" (L8,000, Tuesday–Saturday 9:00–17:30, Sunday 9:00–12:30, closed Monday, Via Brera 28, Metro: Lanza, tel. 02/722-631).

The gallery's highlights include works by: Gentile da Fabriano (room IV), the Bellini brothers and Mantegna (his textbook example of feet-first foreshortening, *The Dead Christ*, room VI), Crivelli (for someone new, in room XXI), Raphael (*Wedding of the Madonna*, room XXIV), and Michelangelo Merisi (a.k.a. Caravaggio, *Supper at Emmaus*, room XXIX).

▲**Risorgimento Museum**—You'll learn the interesting story (if you speak Italian or luck out as I did with a bored and talkative English-speaking guard) of Italy's rocky road to unity:

from Napoleon (1796) to the victory in Rome (1870). It's just around the block from the Brera Gallery at Via Borgonuovo 23 (free, 9:30–17:30, closed Monday; Metro: Montenapoleone).

Poldi Pezzoli Museum—This classy house of art features top Italian paintings of the 15th through 18th centuries and lots of interesting decorative arts like a roomful of old sundials and compasses (L10,000, Tuesday–Sunday 9:30–12:30, 14:30–18:00, closed Monday, Via Manzoni 12, Metro: Montenapoleone, tel. 02/794-889).

Bagatti Valsecchi Museum—This unique 19th-century collection of Italian Renaissance treasures was assembled by two aristocratic brothers who spent a wad turning their home into a Renaissance mansion (L10,000, Tuesday–Sunday 13:00–17:00, closed Monday, half-price on Wednesday, good English descriptions, Via Santo Spirito 10).

▲**Sforza Castle (Castello Sforzesco)**—This immense, much-bombed-and-rebuilt brick fortress is exhausting at first sight. It can only be described as heavy. But its courtyard has a great lawn for picnics and siestas, and its free museum is filled with interesting medieval armor, furniture, early Lombard art, an Egyptian collection, and, most important, Michelangelo's unfinished *Rondanini Pietà*. Michelangelo died while still working on this piece, which hints at the elongation of the mannerist style that would follow. This is a rare opportunity to enjoy a Michelangelo with no crowds (free, Tuesday–Sunday 9:30–17:30, closed Monday, Metro: Cairoli).

▲**Leonardo da Vinci's *Last Supper* (Cenacolo)**—This Renaissance masterpiece is in the refectory of the church of Santa Maria delle Grazie. It captures the emotional moment when Jesus says to his disciples, "One of you will betray me," and 11 wonder nervously, "Lord, is it I?" Notice Judas with his 30 pieces of silver, looking pretty guilty. This ill-fated masterpiece suffers from Leonardo's experimental use of oil rather than the normal fresco technique. Deterioration began within six years of its completion. The church was bombed in WWII, but the *Last Supper* survived. Now undergoing extensive restoration, it's a faded mess with most of the original paint gone and much of the rest behind scaffolding (L12,000, Tuesday–Sunday 8:00–13:45, closed Monday; Metro: Cadorno).

▲**National Leonardo da Vinci Science and Technology Museum (Museo Nazionale della Scienza e Tecnica)**— The spirit of Leonardo lives here. Most tourists visit for the hall of Leonardo designs illustrated in wooden models, but Leonardo's mind is just as easy to appreciate by paging through a coffee-table edition of his notebooks in any bookstore. The rest of this immense collection of industrial cleverness is fascinating, with plenty of push-button action (and no English descriptions): trains, radios, old musical instruments, computers, batteries, telephones, chunks of the first transatlantic cable, and on and on (L10,000, Via San Vittore 21, bus #50 or #58 from the Duomo, or Metro: San Ambrogio, Tuesday–Sunday 9:30–16:50, until 18:30 weekends, closed Monday).

Nightlife—For evening action, check out the arty, student-oriented Brera area in the old center and Milan's formerly Bohemian, now gentrified "Little Venice," the Navigli neighborhood. Specifics change so quickly that it's best to rely on the entertainment information in periodicals from the TI.

Soccer—The Milanese claim their soccer team is the best in Europe. For a dose of Europe's soccer-mania (which many believe provides a necessary testosterone vent to keep Europe out of a third big war), catch a match in Milan. Games are held in the 85,000-seat Meazza stadium most Sundays, September through June (tickets from L20,000–75,000 sold at several downtown outlets, tel. 02/48707123, Metro: Lotto or tram 24 from Duomo directly to stadium).

Sleeping in Milan
(L1,600 = about $1, tel. code: 02)
Sleep Code: **S**=Single, **D**=Double/Twin, **T**=Triple, **Q**=Quad, **b**=bathroom, **t**=toilet only, **s**=shower only, **CC**=Credit Card (Visa, MasterCard, Amex), **SE**=Speaks English, **NSE**=No English.

I have tried to minimize traffic noise problems in my listings. All are within a few minutes walk of Milan's subway system. With Milan's fine Metro, you can get anywhere in town in a flash. Anytime in February, April, May, September and October, the city can be completely jammed by conventions; summer is usually wide open. Hotels cater more to business travelers than to tourists.

Sleeping in the City Center (near the Duomo)
The Duomo (cathedral) area is thick with people-watching, reasonable eateries, and the major sightseeing attractions (from

the central train station, it's just four stops on the Metro, direction S. Donato, to Metro: Duomo). There is no self-service laundry in the center.

Hotel Speronari is perfectly located, safe, quiet, with 32 bright, clean, and newly renovated rooms on a great pedestrian street full of delis and food shops (S-L65,000, Sb-L80,000, D-L90,000, Ds-L120,000, Db-L130,000, T-L120,000, Tb-L170,000, Qb-L200,000, prices promised through 1998 with this book, no breakfast, CC:VM, lots of stairs, ceiling fans; just off Via Torino, 1 block off far left end of Piazza Duomo with back to church, Via Speronari 4, 20123 Milano, tel. 02/864-61125, fax 02/720-03178, run by the Isoni family: father Paolo and John Paul, Maurizio, Carla, Carolina, and Fara). Enjoy a free *cappuccino di benvenuto* upon arrival. Consider breakfast at the Flut Bar across the intersection (from 7:00, closed Sunday).

London Hotel is a fine little hotel (closed in August) with all the comforts on a handy quiet street in the center, run by the friendly Gambino family (30 rooms, Sb-L130,000, D-L160,000, Db-L200,000, Tb-L240,000, breakfast-L12,000, CC:VM; elevator, TVs, telephones, air-conditioned; near Metro: Cairoli at Via Rovello 3, 20121 Milano, tel. 02/720-20166, tel. & fax 02/805-7037, SE). **Hotel Giulio Cesare**, across the street, is bigger, basic, and impersonal but works in a pinch (Db-L180,000, CC:VMA; Via Rovello 10, 20121 Milano, tel. 02/72003915, fax 02/72002179).

Hotel Grand Duca di York is a real hotel with 33 simple rooms and lavish public spaces stuck in the middle of banks and big-city starkness 3 blocks off the Duomo square (two tiny Sb-L90,000, Sb-L160,000, Db-L220,000, Tb-L290,000, with breakfast, summer discounts, CC:VMA, air-con, elevator; near Metro: Piazza Cordusio at Via Moneta 1, 20123 Milano, tel. 02/874-863, fax 02/869-0344, SE).

Hotel Gritti is your best splurge near the Duomo. Facing a quiet square just off Via Torino, it's a bright, classy, professionally-run three-star hotel (48 rooms, Sb-L150,000, Db-L220,000, Tb-L320,000 including breakfast, same price all seasons, family deals, CC:VMA, elevator, air-con; Piazza S. Maria Beltrade 4, 20123 Milano, tel. 02/801056, fax 02/89010999, SE, e-mail: hotel.gritti@iol.it).

One-star hotels near the center with rooms in the L90,000 range include: **Alba d'Oro** (Metro: Porta Venezia, 5 Viale

Piave, tel. 02/760-23880, fax 02/381-01786), **Hotel Kent**
(Metro: San Babila, Via F. Corridoni 2, tel. 02/551-87635),
and **Hotel Roma** (Metro: Porta Romano, 4 Corso Lodi,
tel. 02/583-09560, fax 02/583-05606).

Sleeping near the Train Station
For pure convenience and price, this is a handy, if dreary,
area. The area between the train station and Corso Buenos
Aires, in spite of its seedy, shady-characters-in-the-park
and 55-year-old-prostitutes-after-dark, is reasonably safe.
Corso Buenos Aires is a bustling main shopping and people-
watching drag.

All listings below are within two subway stops or a ten-
minute walk of the station. The street named Via Scarlatti leads
to the first five listings—leave the station's upper hall (with your
back to the tracks) to the left. Across the parking lot, Hotel
Bristol marks the start of Via Scarlatti. Business hotels employ
sleazy hustlers in fake police uniforms to sell their push-list
rooms. The deals are good, but honor (or at least cancel) any
reservations you've made elsewhere. Ibrahim, a hard-working
Egyptian hotel shark with a cellular phone in his pocket and
a line on which fancy L240,000 hotels have rooms on the
L100,000 push list, can often find rooms (tel. 033-636-7377).

The self-service Lavanderia Ondablu washes and dries
a 6.5-kilo load in an hour for L12,000 (19 Via Scarlatti, 8:00–
22:00 daily). The bar on the corner of Scarlatti and Settala is
good for breakfast (cheap ham toasties and good seats).

"The Best" Hotel offers a homey lounge and fine
rooms overlooking either a garden or an ugly car-filled
square that becomes an open-air market on Tuesday and
Saturday (Sb-L90,000, Db-L120,000, no breakfast, elevator,
phones in the room, free parking on square; Via B. Marcello
83, 20124 Milano, tel. 02/294-04757, fax 02/201-966,
Luciana and Peter SE). Request a *tranquillo giardino* room.
From the station, walk straight down Via Scarlatti; at Piazza
Hanky Panky turn right, and you'll see it. (Don't miss it.
On the next corner is a home for prostitutes having a hard
time retiring.) In a sad battle of self-congratulatory names,
the tired and dingy **Hotel Paradiso** next to "The Best"
is sleepable, but fails to live up to its name (D-L80,000,
Db-L100,000, hourglass-shaped elevator; Via B. Marcello 85,
tel. 02/204-9448).

Hotel Andreola, a four-star business hotel, hires hustlers to bring in travelers during slow times when it has door-breaker prices. The rooms are basic, but the location—a block from the station—is ideal. The lounge-lizard public places make you feel like you're in the U.S.A. While not worth its regular rates, from mid-June through August you can telephone and deal. Call three days in advance (maximum low season prices: Sb-L120,000, Db-L160,000, Tb-L210,000 with breakfast, use breakfast as a bargaining chip, hustlers sell the rooms for even less, CC:VMA, air-con, elevator, request *tranquillo* back side; Via Scarlatti 24, tel. 02/670-9141, fax 02/667-13198, SE).

Hotel Due Giardini is a plain, simple, and musty flophouse with a peaceful garden (S-L70,000, D-L100,000, T-L140,000, prices promised through 1998 with this book, CC:VM; walk 5 blocks down Via Scarlatti, right to Via Settala 46, 20124 Milano, tel. 02/295-21093, fax 02/295-16933, Anne-Maria and De Filippo Pellegrino).

Hotel Valley is a dark and quiet little 12-room place a five-minute walk from the station (Db-L100,000–120,000, CC:VM; Via Soperga 19, tel. & fax 02/668-2777, SE). Across the street the **Hotel Soperga** hides uninspired but air-con rooms above a slick business class lobby (Db-L200,000, lower in summer, CC:VMA; Via Soperga 24, 20127 Milano, tel. & fax 02/669-0541, SE).

Hotel Serena is plain, quiet, and handy with lot of stairs (Db-L140,000 with breakfast, CC:VMA; a block off Corso Buenos Aires near the Lima Metro stop, Via Boscovich 59, tel. 02/295-22152, fax 02/294-04958).

Hotel Virgilio is dark and designed for businessmen, but a good value for someone looking for a real hotel near the station (46 rooms, S-L50,000, Sb-L80,000, D-L80,000, Db-L120,000, breakfast L10,000, CC:VMA, elevator, air con L10,000 extra; from the station backtrack 2 blocks and turn right, Via P.L. da Palestrina 30, 20124 Milano, tel.02/669-1337, fax 02/669-82587, SE).

Eating in Milan

This is a fast-food city, but fast food in a fashion capital isn't a burger and fries. The bars, delis, rosticcería, and self-services cater to people with plenty of taste and more money than time.

You'll find delightful eateries all over town. Free

munchies appear late in the afternoon in many bars. A L3,000 beer (if you're either likable or discreet) can become a light meal.

Breakfast is a bad value in hotels and fun in bars. It's OK to quasi-picnic. Bring in a box of juice (*plastica bicchiere* = plastic cup) and some bananas (or whatever) and order a toasted ham-and-cheese panino (*calda* = hot/toasted) or croissant with your cappuccino.

Eating near the Duomo and Recommended Hotels

For a low-stress, affordable lunch facing the Duomo square, eat at **Ciao,** a shiny, modern, second-floor self-serve cafeteria (pasta-L5,000, meatier courses-L7,000, daily 11:30–15:00, 18:00–23:00, view tables from top "terrace" floor, easy public WC). For a more challenging adventure in eating Milanese, assemble an elegant dinner picnic by hitting the colorful shops on Via Speronari (off Via Torino, a block southwest of Piazza Duomo: *rosticcería;* classy cheese, bread, and produce shops). The newly pedestrian-only Via Dante offers several good self-service restaurants with peaceful outdoor seating.

Peck makes a winning trio 2 blocks from the Duomo. Glide royally through Peck's gourmet grocery (8:30–13:00, 15:00–19:00, closed Sunday and Monday morning, Via Spadari 9, peek into the back where food is being prepared, downstairs—fancy wine tasting, upstairs—fancy coffee shop). Peck's elegant *rosticcería* is nearby (Via G. Cantu, off Via Orefici). At the **Peck Snack Bar,** a classy cafeteria, you order at the bar, take the bill to the cashier, pay, pick up your food, and find a stool surrounded by the local office crowd (pasta-L9,000, veggies-L6,000, Monday–Saturday 7:30–21:00, closed Sunday, a block toward the Duomo, just off Via Orefici at Via Victor Hugo 4).

Fast-food cheapskates enjoy the best people-watching in Milan inside the Galleria at McDonalds (salad/pasta plate and tall o.j. for L9,000). The **Pizzeria Dogana** offers L12,000 pizzas and indoor/outdoor seating (closed Monday, a block off Duomo at Via Dogana 3). Worth the 2-blocks-farther walk, the local favorite, **Ristorante Pizzeria Calafuria Unione,** serves tasty L10,000 pizzas in a nonsmoking room (closed Sunday, where Via Falcone hits Via dell' Unione at Via dell' Unione 8, tel. 02/864-62091).

At **Ristorante Familiare della Cimbraccola** the atmosphere is more memorable than the food. Stefanini Arnaldo, with his imaginary mother still in the kitchen (she's 85 and still prepares through the afternoon), merrily throws his entire menu at his guests with a series of uninspired appetizers, pastas, and entrees, with endless wine, water, coffee, *grappa* (firewater), and three desserts—all for L30,000. Stefanini's found his niche and you're at his mercy. The food is Tuscan and plain. Eat what you like. Some of the antipasti come mushy or dry. After six or eight courses you'll get a big plate of meats. The walls are plastered with model ships, pipes, dusty paper money, and pins for each hungry client on a U.S.A. map (closed Sunday, an olive toss off Via Dante, midway between the Duomo and the Fortress at Via S. Tomaso 8, tel. 02/869-2250).

Trattoria Milanese, a classy local-style family-run place, is ideal for a L50,000 splurge. It has an extremely enthusiastic and local clientele (the restaurant didn't even bother to get a phone until 1988) and a wonderfully Milanese ambience (pasta-L15,000, meat-L20,000, open at 19:30, reservations necessary after 20:30, closed Tuesday, Via Santa Marta 11, 5-minute walk from Duomo near Piazza Borromei, tel. 02/864-51991).

Floodlit Mary gazes down from the top of the Duomo on the **Odeon Gelateria** for good reason (next to Burghy on Duomo square, open nightly until 1:00).

Eating near the Train Station and Recommended "Best" Hotel

Brek is a bright, self-serve marketplace festival of healthy food (pasta-L5,000, meat-L8,000, vegetable-L3,000, 2 blocks towards recommended hotels from station at Via Lepetit 20, 11:30–15:00, 18:30–22:30, closed Sunday). **Ristorante Salernitano** (at the intersection of Via Vitruvio and Via Tadino), **Trattoria Torre dei Corsari**, and several places on Via Tadino are reasonable, friendly, and relaxed.

Transportation Connections—Milan

By train to: Venice (departures 5 minutes after each hour, 3 hrs), **Florence** (hourly, 3 hrs), **Genoa** (hourly, 2 hrs), **Rome** (hourly, 5 hrs), **Brindisi** (4/day, 10–12 hrs), **Cinque Terre** (hourly, 3–4 hrs to La Spezia, some direct trains to Monterosso, sometimes changing in Genoa; trains from La Spezia to the villages go hourly), **Varenna** on Lago di Como (the small line to Lecco/Sondrio/Tirano leaves every 2 hours for the 1-hour trip to Varenna—maybe 9:15, 12:15, 14:15, 16:15, 18:00, 19:10, 20:15), **Como** (maybe :25 after each hour, 30 min, ferries go from Como to Varenna).

International destinations: Amsterdam (4/day, 14 hrs), **Barcelona** (2 changes, 17 hrs—before paying extra for the Pablo Casals express, consider flying), **Bern** (7/day, 3 hrs), **Frankfurt** (5/day, 9 hrs), **London** (2/day, 18 hrs), **Munich** (5/day, 8 hrs), **Nice** (5/day, 7–10 hrs), **Paris** (4/day, 6–7 hrs), **Vienna** (4/day, 14 hrs). Train info: tel. 1478-88088.

Driving in Milan: Driving is bad enough in Milan to make the L40,000/day fee for a downtown garage a blessing. If you're driving, do Milan (and Lake Como) before or after you rent. If you have a car, use the well-marked suburban Parcheggi, which offer affordable and safe parking at city-edge subway stations.

Milan's Airports

Most international flights land at Milan's surprisingly cozy **Malpensa** airport, 30 miles northwest of the city. Customs guards fan you through, and even the sniffing dog seems friendly. The airport bank has fine rates (Banco di Milano, 8:00–20:00). Visit the bus/train information and ticket office; this is a convenient chance to buy train tickets and check departure times for train trips from Milan. Buy a L10,000 telephone card and confirm your hotel reservations.

A shuttle-bus connects Malpensa and Milan's central train station (L14,000, 2/hr, 45-min ride, tel. 400-9928-0038). A shuttle bus also runs between Malpensa airport and Piazza Castello, near the Duomo (L14,000, departures at 7:00, 8:00, 9:00, 10:00, 11:00, 13:00, 15:00, and 17:00, 45-min ride). Taxis into Milan cost L120,000 ($70).

Most European flights use Milan's second airport, **Linate,** 5 miles east of the city. The Bank Popular Milano, just past customs, has fine rates. Linate is linked by regular STAM shuttle buses with the central train station (Piazza Luigi di Savoia, L4,500 tickets from driver, 3/hr, 5:40–21:00, tel. 02/669-84509). To get from Linate to the Duomo area, catch bus #73 (get L1,500 ticket from newsstand; for Hotel Speronari, change to #12 or #27 and ask for Via Mazzini). Taxis from Linate to the Duomo cost L25,000.

To get flight information for either airport or the current telephone number of your airline, call 02/748-52200.

LAKE COMO (LAGO DI COMO)

Commune with nature where Italy is welded to the Alps, in the lovely Italian Lakes District. The million-lire question is: Which lake? For the best mix of accessibility, scenery, offbeatness, and a complete dose of Italian-lakes wonder and aristocratic-old-days romance, Lake Como is my choice. And the sleepy midlake town of Varenna, one hop away by ferry, is my home base. Bustling Milan, just an hour away, doesn't even exist. Now it's your turn to be *chiuso per ferie* (closed for vacation).

Lake Como, lined with elegant 19th-century villas, crowned by snowcapped mountains, and buzzing with ferries, hydrofoils, and little passenger ships, is a good place to take a break from the intensity and obligatory turnstile culture of central Italy. It seems half the travelers you'll meet have tossed their itineraries into the lake and are actually relaxing.

Today the hazy, lazy lake's only serious industry is tourism. Thousands of lakeside residents travel daily to nearby Lugano, in Switzerland, to find work. The lake's isolation and flat economy have left it pretty much the way the 19th-century Romantic poets described it.

Planning Your Time

If relaxation's not on your agenda, Lake Como shouldn't be either. Even though there are no essential activities, plan for at least two nights, so you'll have an uninterrupted day to see how slow you can get your pulse.

Lake Como

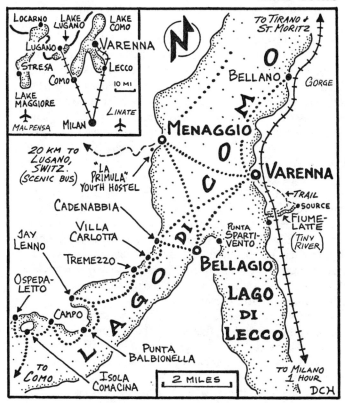

Lake Como is Milan's quick getaway, and the village of Varenna is the gateway. With its handy connections to Milan and midlake destinations, Varenna is my favorite home base.

Arrival in Varenna

I zip directly to Varenna by train from Milan, set up, and limit my activities to midlake (Varenna, Bellagio, and Menaggio). From Milan's Central Station, catch a train heading for Sondrio (but be certain it stops in Varenna). Trains leave about every two hours. Sit on the left for great lake views. Get off at Varenna-Esino.

You can also get to Varenna from Milan via the town of Como. Trains take you from Milan to Como (50-minute rides

usually leaving at :25 past each hour) where you'll catch the
two-hour boat ride (L10,000) up the lake to Varenna.

Getting Around Lake Como

By Boat: Lago di Como is well served by boats and hydrofoils.
The lake service is divided into three parts: north-south from
Como to Colico; midlake between Varenna, Bellagio, Menaggio, and Cadenabbia (Villa Carlotta); and the southeastern arm
to Lecco. Unless you're going through Como, you'll probably
limit your cruising to the midlake service (info: tel. 031/579-
211). Boats go about hourly between Varenna, Menaggio, and
Bellagio (15 min, L4,500 per hop).

Passengers pay the same for car or passenger ferries, but
50 percent more for the enclosed, stuffy, less scenic but very
quick hydrofoil. The free schedule (at tourist office, hotel, or
boat dock) lists times and prices. Stopovers aren't allowed, and
there's no break for round-trips, so buy a ticket for each ride.
The one-day L12,000 midlake pass saves you money if you
make three rides. (Boat-schedule literacy tips: *Feriale* = work-
days, Monday–Saturday. *Festivo* = Sunday and holidays.
Partenze da = departing from.)

By Car: With the parking problems, constant traffic jams,
and expensive car ferries, this is no place to drive if you don't
need to. While you can easily drive around the lake, the road is
narrow, congested, and lined by privacy-seeking walls, hedges,
and tall fences. It costs L13,000 to take your car onto a ferry.
And parking is rarely easy where you need it, especially in Bellagio. Park in Varenna (free by the ferry dock or on the main
road south of town) and cruise.

Sights—Lake Como

▲▲▲Varenna—This town (of 800 people) is the best of all
lake worlds. Easily accessible by train, on the less-driven side
of the lake, Varenna has a romantic promenade, a tiny harbor,
narrow lanes, and its own villa. It's the right place to savor a
lakeside cappuccino or *aperitivo*. This place is quiet at night.
The *passerella* (lakeside walk) is adorned with caryatid lovers
pressing silently against each other in the shadows.

There's wonderfully little to do in Varenna. A tiny public
beach is just past the ferry dock, and a tiny private one (L2,000
entry, showers, rentable chairs and cabins, bar, open only in
summer) is just beyond that. The ladies in the harborfront

Varenna

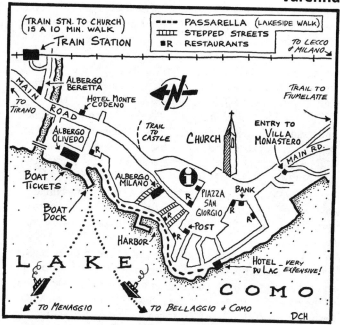

dress shop overcharge for their rental boats. The cooper welcomes gawkers in his *grappa* keg-making shop. Varenna's TI is on the main square (Pro Local, open daily May 15–October 1, 9:00–12:00 and 15:00–18:00, Sunday 10:00–12:30 and 15:00–18:00, off-season mornings only, tel. 0341/830-367). For accommodations, see Sleeping, below.

A steep trail leads to Varenna's ruined hill-top castle (L2,000 entry, look for yellow signs from the main road in Varenna to Castello Vezio). It's as intriguing as a locked-up castle can be. While you can't get in, there's a fine view café at its entrance and a peaceful, traffic-free, one-chapel, town behind it. A kilometer south of Varenna, the town of Fiumelatte is named for its milky river. It's the shortest in Italy (800 feet) and runs only during the tourist season. Local brochures lay out a walk from Varenna to the Fiumelatte to the castle and back.

▲**Bellagio**—The self-proclaimed "Pearl of the Lake" is a classy combination of tidiness and Old World elegance. If you don't mind that "tramp in a palace" feeling, it's a fine place to surround yourself with the more adventurous of the posh travelers and shop for umbrellas and ties. The heavy curtains between the arcades keep the visitors and their poodles from sweating. Steep-stepped lanes rise from the harborfront, and the shaded promenade leads to the Lido (beach). While Johnny Walker and jewelry sell best at lake level, the locals shop up the hill. The town has a tourist office on Piazza Chiesa next to the church (loosely open 9:00–12:00, 15:00–18:00, tel. 031/950-204), a worth-a-look church, and some surprisingly affordable funky old hotels (listed below). For something offbeat to do in Bellagio, clink glasses with **Tony the Wine King**. He runs a wild little cantina behind the camera shop near the ferry dock (11:00–13:00, 14:00 or 15:00–19:30, Salita Genazzini 3, tel. 031/950-935). Tony, who speaks English, greets you with an empty glass and ten or 15 open bottles of wine and booze to taste. The tasting's free. After 50 years in his cantina, he looks darn good.

Bellagio, the administrative capital of the midlake region, is located where the two southern legs of the lake split off. For an easy break in a park with a great view, wander right on out to the crotch. Meander past the rich and famous Hotel Villa Serbelloni, past the little Ortofrutta market (get fruit and juice for the viewpoint, 8:00–12:30, 13:30–18:30, closed all day Monday and Wednesday afternoon), and walk five minutes to the Punta Spartivento, literally "the point that divides the wind." You'll find a Renoir atmosphere complete with bar, tiny harbor, and a chance to sit on a bench and gaze north past Menaggio, Varenna, and the end of the lake to the Swiss Alps.

▲**Menaggio**—Just 8 miles (12 km) from Lugano in Switzerland, Menaggio has more urban bulk than its neighbors. Since the lake is getting a bit dirty for swimming, consider its fine public pool. This is the starting point for a few hikes. Only 25 years ago, these trails were used by cigarette smugglers. As many as 180 people a night would sneak through the darkness from Switzerland back into Italy with tax-free cigarettes. The hostel (see Sleeping, below) has information about catching the bus to trailheads on nearby Mount Grona. The hostel also rents bikes for a 40-kilometer, four-hour bike trip: pedal 15 level kilometers from the hostel to Argegno, catch the lift to 2,500-foot-high Pigra (L5,000 with bike), and coast scenically back to Lake Lugano and then 10 km along the traffic-filled road home to Menaggio. This is a physically demanding ride and can be scary because of traffic.

Villa Carlotta—This is the best of Lake Como's famed villas. I see the lakes as a break from Italy's art, but if you're in need of a place that charges admission (L10,000, 9:00–18:00 daily in season), Villa Carlotta offers an elegant neoclassical interior, a famous Canova statue, and a garden (its highlight, best in spring). If you're touring one villa on the lake, this is probably the best. Nearby Tremezzo and Cadenabbia are pleasant lakeside resorts an easy walk away. Boats serve all three places.

Como—On the southwest tip of the lake, Como has a good, traffic-free old town, an interesting Gothic/Renaissance cathedral, and a pleasant lakefront with a promenade (TI tel. 031/274-064). It's an easy walk from the boat dock to the train station (from Milan in 30 minutes, usually leaving at :25 past each hour). Boats leave Como about hourly for midlake (ferries take two hours and cost L10,000; hydrofoils do the trip in an hour for L15,000; tel. 031/304-060).

Sleeping and Eating on Lake Como
(L1,600 = about $1)

Sleep Code: **S**=Single, **D**=Double/Twin, **T**=Triple, **Q**=Quad, **b**=bathroom, **t**=toilet only, **s**=shower only, **CC**=Credit Card (**V**isa, **M**asterCard, **A**mex), **SE**=Speaks English, **NSE**=No English.

The area is tight in August, snug in July, and wide open most of the rest of the year. Many places close in winter. All places listed are family-run, have lake-view rooms, and some English is spoken. View rooms are given (sometimes for no extra cost) to those who telephone reservations and request *"camera con vista."* If ever I were to kill, it would be here . . . for the view. Prices go soft in the off-season. Shop around by phone to confirm the view and price. If you fail, ask to get a view balcony for your second night.

Sleeping in Varenna
(tel. code: 0341, zip code: 23829)

Albergo Olivedo, facing the ferry dock, is a neat and tidy old hotel. Each room has squeaky hardwood floors, World War II furniture, and Art Nouveau mattresses. Many rooms have glorious little lake-view balconies. It's a fine place to hang out and watch the children, boats, and sun come and go (prices vary with season and views: S-L70,000–83,000, D-L80,000–110,000, Db-L100,000–135,000, includes breakfast, sit-down tubs with "telephone showers," tel. & fax 0341/830-115, Laura SE and runs a good restaurant). In summer, you'll pay extra for the required half-pension (dinner at hotel). Reserve with a phone call and give your credit-card number for security or send a $50 traveler's check.

Albergo Milano, located right in the old town, is your best splurge. Friendly but non-English-speaking Amelia obviously loves serving people. Her son, Giovanni, speaks English. Each of the eight rooms is comfortable and comes with great plumbing (Sb-L145,000, Db-L170,000, meager L5,000 total discount for three-night stay in off-season and with a side view, CC:VM; Via XX Settembre 29, tel. & fax 0341/830-298, ideally reserve with a fax and credit-card number). Lakeside rooms 1 and 2 are smaller with royal balconies (best in sunny weather). Lakeside rooms 5 and 6 are bigger with small balconies. This place whispers *luna di miele* (honeymoon).

Albergo Beretta, off the water on the main road below the station, has good beds but minimal character (D-L85,000, Db-L100,000, includes small breakfast, rooms 5 and 9 have view balconies; Via per Esino 1, tel. & fax 0341/830-132).

Albergo del Sole is a six-room, one-tub place on the main square offering decent cheap beds (D-50,000; Piazza San Giorgio 17, tel. 0341/830-206, NSE).

Hotel Monte Codeno is a friendly, family hotel on the main road between the train station and lake. All rooms have bathrooms and phones (Sb-L110,000, Db-L140,000, includes breakfast buffet, CC:VMA, attached restaurant serves seafood; Via della Croce 2, tel. 0341/830-123, fax 0341/831-041, Marina Castelli SE).

Villa Cipressi, in a huge quiet garden, has all the amenities and is a fine splurge (Sb-L103,000, Sb with view-L115,000, Db-L136,000, Db with view-L150,000, includes breakfast; Via IV Novembre 18, tel. 0341/830-113, fax 0341/830-401, SE).

Eating in Varenna

The best cheap meals in Varenna are at the *pizzeria* (19:00–24:00, closed Monday, Piazza San Giorgio 1, below Hotel Royal Victoria, across from the church). **Ristorante del Sole** serves tasty Naples-style pizzas across the square at Piazza San Giorgio 17 (tel. 0341/830-206, closed Wednesday). The royal **Hotel du**

Lac serves an elegant-yet-affordable lunch with lakeside splendor. The **Vecchia Varenna** restaurant is romantic, but disappointing. Try the **Albergo Olivedo** more for its fine food (L40,000 meals) than its ambience. For the same great view but much cheaper eating, the harborfront **Nilus Bar** serves dinner crepes, salads, and hot sandwiches with a smile. For cold, sweet, and fruity treats, check out the harborfront **frulleria/ frapperia.** The grocery stores near the main square have all you need for a classy balcony or breakwater picnic dinner.

Sleeping in Bellagio
(tel. code: 031, zip code: 22021)

Hotel du Lac is your best splurge. Right on the harbor with a roof garden, it's completely remodeled (air conditioning, TVs, mini-bars) and gives you the old flavor with absolutely no loss of comfort (prices vary with season, Db-L195,000–210,000, includes breakfast, CC:VM, L15,000 garage; Piazza Mazzini 32, Leoni family SE, tel. 031/950-320, fax 031/951-624, web site: www.fromitaly.it/Bellagio/H3/DULAC, e-mail: dulac@mbox.vol.it).

A few doors away, the cozier **Hotel Florence** is hardwood, pastel, and family-run, with a rich touch of Old World elegance (Sb-L155,000, Db-L210,000 with breakfast, closed November–March, CC:VMA, elevator, hand-held showers only, tel. 031/950-342, fax 031/951-722, SE, e-mail: hotflore@mbox.vol.it).

Hotel Suisse somehow landed right on the harbor next to the stuffy places. It's frumpy with simple rooms, hardwood floors, fine bathrooms, variable beds, and some great views and balconies (Db-L80,000, Db with view-L90,000, optional L10,000 breakfast, CC:VM; Piazza Mazzini 8, tel. 031/950-335, fax 031/951-755, SE).

The simpler and friendlier one-star **Hotel Roma** cranes its well-worn neck behind and above Hotel Suisse. The fifth floor has the cheapest rooms (shower down the hall) with great view balconies (D-L77,000, Db-L92,000, with breakfast, closed off-season, CC:VMA, elevator; Via Grandi 6, tel. 031/950-424, fax 031/951-966, Isabelle SE).

Hotel Giardinetto, near the TI and about 100 steps above the waterfront, offers squeaky-clean, cool, and quiet rooms—some with a balcony, above a breezy and peaceful garden. It's run by the Ticozzi family (D-L65,000, Db-L85,000,

breakfast-L10,000; Via Roncati 12, tel. 031/950-168, Eugene
and Laura SE). For a good back-street L26,000 dinner, try
Trattoria S. Giacomo (closed Tuesday, Salita Servelloni 45,
tel. 031/950-329).

To escape the tourism and crowds of Bellagio, take the
15-minute walk to the five-building hamlet of Pescallo and
relax at the lakeside **Hotel Ristorante La Pergola**, which has
a fine reputation for dining and also offers eight simple rooms
in a tranquil setting (D-L90,000, Db-L105,000, includes
breakfast, tel. 031/950-263, NSE).

Sleeping in Menaggio

La Primula Youth Hostel is a rare hostel. Family-run
for 15 years by Ty and Paola (and their Australian sidekick,
Paul), it caters to a quiet, savor-the-lakes crowd and offers
the only cheap beds in the area. Located just south of the
Menaggio dock (you'll see the sign from the boat), it has a
view terrace; lots of games; a members' kitchen; a washing
machine; bike, canoe, and kayak rentals (L15,000 a day,
L30,000 for non-hostelers); discount tickets to Villa Carlotta;
discount boat passes; easy parking; and a creative and hard-
working staff. You'll need a hostel membership card to stay
here; cards are available at the hostel but handy to bring
from home. (Closed 10:00–17:00 daily and from mid-
November–mid-March, L17,000 per night in a four- to six-
bed room with sheets and breakfast, L19,000 with private
plumbing, no twins or doubles, hearty dinners with a local
flair and wine are only L15,000, vegetarian options available;
reserve dinner by 18:00—because of ferry schedules, this
is practical only for people staying in Menaggio.) Ty and
Paola print a newsletter to advertise their activities programs
(inexpensive 14-day Italian language, three- to seven-day
hikes, bike trips, cooking classes). The bike ride described
under Sights—Menaggio, above, is a favorite with hostelers.
Show your copy of this book and receive a free La Primula
recipe book. (Ostello La Primula, Via IV Novembre 86,
22017 Menaggio, tel. & fax 0344/32356.) Reserve ahead
for this popular place; they'll hold a reservation until 17:00.
They also offer a couple of apartments in the nearby village
of Barna for week-long stays (L500,000 per person,
maximum four people).

There is also a hostel at the south end of the lake (Como's Villa Olmo, tel. 031/573-800) and in the north (Domaso, tel. 0344/96094).

Transportation Connections—Varenna

From any destination covered in this book you'll get to Lake Como via Milan. The quickest Milan connection to any point at midlake (Bellagio, Menaggio, or Varenna) is via the train to Varenna (called: Varenna/Esino). If leaving Varenna by train, please note that the Varenna train station no longer sells tickets. They must be purchased at the nearby Hotel Monte Codeno, then stamped in the machine at the station before boarding.

Milan to Varenna: Catch a train at Milano Centrale (last year's schedule: 9:15, 12:15, 14:15, 16:15, 18:00, 19:10, and 20:15, 60 min, L6,500). Milan train schedules list Sondrio, Lecco, and Tirano, but often not Varenna; Varenna is a small stop. Some cars on long trains don't even get a platform. Ask for help so you don't miss the stop. You may have to open the door yourself. (Look for the handle.)

Varenna to Milan: Trains leave Varenna for Milano Centrale at 5:30, 6:19, 7:27, 8:27, 10:27, and every two hours until 22:27. (Confirm schedule at train station.) A few daily trains end at outlying stations in Milan; you want the Milano Centrale station. Varenna makes a comfy last stop before catching the shuttle from Milan's station to the airport.

Varenna to St. Moritz: From Varenna, you have fantastic access to the Bernina Express and scenic train to St. Moritz. First take the train to Tirano, then transfer to St. Moritz (3/day, allow 6 hrs with transfer).

THE DOLOMITES

Italy's dramatic limestone rooftop, the Dolomites, offers some of the best and most unique mountain thrills in Europe. Bolzano is the gateway to the Dolomites, and Castelrotto is a good home base for your exploration of Alpe di Siusi, Europe's largest alpine meadow.

The sunny Dolomites are well developed, and the region's famous valleys and towns suffer from *après*-ski fever. The cost for the comfort of reliably good weather is a drained-reservoir feeling. Lovers of the Alps may miss the lushness that comes with the unpredictable weather farther north. But the bold limestone pillars, flecked with snow over green meadows under a blue sky, offer a worthwhile mountain experience.

A hard-fought history has left the region bicultural, with an emphasis on the German. Locals speak German first, and some wish they were still part of Austria. In the Middle Ages, the region faced north, part of the Holy Roman Empire. Later they were firmly in the Austrian Hapsburg realm. By losing WWI, Austria's South Tirol became Italy's Alto Adige. Mussolini did what he could to Italianize the region, including giving each town an Italian name. But even in the last decade, secessionist groups have agitated violently for more autonomy.

The government has wooed locals with economic breaks that make it one of Italy's richest areas (as local prices attest), and today all signs and literature in the province of Alto Adige/Süd Tirol are in both languages. Many include a third language, Ladin, the ancient Latin-type language still spoken in a few traditional areas. (I have listed both the Italian and German so the confusion caused by this guidebook will match that caused by your travels.)

In spite of all the glamorous ski resorts and busy construction cranes, the local color survives in a warm, blue-aproned, ruddy-faced, long-white-bearded way. There's yogurt and yodeling for breakfast. Culturally as much as geographically, the area reminds me of Austria. The Austrian Tirol is named for a village that is now part of Italy.

Planning Your Time

Train travelers should side trip in from Bolzano (90 minutes north of Verona). To get a feel for the Alpine culture here, spend a night in Castelrotto. With two nights in Castelrotto, you can actually get out and hike. Tenderfeet ride the bus, catch a chairlift, and stroll. For mountain thrills, do a six-hour hike. And for a mountain thrill that won't soon fade away, avid hikers will want to spend a night in a mountain hut. This means two nights in Castelrotto straddling a night in a hut.

Car-hikers with a day can drive the three-hour loop from Bolzano or Castelrotto (Val Gardena–Sella Pass–Val di Fassa) and ride one of the lifts to the top for a ridge walk. Connecting Bolzano and Venice by the Great Dolomite Road takes two hours longer than the *autostrada* (via Verona) but is more scenic (see below).

Hiking season is mid-June through mid-October. The region is packed and booming from mid-July through mid-September. Spring is dead, with no lifts running, huts closed, and the most exciting trails still under snow. Ski season is busiest of all.

Helpful Hints

Sleeping: Most towns offer hotels, which charge at least L35,000 per person, and private homes, which offer beds for as low as L25,000 but are often a long walk from the town centers. Beds nearly always come with a hearty breakfast. Those traveling in peak season or staying for only one night are often penalized. Local TIs can always find budget travelers a bed in a private home *(Zimmer)*. Drivers on a tight budget should pick remote Zimmers. Most mountain huts offer reasonable doubles, cheap dorm *(lager)* beds, and inexpensive meals. Telephone any hut to secure a spot before hiking there. Most huts are open mid-June through September only.

Dolomites and Northeast Italy

Eating: In local restaurants there is no cover charge, and tipping is not expected. If you're low on both money and scruples, Süd Tirolian breakfasts are the only ones in Italy big enough to steal lunch from. A *Jausenstation* is a place that serves cheap, hearty, and traditional mountain-style food to hikers.

BOLZANO (BOZEN)

Willkommen to the Italian Tirol! If it weren't so sunny, you could be in Innsbruck. This enjoyable old town of 100,000 is the most convenient gateway to the Dolomites, especially if you're relying on public transportation. It's just the place to gather Dolomite information and take a Tirolean stroll.

Bolzano is easy. Everything mentioned in Bolzano is within 3 blocks of Piazza Walther. Leaving the train station, veer left up the tree-lined Viale Stazione (Bahnhofsallee) and walk past the bus station (on your left) 2 blocks to Piazza Walther, where you'll find the city TI on your right (9:00–12:00 and 14:00–17:30, closed Saturday afternoon and Sunday, tel. 0471/993-808). The excellent—as if your safety depended on it—Dolomites information center is a block past the big church down Via Posta/Postgasse (Monday–Friday 9:00–12:00, 15:00–17:00, Parrocchia 11, tel. 0471/993-809). The medieval heart of town is just beyond Piazza Walther. Choose your favorite Italian and bunny-hop down the arcaded Via dei Portici to the Piazza Erbe, with its ancient and still thriving open-air produce market.

Mediocre Side Trip: Many are tempted to wimp out on the Dolomites and see them from a distance by making the quick trip into the hills above Bolzano (cable car from near the Bolzano station to the touristy village of Oberbozen, where you'll take a long, pastoral walk to the Pemmern chairlift; ride to Schwarzseespitze and walk 45 more minutes to the Rittner Horn). You'll be atop a 7,000-foot peak with distant but often hazy Dolomite views. It's not worth the trouble.

Sleeping in Bolzano
(L1,600 = about $1, tel. code: 0471, zip code: 39100)
Sleep Code: **S**=Single, **D**=Double/Twin, **T**=Triple, **Q**=Quad, **b**=bathroom, **t**=toilet only, **s**=shower only, **CC**=Credit Card (**V**isa, **M**asterCard, **A**mex), **SE**=Speaks English, **NSE**=No English.

Gasthof Weisses Kreuz is your best value, but it's usually booked up (ten rooms, D-L58,000, Db-L75,000, without breakfast; 1 block off Piazza Walther in the old town at Kornplatz 3, tel. 0471/977-552, fax 0471/972-273, NSE). It couldn't be better located or more German—or at least anti-English. Hotel signs and cards are quadrilingual, and English didn't make it. The quirky Hotel Figl has more character than value (D-L65,000, Db-L100,000, without breakfast, CC:VMA, elevator; Kornplatz 9, tel. & fax 0471/978-412).

The modern, clean, church-run **Kolpinghaus Bozen** has plenty of rooms with twin beds, all the comforts, and makes one feel thankful (Sb-L60,000, Db-L100,000, Tb-L145,000, includes breakfast, confusing elevator; in the center, 2 blocks beyond the Dolomites information center at Spitalgasse 3, tel. 0471/971-170, fax 0471/973-917, SE). Its institutional cafeteria is open to all (L15,000 dinners, Monday–Friday 18:30–19:30).

Transportation Connections—Bolzano
By train to: Milan (2/day, 4 hrs), **Verona** (hourly, 1.5 hrs), **Trento** (hourly, 40 min), **Merano** (hourly, 40 min), **Venice** and **Florence** (via Verona, 3–4 hrs), **Innsbruck** (hrly, 2.5 hrs). Train info: tel. 0471/974292. **By bus to: Castelrotto** (hourly, 40 min).

CASTELROTTO (KASTELRUTH)
Castelrotto (population 5,000, altitude 1,060 m), the ideal home base for exploring the Alpe di Siusi, has more village character than any town I saw in the region. Friday morning is the farmers' market, and a crafts market fills the town square on Tuesday mornings. It's touristy but not a full-blown resort—it's full of real people. Pop into the church to hear the choir practice or be on the town square at 15:00 as the bells peal and the moms bring home their kindergartners. The TI is on the main square (Monday–Saturday 8:30–12:30, 14:00–18:00, Sunday 9:00–12:00, tel. 0471/706-333).

Sleeping in Castelrotto
(L1,600 = about $1, tel. code: 0471, zip code: 39040)
Albergo Torre (in German, Gasthof Zum Turm) is comfortable, clean, and traditional with great beds and modern bathrooms (prices vary with season, Db-L112,000–130,000, Tb-L168,000–195,000, includes breakfast, L5,000 extra for one-night stays, CC:VM; behind the TI at Kofelgasse 8, tel. 0471/706-349, fax 0471/707-268, Gabi and Günther SE). If you're driving, go right through the traffic-free town center (very likely with a police escort). Under the bell tower, go through the white arch to the right of the TI and park (free for guests) in the lot opposite the front door.

Gasthof Zum Wolf (in Italian, Al Lupo) is newly-remodeled Tirolean with all the comforts (prices vary with season and view, Sb-L90,000–115,000, Db-L160,000–210,000, breakfast-L15,000; a block below the square at Wolkensteinstrasse 5, tel. 0471/706-332, fax 0471/707-030, Arno SE).

Hotel Cavallino D'Oro (in German, Goldenes Rossl), next door, has plenty of Tyrolean character and is run by friendly and helpful Stefan. Every room is different and locals frequent the bar. If you love antiques by candlelight (or have only credit cards) this 600-year-old hotel is the best in town (Sb-L100,000–130,000, Db-L150,000–180,000, depending on the season, discount for three nights or longer, CC:VMA; no elevator; on Krausplatz, tel. 0471/706-337, fax 0471/707-172, SE, web site: www.cavallino.it, e-mail: cavallino@cavallino.it).

Just below the Pensione Castelrotto, **Haus Harderer** rents out three rooms (Db-84,000, includes breakfast, minimum two nights in summer; Plattenstrasse 20, tel. 0471/706-702). For week-long stays, ask about their apartment.

Tirler Hof, the storybook Jaider family farm, has 35 cows, one friendly *hund*, four Old World-comfy guest rooms, and a great mountain view (D-L70,000, includes breakfast; practical only for drivers, it's the first farm outside of town on the right on the road to St. Michael, Paniderstrasse 44, tel. 0471/706-017, NSE). The ground-floor double has a private bath. The top-floor rooms share a bathroom and a great balcony. Take a stroll before breakfast.

Transportation Connections—Castelrotto

Catch buses to get into the heart of the Alpe de Siusi.

By bus to: Saltria (4-8/day, toll free info tel. 167-846047 or tel. 0471/706-633), **Val di Fassa, Vigo di Fassa,** and **Canazei** (2/day, 4/day in summer, 2 hrs), and **Val Gardena, Ortisei/St. Ulrich,** and **St. Cristina** (4/day, 1 hr).

Summer Shuttle Buses: From June through mid-October, "Buxi" shuttle buses go about twice an hour from Castelrotto through the Alpe di Siusi to Saltria (8:00–17:00, discounted return tickets). Off-season there's one "sad" 9:10 bus from Castelrotto to Saltria and a 15:50 bus coming back.

ALPE DI SIUSI (SEISER ALM)

Europe's largest high alpine meadow, Alpe di Siusi, separates two of the most famous Dolomite ski-resort valleys. Measuring

5 kilometers by 12 kilometers, and soaring from 1,800 to 2,000 meters high, Alpe di Suisi is dotted by farm huts and wildflowers, surrounded by dramatic (if distant) Dolomite peaks and cliffs, and much appreciated by hordes of walkers.

The Sasso Lungo (Langkofel) mountains at the head of the meadow provide a storybook Dolomite backdrop, while the spooky Schlern stands boldly looking into the haze of the Italian peninsula. Not surprisingly, the Schlern, looking like a devilish *Winged Victory*, gave ancient peoples enough willies to spawn legends of supernatural forces. The Schlern witch, today's tourist brochure mascot, was the cause of many a broom-riding medieval townswoman's fiery death.

The Alpe di Siusi is my recommended one-stop look at the Dolomites because of Castelrotto's charm as a home base, because it's equally accessible to those with and without cars, because of its variety of walks and hikes, and because of its quintessentially Dolomite mountain views.

A natural preserve, Alpe di Siusi is closed to cars past Compatsch. The meadow is virtually car-free. The Buxi park bus service shuttles hikers to and from key points along the tiny road all the way to Saltria at the foot of the postcard-dramatic Sasso peaks (Sasso Lungo, 3,180 meters). Meadow walks, for flower lovers and strollers, are pretty— or maybe pretty boring. Chairlifts provide springboards for more dramatic and demanding hikes. A few tiny service roads are technically closed, but people with reservations in distant chalets and huts drive them. Off-season you may get away with some "car hiking."

Trails are well marked, and the brightly-painted numbers are keyed into local maps. The Kompass Bolzano map #54 covers everything in this chapter (scale 1:50,000, L8,000). The Gardena/Alpe di Siusi "Tobacco" map offers more detail on the Alpe di Siusi (scale 1:25,000, L5,000).

Compatsch, a kilometer into the park and as far as you're allowed to drive, is the park tourist village (1,870 m), with a tourist information office (tel. 0471/727-904), grocery store, mountain bike rentals (L10,000/one hour, L25,000/four hours), tour bus corral, car park (L6,000/day), hotels, restaurants, shops, lifts, and so on.

Sleeping near the park entrance: Gasthof/Albergo Frommer offers handy, comfortable, budget beds at the edge

The Western Dolomites

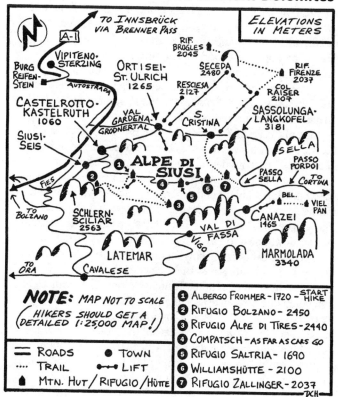

TO INNSBRÜCK
VIA BRENNER PASS

ELEVATIONS
IN METERS

RIF.
BROGLES
2045

A-1

VIPITENO-
STERZING

ORTISEI-
ST. ULRICH
1265

SECEDA
2480

RIF.
FIRENZE
2037

BURG
REIFEN-
STEIN

AUTOSTRADA

RESCIESA
2127

COL
RAISER
2107

CASTELROTTO-
KASTELRUTH
1060

VAL
GARDENA-
GRÖDNERTAL

S.
CRISTINA

SASSOLUNGA-
LANGKOFEL
3181

SIUSI-
SEIS

SELLA

FIES

❶

ALPE DI
SIUSI

PASSO
PORDOI

PASSO
SELLA

TO
CORTINA

❷

❹

TO
BOLZANO

SCHLERN-
SCILIAR
2563

❸

❺

❻ ❼

BEL.

VIEL
PAN

CANAZEI
1465

VAL DI
FASSA

LATEMAR

VIGO

TO
ORA

CAVALESE

MARMOLADA
3340

NOTE: MAP NOT TO SCALE
(HIKERS SHOULD GET A)
(DETAILED 1:25,000 MAP!)

❶ ALBERGO FROMMER – 1720 – START HIKE
❷ RIFUGIO BOLZANO – 2450
❸ RIFUGIO ALPE DI TIRES – 2440
❹ COMPATSCH – AS FAR AS CARS GO
❺ RIFUGIO SALTRIA – 1690
❻ WILLIAMSHÜTTE – 2100
❼ RIFUGIO ZALLINGER – 2037

══ ROADS   ● TOWN
···· TRAIL   ●━━● LIFT
⬟ MTN. HUT / RIFUGIO / HÜTTE

DCH

of the Alpe di Siusi (Db-L135,000, tel. 0471/727-917, NSE). Arthur would heartily recommend this place. This rustic but classy old inn 100 meters from the Spitzbühl chairlift has good meals, free parking, the Schlern peak out its window, and the Bolzano/Castelrotto/Buxi bus stop at its door. This is a good choice for serious hikers who don't want to sleep in a mountain hut. Easy to find, it's a landmark place at the entry of the park about a kilometer before Compatsch.

Pension Seelaus, a ten-minute walk from Compatch, is a cozy, friendly, family-run place with a Germanic feel and down comforters (prices vary with season, Sb-L75,000–92,000, Db-L140,000–172,000, includes breakfast and dinner; Via Compatsch 8, tel. 0471/727-954, fax 0471/727-835, Roberto SE).

Hikes in the Alpe di Siusi

Easy meadow walks abound, giving tenderfeet classic Dolomite views from baby-stroller trails. Experienced hikers should consider the tougher and more exciting treks. Before attempting a hike, call or stop by the local tourist information office to confirm your understanding of the time and skills required. Many lifts operate mid-June through late September and during the winter ski season. From Compatsch, the Panorama and Puflatsch lifts run further into the off-season.

Summit hike of Sciliar (Schlern): For a challenging 12-mile, seven-hour hike with a possible overnight in a traditional mountain refuge, consider hiking to the summit of Sciliar (Schlern) and spending a night in Rifugio Bolzano (Schlernhaus). Start at the Spitzbühl lift and Albergo Frommer (1,725 m, free car-park, first bus stop in the park). The Spitzbühl chairlift drops you at Spitzbichl (1,935 m). Trail #5 takes you through a high meadow, down to the Saltner Schwaige dairy farm (1,830 m), across a stream, and steeply up the Schlern mountain. You'll meet trail #1 and walk across the rocky tabletop plateau of Schlern to the mountain hotel, Rifugio Bolzano/Schlernhaus, three hours into your hike (2,450 m, D-L55,000, dorm beds-L15,000, tel. 0471/612-024, call for a reservation). From this dramatic setting you get a great view of the Rosengarten range. Hike 20 more minutes up the nearby peak (Mt. Pez, 2,560 m) for a 360-degree Alpine panorama. From the Schlernhaus you can hike back the way you came or walk farther along the Schlern (12 km, two hours, past the Rifugio Alpe di Tires, tel. 0471/727-958, D or dorm beds, 2,440 m) and descend back into the Alpe di Siusi and the road where the Buxi bus will return you to your starting point or hotel.

Loop around Sasso Lungo: Another dramatic but not difficult hike is the six-hour walk around Sasso Lungo (Langkofel). You can ride the bus to Saltria (end of the line), take the chairlift to Williamshütte, walk past the Zallingerhütte (overnight possible, tel. 0471/727-947), and circle the Sasso group. **Three Easy Walks:** From Compatsch, consider a two-hour loop north to Arnikahütte and back via Puflatsch (elevation gain about 200 m).

Or: From Compatsch, ride the lift to Panorama, hike 90 minutes to Molignonhütte (2,050 m) and back down to Compatsch; or continue 2.5 hours (fairly level) to Zallingerhütte (2,050 m) and another 90 minutes to Saltria and the Buxi bus stop.

Alpe di Siusi

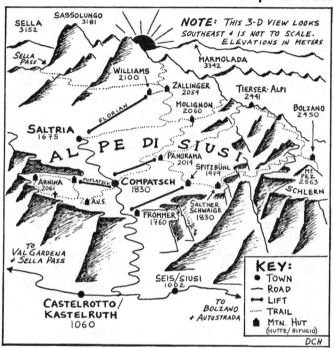

NOTE: THIS 3-D VIEW LOOKS SOUTHEAST & IS NOT TO SCALE. ELEVATIONS IN METERS

SELLA 3152
SASSOLUNGO 3181
SELLA PASS
WILLIAMS 2100
MARMOLADA 3342
ZALLINGER 2054
MOLIGNON 2060
TIERSER-ALPI 2441
BOLZANO 2450
SALTRIA 1675
FLORIAN
A L P E · D I · S I U S I
PANORAMA 2014
SPITZBÜHL 1979
MT. PEZ 2563
ARNIKA 2061
PUFLATSCH
COMPATSCH 1830
SCHLERN
A.V.S.
FROMMER 1760
SALTNER SCHWAIGE 1830
TO VAL GARDENA & SELLA PASS
SEIS/SIUSI 1002
TO BOLZANO & AUTOSTRADA
CASTELROTTO/ KASTELRUTH 1060

KEY:
● TOWN
— ROAD
•—• LIFT
····· TRAIL
▪ MTN. HUT (HUTTE/RIFUGIO)

DCH

Or: Bus to Saltria and hike the 2.5-hour loop to Zallingerhütte (2,050 m, 200-m altitude gain).

MORE SIGHTS IN THE DOLOMITES

▲**Great Dolomite Road**—This is the definitive Dolomite drive (Belluno/Cortina/Pordoi Pass/Sella Pass/Val di Fassa/Bolzano). Connecting Venice with Bolzano this way (the Belluno–Venice autostrada is slick) takes two hours longer than the Bolzano–Verona–Venice autostrada. No public transit does this trip. In spring and early summer, passes labeled "closed" are often bare, dry, and, as far as local drivers are concerned, wide open. While Cortina is the most famous resort in the region, it has more diamonds than charm.

▲▲**Abbreviated Dolomite Loop Drive**—See the biggies in half the miles (allow three hours, Bolzano/Castelrotto/Val Gardena/Sella Pass/Val di Fassa/Bolzano). **Val Gardena**

(Grodner Tal) is famous for its skiing and hiking resorts, traditional Ladin culture, and woodcarvers (ANRI is from the Val Gardena town of St. Cristina). It's a bit overrated, but even if its culture has been suffocated by the big bucks of hedonistic European fun-seekers, it remains a good jumping-off point for trips into the mountains. Within an hour you'll reach the **Sella Pass** (2,240 m) viewpoint. After a series of tight hairpin turns a mile or so over the pass, you'll see some benches and cars. Pull over and watch the rock-climbers. **Val di Fassa** is Alberto Tomba country. The town of **Canazei**, at the head of the valley and the end of the bus line, has the most ambience and altitude (4,600 feet). From there a lift takes you to Col dei Rossi Belvedere, where you can hike the Bindelweg trail past the Rifugio Belvedere along an easy but breathtaking ridge to the Rifugio Viel del Pan. This is a three-hour round-trip hike with views of the highest mountain in the Dolomites, the Marmolada, and the Dolo-mighty Sella range along the way.

▲▲**Reifenstein Castle**—For one of Europe's most intimate looks at medieval castle life, let the friendly lady of Reifenstein (Frau Blanc) show you around her wonderfully preserved castle. She leads tours on the hour, in Italian and German, squeezing in whatever English she can.

Just before the Austrian border, leave the *autostrada* at Vipiteno (Sterzing); follow signs toward Bolzano, then over the freeway to the base of the castle's rock. It's the castle on the west. While this is easy by car, it's probably not worth the trouble by train (from Bolzano, 6/day, 70 min). The park beside the drawbridge is a good spot for a picnic; remember to pack out your litter (L4,000, tours offered offered Easter– November at 9:30, 10:30, 14:00, and 15:00, closed Friday, tel. 0472/765-879).

▲**Glurns**—Drivers deciding to connect the Dolomites and Lake Como by the high road via Meran and Bormio or the southwest of Switzerland should spend the night in the amazing little town of Glurns (45 minutes west of touristy Meran between Schluderns and Taufers). Glurns still lives within its square wall on the Adige River, with a church bell tower that has a thing about ringing, and real farms, rather than boutiques, filling the town courtyards. This is a break after so many tourist towns. There are several small hotels in the town, but I'd stay in a private home 100 yards from the town square, near the church, just outside the wall on the river (Family Hofer, six rooms, Db-L60,000 with breakfast, less for two nights, tel. 0473/831-597).

NAPLES, AMALFI COAST, AND POMPEII

If you like Italy as far south as Rome, go farther south. It gets better. If Italy is getting on your nerves, think twice about going farther. Italy intensifies as you plunge deeper. Naples is a barrel of cultural monkeys, Italy in the extreme—its best (birthplace of pizza and Sophia Loren) and its worst (home of the Camorra, Naples' "family" of organized crime). Serene Sorrento, without a hint of Naples and just an hour to the south, makes a great home base. It's the gateway to the much-loved Amalfi Coast. From the jet-setting island of Capri to the stunning scenery of the Amalfi Coast, from ancient Pompeii to even more ancient Paestum, this is Italy's Coast with the Most.

Planning Your Time

On a quick trip, give the area three days. With Sorrento as your sunny springboard, spend a day in Naples, a day on the Amalfi Coast, and a day split between Pompeii and the town of Sorrento. While Paestum, the crater of Vesuvius, Herculaneum, and the island of Capri are decent options, these are worth-while only if you give the area more time. Consider a night train in or out of the area.

For a blitz tour, you could have breakfast on the early Rome–Naples express (7:10–9:10), do Naples and Pompeii in a day, and be back in Rome in time for Letterman. That's exhausting but more interesting than a third day in Rome. Remember that in the afternoon, Naples' street life slows and many sights close as the temperature soars. Then things pick up again in the early evening.

For a small-town vacation from your vacation, spend a few more days on the Amalfi Coast, sleeping in Positano, Atrani, or Marina del Cantone.

Driving south of Rome is not only stressful, it's impractical for most. Take advantage of the wonderful public transportation: the slick two-hour Rome–Naples express trains; the handy Circumvesuviana lacing together Naples, Pompeii, and Sorrento; and the regular bus service from Sorrento into the Amalfi region (where parking and car access are severely limited).

NAPLES (NAPOLI)

Italy's third-largest city (with more than 2 million people), has almost no open spaces or parks, which makes its position as Europe's most densely populated city plenty evident. Watching the police try to enforce traffic sanity is almost comical in Italy's grittiest, most polluted and crime-ridden city. But Naples surprises the observant traveler with its impressive knack for living, eating, and raising children in the streets with good humor and decency. Overcome your fear of being run down or ripped off long enough to talk with people—enjoy a few smiles and jokes with the man running the neighborhood tripe shop or the woman taking her day-care class on a walk through the traffic.

Twenty-five hundred years ago, Neapolis ("new city") was a thriving Greek commercial center. It remains southern Italy's leading city, offering a fascinating collection of museums, churches, eclectic architecture, and volunteers needing blood for dying babies. The pulse of Italy throbs in Naples. Like Cairo or Bombay, it's appalling and captivating at the same time, the closest thing to "reality travel" you'll find in Western Europe. But this tangled mess still somehow manages to breathe, laugh, and sing—with a captivating Italian accent.

Orientation (tel. code: 081)

For a quick visit, start with the museum, do the Slice-of-Neapolitan-Life Walk (see Sights, below), and celebrate your survival with pizza. Of course, Naples is huge. But with limited time, if you stick to the described route and grab a cab when you're lost or tired, it's fun. Treat yourself well in Naples; the city is cheap by Italian standards.

Bay of Naples

Tourist Information: At the TI in the central train
station (opposite track #16), pick up a map and the Qui Napoli
booklet—if they say they're "finished," ask for an old one
(Monday–Saturday 9:00–19:00, Sunday 9:00–13:00, tel.
081/268-779 or 081/405-311).

Arrival in Naples: There are several Naples stations.
Naples Centrale is the main one (facing Piazza Garibaldi;
has Circumvesuviana stop for commuter trains to Sorrento
and Pompeii, baggage check, and TI). Since Centrale
is a dead-end station, through trains often stop at Piazza
Garibaldi (actually a subway station just downstairs from
Centrale) or at the Napoli Mergellina station across town
(equipped with a TI; a direct ten-minute subway ride to
Centrale, a railpass or train ticket to Napoli Centrale
covers you for the connecting ride to Centrale, subway
trains depart about every ten minutes). As you're coming
in, ask someone which stations your train stops at. Get
off at Mergellina only if your train doesn't stop at
Centrale or Garibaldi.

Helpful Hints

Traffic: In Naples red lights are discretionary, and mopeds can mow you down from any place at any time.

Theft Alert: Don't venture into neighborhoods that make you uncomfortable. Walk with confidence, as if you know where you're going and what you're doing. Assume able-bodied beggars are thieves. Give your money belt an extra half-hitch and keep it completely hidden. Stick to busy streets and beware of gangs of young street hoodlums. Remember, a third of the city is unemployed, and past local governments set an example the Mafia would be proud of. Assume con artists are more clever than you. Any jostle or commotion is probably a thief team smoke screen. Lately Naples, under a new activist mayor, has been occupied by an army of police which has made it feel safer. Still, err on the side of caution. Any bags you have are probably safest checked at the central train station (L5,000, Deposito Bagagli in front of track #24).

Getting Around Naples

Naples' simple one-line subway, the Servizio Metropolitano, runs from the Centrale station through the center of town (direction: Pozzouli), stopping at Piazza Cavour (Archaeology Museum) and Montesanto (top of Spanish Quarter and Spaccanapoli). L1,300 tickets are good for 90 minutes. All-day tickets cost L4,000. If you can afford a taxi, don't mess with the buses. A short taxi-ride costs L4,000–6,000 (insist on the meter).

Sights—Naples

▲▲▲**Museo Archeologico**—For lovers of antiquity, this museum alone makes Naples a worthwhile stop; it offers the only possible peek into the artistic jewelry boxes of Pompeii and Herculaneum. The actual sights are impressive but barren; the best art ended up here.

Paintings and artifacts: Climb the grand stairs to the top floor, and from the grand ballroom, go left into a Pompeiian art gallery lined with paintings, bronze statues, artifacts, and an impressive model of the town of Pompeii (room LXXXIII), all of which make the relative darkness of medieval Europe obvious and clearly show the seeds of inspiration for the Renaissance greats.

Mosaics: From the same staircase, one floor (several flights) down, on the opposite side, you'll find a smaller but

Naples

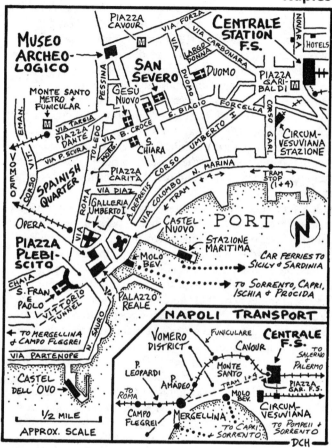

exquisite collection of Pompeiian mosaics (especially the fourth-century B.C. Battle of Alexander showing the Macedonians defeating the Persians).

Farnese Collection: The ground floor (on the distant left as you leave the stairs) has enough Greek, Roman, and Etruscan art to put any museum on the map, but its highlight is the Farnese Collection—a giant hall of huge, bright, and wonderfully restored statues excavated from Rome's Baths of Caracalla. You can almost hear the *Toro Farnese* snorting. This largest intact statue from antiquity (a third-century copy of a Hellenistic original) was carved out of one piece of marble and restored by Michelangelo. Read the worthwhile descriptions on the walls (L12,000, Wednesday–Monday 9:00–14:00, maybe until 19:00 July–September, closed Tuesday, tel. 081/440-166, call to confirm times if visiting in the afternoon.)

To get to the museum from the Centrale train station, follow signs to Metropolitano (tickets from window on left, ask which track—*"Che binario?"*—to Piazza Cavour, and ride the subway one stop). As you exit, turn right and head gradually uphill. At the end of cluttered Piazza Cavour, you'll see the museum, a huge pink-brick building. The WC below and behind the main stairway is uncharacteristically pleasant.

▲▲▲The Slice-of-Neapolitan-Life Walk—Walk from the museum through the heart of town and back to the station (allow at least two hours plus lunch and sightseeing stops). Sights are listed in the order you'll see them on this walk.

Naples, a living medieval city, is its own best sight. Couples artfully make love on Vespas surrounded by more fights and smiles per cobble here than anywhere else in Italy. Rather than seeing Naples as a list of sights, see the one great museum, then capture its essence by taking this walk through the core of the city. Should you become overwhelmed or lost, step into a store and ask for help (*"Dové il stazione centrale?"*) or point in this book to the next sight.

Via Toledo and the Spanish Quarter (city walk, first half): Leaving the Archaeological Museum at the top of Piazza Cavour (Metro: Piazza Cavour), cross the street, and dip into the ornate galleria on your way to Via Pessina. The first part of this walk is a straight 1-mile ramble down the boulevard to Galleria Umberto I near the Royal Palace. Coffee will be waiting.

Busy Via Pessina leads downhill to Piazza Dante. After 2 blocks, a tiny pedestrian street (Via Micco Spadaro) leads to the Academy of Fine Arts (Belle Arti). Sneak a peek inside. Isn't that Michelangelo's *David*?! (The bar/pizzeria in front serves a decent quick lunch with pleasant outdoor seating.)

At Piazza Dante, notice poor old Dante in the center, looking out over the chaos with a hopeless gesture. Past the square, Via Pessina becomes Via Toledo, Naples's principal shopping street. About 5 blocks below Piazza Dante, at Via Maddaloni,

Naples Walk

1/4 MILE

MUSEO ARCHEOLOGICO

ONE STOP ON SUBWAY TO PIAZZA GARIBALDI & CENTRAL STATION

PIAZZA CAVOUR

CAVOUR METRO STOP

Start

VIA PESSINA →

PIAZZA BELLINI

VIA FORCA

SAN SEVERO

DUOMO

VIA DUOMO

COLLETTA

VICARIA

PIAZZA DANTE

VIA PORTA ALBA

SAN DOM.

CROCE

PIZZA

GESU NUOVO

CAPITELLI

"SPACCA-NAPOLI"

TO PIAZZA GARI-BALDI (10 MIN. WALK)

VIA TOLEDO →

SANTA CHIARA

CORSO UMBERTO

PIAZZA CARITA

VIA MORGANTINA

VIA DIAZ

SPANISH QUARTER

GALLERIA UMBERTO I

BAY

PIAZZA MUNICIPIO

STAZIONE MARITTIMA

CASTEL NUOVO

OF

SAN CARLO →

ROYAL PALACE

BEVERELLO PORT (BOATS TO SORRENTO) & CAPRI

S. FRAN. DI PAOLA

PIAZZA PLEBISCITO

DCH

NAPLES

you cross the long straight *Spaccanapoli* (literally, "split Naples"). Look left and right. Since ancient times, this thin street (which changes names several times) has bisected the city. (We'll be coming back to this point later. To abbreviate this walk, turn left here and skip down to the Spaccanapoli section.)

Via Toledo runs through Piazza Carita. You may meet a Fascist here eager to point out the Mussolini photo in his wallet and the Fascist architecture (from 1938) overlooking the square. Wander down Via Toledo a few blocks past the Fascist architecture of two banks (both on the left). Try robbing the second one (Banco di Napoli, 178 Via Toledo).

Up the hill to your right is the Spanish Quarter, Naples at its rawest, poorest, and most historic. Thrill-seekers (or someone in need of a $20 prostitute) will take a stroll up one of these streets and loop back to Via Toledo. The only thing predictable about this Neapolitan tidepool is the ancient grid plan of its streets, the friendliness of its shopkeepers, and the boldness of its mopeds. Concerned locals will tug on their lower eyelid, warning you to be wary. Pop into a grocery shop and ask the man to make you his best ham and mozzarella sandwich. Trust him for the price—it shouldn't be more than L5,000.

Continue down Via Toledo to the Piazza Plebiscito. From here you'll see the church of **San Francesco di Paola** with its Pantheon-inspired dome and broad, arcing colonnades. Opposite is the **Royal Palace**, which has housed Spanish, French, and even Italian royalty. The lavish interior is open for tours (L8,000, Tuesday–Sunday 9:00–13:30, closed Monday). Next door, peek inside the neoclassical **Teatro San Carlo**, Italy's second-most-respected opera house (after Milan's La Scala). The huge castle on the harborfront just beyond the palace houses government bureaucrats and is closed to tourists.

Under the Victorian iron and glass of the 100-year-old Galleria Umberto I, enjoy a coffee break or sample a unique Neapolitan pastry called *sfoigliatella* (with sweet ricotta cheese with nuggets of candied fruit). Go through the tall yellow arch at the end of Via Toledo or across from the opera house. Gawk up.

Spaccanapoli back to the station (city walk, second half): To continue your walk, double back up Via Toledo past Piazza Carita to Via Maddaloni. (Consider going via the back streets.) Look east and west to survey the straight-as-a-Roman-arrow Spaccanapoli. Formerly the main thoroughfare of the Greek city of Neapolis, it starts up the hill near the Monte santo funicular (a colorful and safer Spanish Quarter neighborhood from where you can see how strictly Spaccanapoli splits Naples' historic center).

Turn right off Via Toledo and walk down Via Maddaloni to two bulky old churches (and a TI, open until 19:00) on Piazza Gesu Nuovo. Check out the austere, fortresslike church of **Gesu Nuovo** with its peaceful but brilliant Baroque interior. Across the street, the simpler Gothic church of **Santa Chiara** offers a stark contrast (churches usually close 13:00–16:30).

The rest of this walk is basically a straight line (all of which locals call Spaccanapoli). Continue down traffic-free Via B. Croce to the next square, Piazza S. Domenico Maggiore. Detour behind the castlelike **San Domenico Maggiore** church (to the right as you face the church, take the first right after that), following yellow signs to the **Capella Sansevero** (L6,000, Wednesday–Sunday 10:00–17:00, closed Tuesday, Via de Sanctis 19). This small chapel is a Baroque explosion mourning the body of Christ, lying on a soft pillow under an incredibly realistic veil—all carved out of marble. It's like no statue I've seen (by Giuseppe "howdeedoodat" Sammartino, 1750). Lovely statues, carved from a single piece of marble, adorn the altar. *Despair* struggles with a marble rope net (on the right, opposite *Chastity*). Then, for the ghoul in all of us, walk down the stairway to the right for a creepy look at two 200-year-old studies in varicose veins. Was one decapitated? Was one pregnant?

Back on Via B. Croce, turn left and continue the Spaccanapoli cultural scavenger hunt. As Via B. Croce becomes Via S. Biagio dei Librai, notice the gold and silver shops and the tidy little shop at #34. Poke into the Ospedale delle Bambole (doll hospital) at #81.

Cross busy Via Duomo. The street and side-street scenes along Via Vicaria intensify. Paint a picture with these thoughts: Naples has the most intact street plan of any ancient Roman city. Imagine life here as in a Roman city (retain these images as you visit Pompeii) with street-side shop-fronts that close up to form private homes after dark. Today is just one more page in a 2,000-year-old story of city activity: all kinds of meetings, beatings, and cheatings; kisses, near misses, and little-boy pisses. You name it, it occurs right on the streets today, as it has since Roman times. People ooze from crusty corners. Black-and-white death announcements add to the clutter on the walls. Widows sell cigarettes from buckets. For a peek behind the scenes in the shade of wet laundry, venture down a few side streets (2 blocks before the Y in the road). Buy two carrots as a gift for the woman on the fifth floor if she'll lower her bucket down to pick them up.

At the tiny fenced-in triangular park, veer right onto Via Forcella. Turning right on busy Via Pietro Colletta, you can step right into the North Pole. Reward yourself for surviving this safari with a stop at the Polo Nord Gelateria (Via Pietro Colletta 41, sample their Kiss flavor before ordering). Via Pietro Colletta leads past Napoli's two most competitive pizzerias (see Eating, below) to Corso Umberto.

To finish the walk, turn left on the grand-boulevardian Corso Umberto, and walk through all kinds of riffraff to the vast and ugly Piazza Garibaldi. On the far side is the Central Station. Run for it! (If you're tired or late, any bus coming down the meridian is Central Station-bound.)

Naples has many more museums, churches, and sights that some consider important. For a rundown on these, refer to the TI's free *Qui Napoli* publication.

Sleeping in Naples
(L1,600 = about $1, tel. code: 081)
Sleep Code: **S**=Single, **D**=Double/Twin, **T**=Triple, **Q**=Quad, **b**=bathroom, **t**=toilet only, **s**=shower only, **CC**=Credit Card (**V**isa, **M**asterCard, **A**mex), **SE**=Speaks English, **NSE**=No English. Breakfast is normally included only at the expensive places.

With Sorrento just an hour away, I can't imagine why you'd sleep in Naples. But if needed, here are two safe, clean places (200 yards from the station) and a hostel. For the hotels, turn right out of the station and walk under an elevated road 1 block up Corso Novara. The area is thoroughly ugly but reasonably safe. Still, be careful after dark.

Hotel Ginerva is quiet, bright, and cheery, with new beds, floral wallpaper, and an L8,000-per-load washing machine. Bruno and Anna's son Lello speaks English (13 rooms, S-L36,000, D-L60,000, Db-L70,000, T-L81,000, Tb-L95,000, Q-L102,000, special 10 percent discount with this book, prices promised through 1998, CC:VMA; right off Corso Novara down Via Genova to #116, tel. 081/283-210).

Hotel Eden, not as cozy, is a big old establishment run with panache by English-speaking Nicola (Danny DeVito) and his brother, Vincenzo. Clean, good beds, brown and gray tones, and all the comforts in sterile surroundings, which is exactly what you're after in Naples (Db-L72,000, Tb-L88,000, prices good through '98 with this book, CC:VMA; Corso Novara 9, tel. & fax 285-344 or 285-690). Ask to see the hall lighting ambience.

Ostello Mergellina is well run, cheap, and pleasant (L25,000 beds with sheets and breakfast in small rooms with two to six beds, closed 9:00–16:00 and at 24:00, cheap meals; Metro: Mergellina, Salita della Grotta a Piedigrotta 23, tel. 081/761-2346).

Eating in Naples

Drop by one of the two most traditional pizzerias. Naples, baking just the right combination of fresh dough, mozzarella, and tomatoes in traditional wood-burning ovens, is the birthplace of pizza. A few blocks from the train station, **Antica Pizzeria da Michele** is for purists (Monday–Saturday 8:00–23:00, closed Sunday, cheap, filled with locals, 50 yards off Corso Umberto on Via Cesare Sersale, look for the vertical red "Antica Pizzeria" sign, tel. 081/553-9204). It serves two kinds: Margherita (tomato sauce and mozzarella) or Marinara (tomato sauce, oregano, and garlic, with no cheese). A pizza with beer costs L8,000. Some locals prefer **Pizzeria Trianon** (Monday–Saturday 10:00–13:30, 18:30–23:00, closed Sunday; across the street at Via Pietro Colletta 42, tel. 081/553-9426). Da Michele's arch-rival offers more choices and a cozier atmosphere.

Near the station and recommended hotels, the **Ristorante Grandoni** is a big old traditional eatery serving good food for a good price (closed Sunday, Corso Novara 11, next to Hotel Eden).

Transportation Connections—Naples

By boat to: Sorrento (7/day, 30 min, L12,000), **Capri** (6 hydrofoils/day, 45 min, L16,000).

By train to: Rome (hourly, 2–3 hrs), **Brindisi** (2/day, 7 hrs, overnight possible; from Brindisi, ferries sail to Greece), **Milan** (4/day, 7–9 hrs, overnight possible, more with a change in Rome), **Venice** (4/day, 8–10 hrs), **Nice** (4/day, 13 hrs), **Paris** (3/day, 18 hrs). Naples train information: tel. 081/1478-88088.

The Circumvesuviana: Naples, Herculaneum, Pompeii, and **Sorrento** are all on the handy commuter train, the Ferrovia Circumvesuviana. Catch it in the basement of Naples' Centrale station; it's clearly signposted (get tickets

across from train turnstiles). The Circumvesuviana also
has its own terminal, one stop or a ten-minute walk beyond
the Centrale station. Take your pick. Two trains per
hour marked "Sorrento" get you to Herculaneum (Ercolano)
in 15 minutes, Pompeii in 40 minutes, and Sorrento, the
end of the line, in 70 minutes (L4,200 one-way, no train
passes). When returning to Naples Centrale station on
the Circumvesuviana, get off at the second-to-the-last
station, the Collegamento FS or Garibaldi stop (Centrale
station is just up the escalator).

SORRENTO

Wedged on a ledge under the mountains and over the
Mediterranean, spritzed by lemon and olive groves,
Sorrento is an attractive resort of 20,000 residents and—
in the summer—as many tourists. It's as well-located
for regional sightseeing as it is a pleasant place to stay
and stroll. The Sorrentines have gone out of their way to
create a completely safe and relaxed place for tourists to
come and spend money. Everyone seems to speak fluent
English and work for the Chamber of Commerce. This
gateway to the Amalfi Coast has an unspoiled old quarter,
a lively main shopping street, and a spectacular cliffside
setting. Skip the port and its poor excuse for a beach
unless you're taking a ferry.

Orientation (tel. code: 081)

Sorrento is long and narrow. The main drag, Corso Italia
(50 meters in front of the Circumvesuviana train station), runs
parallel to the sea from the station through the town center
and out to the cape, where it's renamed Via Capo. Everything
mentioned (except the hotels on Via Capo) is within a five-
minute walk of the station.

   Tourist Information: At the TI, or Soggiorno e
Turismo (daily 8:30–14:00, 17:00–20:00, less off-season, tel.
081/807-4033), get a free *Surrentum* magazine with great map
and schedules of boats, buses, and events. To reach the TI
from the station, go left on Corso Italia and walk five minutes
to Piazza Tasso. Turn right at end of square down Via L. de
Maio through Piazza Sant Antonino to the Foreigners' Club
mansion at #35. You'll pass many fake "tourist offices" on the
way (travel agencies selling bus and boat tours).

Sorrento

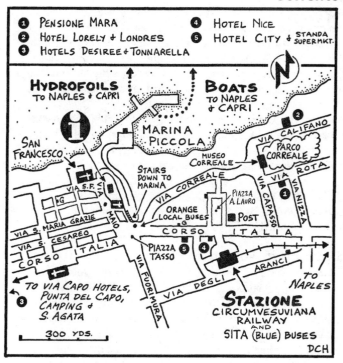

1. PENSIONE MARA
2. HOTEL LORELY & LONDRES
3. HOTELS DESIREE & TONNARELLA
4. HOTEL NICE
5. HOTEL CITY & STANDA SUPERMKT.

HYDROFOILS TO NAPLES & CAPRI

BOATS TO NAPLES & CAPRI

MARINA PICCOLA

SAN FRANCESCO

STAIRS DOWN TO MARINA

MUSEO CORREALE

PARCO CORREALE

VIA CALIFANO

VIA ROTA

VIA NIZZA

VIA CAPASSO

VIA S.F.

VIA CORREALE

PIAZZA A. LAURO

ORANGE LOCAL BUSES

POST

VIA S. MARIA GRAZIE

VIA S. CESAREO

CORSO   ITALIA

CORSO   ITALIA

PIAZZA TASSO

PIAZZA 5 4

VIA FUORIMURA

VIA DEGLI

ARANCI

TO VIA CAPO HOTELS, PUNTA DEL CAPO, CAMPING & S. AGATA

TO NAPLES

STAZIONE CIRCUMVESUVIANA RAILWAY AND SITA (BLUE) BUSES

300 YDS.

DCH

Helpful Hints: The Foreigners' Club provides reasonably priced snacks and drinks, relaxation and views, and a handy place for visitors to meet locals (behind the TI, city discount cards, public WC). It's lively with concerts or dancing on summer evenings. If you need immediate tanning, you can rent a chair on the pier by the port, though the best swimming is at Punta del Capo (see below). There's a handy coin-op laundromat (one load-L15,000, two loads-L25,000) at Corso Italia 30; turn right down the alley for the side entrance.

Getting Around Sorrento

Orange city buses run from the station to the Punta del Capo, and down to the port (L1,000 tickets within the center, sold at *tabacchi* shops). Rental mopeds (L35,000) and Vespas (L50,000, tel. 081/878-1386) are at Corso Italia 210. In summer, forget renting a car unless you enjoy traffic jams.

Sights—Sorrento

▲**Strolling**—Take time to explore the surprisingly pleasant old city between Corso Italia and the sea. Views from the public park next to the Imperial Hotel Tramontano are worth the detour. The evening *passeggiata* (along the Corso Italia and Via San Cesareo) peaks around 22:00. Check out the old-boys' club playing cards, oblivious to the tourism, under their portico at Via San Cesareo and Via Tasso.

▲**Punta del Capo**—For clean water and a pebbly peninsula-tip beach, walk 40 minutes to Punta del Capo (or take the ten-minute bus ride from Piazza Tasso, 2/hour, L1,000). It's a rocky but accessible, traffic-free swimming area with a stunning view of Sorrento and Naples. The ruined Roman Villa di Pollio marks this discovered but beautiful cape. Leave the road at the American Bar, turn right, and amble down the covered walkway to the beach.

Sleeping in Sorrento
(L1,600 = about $1; tel. code: 081, zip code: 80067)

Unlike many resorts, Sorrento offers the whole range of rooms. If you decide to splurge, get a balcony and view. (Ask, *"Con balcon, con vista sul mare."*) *"Tranquillo"* is taken as a request for a room off the street. Hotels listed here are either near the station and city center or out toward the Punta del Capo, a 40-minute walk (or short bus ride) from the station. While many hotels close for the winter, you should have no trouble finding a room any time outside of August when the place is jammed and many hotel prices go way up. Note: The spindly, more exotic, and more tranquil Amalfi Coast town of Positano (see Amalfi Coast, below) is also a good place to spend the night.

Sleeping near the Train Station and in the Town Center

A block in front of the station, turn right onto the Corso Italia, then left down Via Capasso for the first two listings. Turn left on Corso Italia for the next three listings.

   Pension Mara provides simple, clean rooms in a dull building with a good location (S-L30,000, D-L65,000, Db-L70,000, T-L95,000, Tb-L115,000, cheap quads and family room, add L10,000 in August, prices promised through 1998; six of its eight rooms have a balcony; from Via Capasso, turn right onto the unmarked Via Rota just past the police station, Via Rota 5, tel. 081/878-3665, friendly Adelle speaks a little English).

Hotel Loreley is a reasonable exception in an otherwise expensive neighborhood. The setting is drunk with character. This rambling, spacious, colorful old Sorrentine villa is ideal for those wishing to sit on the bluff and stare at the sea. Nineteen of its 27 rooms are quiet with seaview balconies. Eight are cheaper but on a noisy street. An elevator takes you to the hotel's private beach (Sb-L70,000, Db-L120,000 with breakfast and sea-view balcony; from July 15–September 15 half-pension at L90,000 per person is required, but the dinner's great, prices promised with this book through 1998, CC:VM, easy free parking on the street; follow Via Capasso to the water and turn right to see the big rose-colored hotel at Via Califano 2, tel. & fax 081/807-3187).

Hotel City is small and bright but on a busy street with single pane windows and double-pain Vespas. The manager, Gianni, caters to budget English-speaking travelers and runs a newsstand and travel agency in his lobby (Sb-L70,000, Db-L90,000, breakfast-L5,000, cheaper and with breakfast in off-season, CC:VM; very handy near Piazza Tasso at Corso Italia 221, tel. & fax 081/877-2210).

Hotel Nice is a good, basic value very near the station on the busy main drag. Ask for a room off the street (Sb-L75,000, Db-L95,000, includes breakfast, third and fourth roommates-L35,000 each; Corso Italia 257, tel. 081/878-1650, fax 081/807-1154).

Hotel Del Corso, a just-renovated Old World hotel, is clean and comfortable, with spacious rooms and urban noise (D-L90,000, Db-L110,000, breakfast-L10,000; half-pension at L95,000 per person required in August, CC:VMA; in town center, Corso Italia 134, tel. 081/807-3657, fax 081/807-1016). Lucca is very helpful and speaks English.

Ostello di Sorrento La Caffetteria, a tiny hostel run by a bar 5 blocks from the train station, offers the cheapest beds in town (50 L30,000 beds in triples and quads, Sb-L40,000–60,000, Db-L70,000–100,000, includes breakfast; Via degli Aranci 160, tel. & fax 081/877-1371, SE).

Sleeping with a View on Via Capo

These hotels are outside of town near the cape (straight out Corso Italia, which turns into Via Capo; 40 minutes on foot from the center, L15,000 by taxi, or a bus-ride away). The goofy bus situation: there are two competing companies—blue SITA and Orange Circumvesuviana; Orange is more frequent (3/hour) and both kinds of tickets are sold at tobacco shops, not on the bus. It's an easy walk to the Punta del Capo from these hotels. If you're in Sorrento to stay put and luxuriate, these are best (although I'd rather luxuriate on the Amalfi Coast).

Pension La Tonnarella is a Sorrentine villa with several terraces, stylish tiles, sea views, a dreamy chandeliered view dining room, and disinterested owners (Db-L150,000–175,000 with view and breakfast; obligatory L120,000 per person half-pension with dinner in August; many rooms with great view balconies, CC:VMA; Via Capo 31, tel. 081/878-1153, fax 081/878-2169).

Hotel Desiree, run by helpful Ingeborg, Michele and Corinna, is a simpler affair with humbler views but all the comforts and no half-board requirements (Db-125,000 with breakfast promised through 1998, shares La Tonnarella's driveway and beach; at Via Capo 31, tel. & fax 081/878-1563). It's generally booked out in August.

Hotel Minerva is run by friendly, English-speaking owners who have lovingly restored this dream palace. Catch the elevator at Via Capo 32. Getting off at the fifth floor, you'll step into a spectacular terrace with outrageous Mediterranean views and a cliff-hanging swimming pool complementing 54 large tiled rooms (49 have seaview balconies). Peasants sneak in a picnic dinner and enjoy just hanging out here (Sb-L120,000, Db-L190,000, Tb-L220,000, Qb-L260,000 with this book through 1998, includes breakfast, no summer half-pension requirement, CC:VMA; Via Capo 30, tel. 081/878-1011, fax 081/878-1949). The nearby Verdemare restaurant is good.

The humble **Pension Elios**, run by Luigi and Maria, offers simple but spacious rooms, many with balconies and views, and a fine roof terrace (D-L70,000, Db-L76,000, includes breakfast, discounted in low season, special '98 prices with this book; Via Capo 33, tel. 081/878-1812).

Eating in Sorrento

Dining out can be reasonable here. If you fancy a picnic dinner on your balcony, on the hotel terrace, or in the public garden, you'll find many markets and take-out pizzerias in the old town. The supermarket at 223 Corso Italia has it all (8:30–13:00, 16:30–20:30, closed all day Sunday and Thursday afternoons).

In the city center, **Sant Antonino's** offers friendly service, red-checkered tablecloths, an outdoor patio, decent prices, and good pasta (closed Monday, just off the Piazza Sant Antonino on Santa Maria delle Grazie 6, tel. 081/877-1200). The nearby and smaller **Pizzeria Da Gigino** is also good (first road to the right of Sant Antonino as you face it). **Pizzeria Giardiniello** is a family show offering good food, good prices, and seating inside or in a tropical garden (closed Thursday, Via Accademia 7, tel. 081/878-4616). **Osteria Gatto Nero**, a loveable hole-in-the-wall, is a mom-and-pop place that respects its budget eaters (Via Santa Maria della Pieta 36, 1 block off Corso Italia on inland side, closed Monday, tel. 081/878-1582). The restaurant on the terrace of **Hotel Loreley** serves the best reasonably priced great-view meals in town. **La Favorita-O'Parrucchiano** is venerable, expensive, and a decent splurge for fine regional cooking in a cascading garden setting (Corso Italia 71, tel. 081/878-1321). The popular **Davide "il" Gelato** has many repeat customers—so many flavors, so little time (Via P.R. Giuliani 39, off Corso Italia).

Transportation Connections—Sorrento

By boat to: Capri (about hourly, 25 min, L5,000; quicker and pricier by hydrofoil and jet boat: 15 min, L8,500), **Positano** (daily in summer, weekends only in late spring and early fall, 75 min, L8,000–12,000). Sorrento's busy port also launches ferries to **Naples** (7/day, 30 min, L12,000) and **Ischia** (schedules available at TI, walk or shuttle-bus to port from Piazza Tasso). Several lines compete, using boats and hydrofoils. Buy only one-way tickets (there's no round-trip discount) for schedule flexibility, so you can take any company's boat back. Prices are the same. Check times for the last return crossing upon arrival. The first boats leaving Sorrento can be jammed; you may want to leave closer to 10:00.

To the Amalfi Coast by bus: Blue SITA buses depart from Sorrento's train station nearly hourly and stop at all Amalfi Coast towns (Positano in 45 minutes, L2,000; Amalfi in 90 minutes, L3,500), ending up in Salerno at the far end of the coast in just under three hours. Buy tickets at the tobacco shop nearest any bus stop before boarding. (There's a *tabacchi* street level at the Sorrento station.) Leaving Sorrento, arrive early to

Amalfi Coast

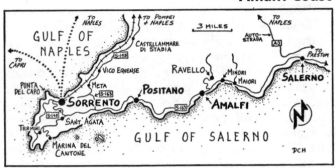

grab a seat on the right for the best views. There are often
two or three buses leaving at the same time. You may have
to change in Amalfi to get to Salerno.

Amalfi Coast tours by taxi: Fun-loving Carmino
Monetti offers four-hour trips from Sorrento along the coast
visiting Positano, Amalfi, and Ravello (L150,000 for two or
three, L200,000 for four people, tel. 033-846-2860). This is
a fine deal for small groups with limited time.

**To Pompeii, Herculaneum, and Naples by
Circumvesuviana train:** This handy commuter train
runs about every 40 minutes between Naples and Sorrento.
From Sorrento, it's 30 minutes to Pompeii, 45 minutes to
Herculaneum, and 70 minutes to Naples (L4,200 one-way).
See Transportation Connections—Naples, above, for tips
on arriving there smartly.

Sights—The Amalfi Coast

▲▲▲**Bus ride along Amalfi Coast**—One of the world's
great bus rides, this trip from Sorrento to Salerno along
the Amalfi Coast will leave your mouth open and your film
exposed. You'll gain respect for the Italian engineers who built
the road—and even more respect for the bus drivers who drive
it. As you hyperventilate, notice that the Mediterranean, a
sheer 500-foot drop below, really twinkles.

Cantilevered garages, hotels, and villas cling to the vertical
terrain, and beautiful sandy coves tease from far below and out
of reach. Gasp from the right side of the bus as you go and
the left on the way back (if you return by bus). Those on the
wrong side really miss out. Traffic is so heavy that in the

summer, local cars are allowed to drive only every other day—even-numbered license plates one day, odd the next. (Buses and tourists foolish enough to drive are exempt from this system.)

The Amalfi Coast towns are pretty but generally touristic, congested, overpriced, and a long hike above tiny beaches. The real thrill here is the scenic drive. Catch a blue SITA bus from the Sorrento train station (see above for details).

▲▲**Positano**—Specializing in scenery and sand, Positano hangs halfway between Sorrento and Amalfi on the most spectacular stretch of the coast. The village, a three-star sight from a distance, is a pleasant (if expensive) gathering of women's clothing stores and cafés, with a good but pebbly beach. There's little to do here but enjoy the beach and views and window-shop. Consider a day trip from Sorrento; take the bus out and the afternoon ferry home.

To minimize your descent, use the last Positano bus stop (on the Amalfi town side, ask for "Sponda;" there are only two scheduled stops in Positano: Sponda and Chiesa). It's a 15-minute stroll/shop/munch from here to the beach. If catching the bus back to Sorrento, remember it may leave from Sponda five minutes before the printed departure; there is no place for the bus to wait, so in case the driver is early, you should be, too. You can also take the orange bus up to the highway and catch the blue SITA bus from the small town square (2/hourly, tickets from the adjacent café). Boats to Sorrento, Amalfi, and Capri depart from Positano (tickets are sold at the far right end of the beach). For accommodations, see Sleeping, below. Positano TI: tel. 089/875-067.

Amalfi—The waterfront of this most famous of the Amalfi Coast villages is dominated by a bus station, a parking lot, and two gas stations. The main street through the village—hard for pedestrians to avoid—is packed with cars and bully mopeds. Neighboring Atrani, a 15-minute walk away, and Minori, a bit farther on, are more pleasant. For accommodations, see Sleeping, below.

▲**Bus ride to Sant Agata and Sorrento Peninsula**—The trip from Sorrento to Sant Agata is a beautiful cliff-hanger punctuated by lemon groves, olive orchards, and wildflowers. Catch the sunset here for the single best view over both sides of the peninsula. From the end of the line, Sant Agata, walk toward Sant Agata's church. Follow signs to the monastery, Il Deserto. Go through the gate and climb into and on top of the

monastery for the views surveying both the Golfo di Napoli
and the Golfo di Salerno (ask for Colle di Fontanelle.) The village of Sant Agata is nothing special, but you'll find it refreshingly unspoiled. It's a decent place for dinner or a *granita caffè
con panna* at the old wooden bar about 100 meters from the bus
stop (departures—2/hourly, 20-minute ride—on blue SITA
buses from the Sorrento station; buy two one-way L1,800
tickets in the Sorrento station café).

This is the gateway to the scenic but ignored Sorrento
Peninsula that stretches 20 kilometers from Sorrento to the
Campanella point. From Sant Agata, the bus continues to
Marina del Cantone and Termini. From Termini a 7-kilometer
walk takes you to the point under a ruined Norman Tower
where you can almost reach out and touch Capri (bring water,
get local directions, not good for swimming).

Marina del Cantone, a tiny fishing village near Nerano
on a Sorrento Peninsula dead-end, is the place to establish a
sleepy, fun-in-the-sun residency (five buses/day from Sorrento
to Nerano, 1 hr, L2,000). Sleep at the friendly **Pensione La
Certosa** which offers a beachfront restaurant, organizes boat
excursions, and can direct you to a number of peaceful little
beaches (16 rooms, Db-L100,000 with breakfast, dinner
required in August, 80068 Massa Lubrense, tel. 081/808-1209,
fax 081/808-1245, run by Alfonso). There's a fine pizzeria next
door. For cheaper beds, try the bungalows at **Camping
Nettuno** (Db-L60,000, Qb-L80,000, tel. 081/808-1051).
A short hike takes you to the quiet beach at Baia di Ieranto.
Alfonso may pick you up by boat in the evening.

Sleeping on the Amalfi Coast
(L1,600 = about $1)

Sleeping in Positano
(tel. code: 089, zip code: 84017)
These hotels are all on Via Colombo, which leads from the
Sponda SITA bus stop down into the village.

Albergo California has great views, spacious rooms,
and a comfortable terrace (Db-L150,000, CC:VMA; Via
Colombo 141, tel. & fax 089/875-382, Maria SE). **Residence
La Tavolozza** is an unassuming eight-room hotel warmly
run by Celeste. Flawlessly restored, each room comes with
view, balcony, fine tile, and silence (Db-L120,000, also a

royal family apartment; Via Colombo 10, tel. 089/875-040).
Hotel Bougainville is spotless with eager-to-please owners
and comfortable rooms (Db-L120,000 with view balcony,
L100,000 without view, breakfast included with this book,
CC:VMA, some traffic noise and fumes; Via Colombo 25,
tel. 089/875-047, fax 089/811-150, Carlo and Luisa SE,
e-mail: bougan@mbox.argosid.it). **Hotel Marincanto** is
worth the extra money (Db-L180,000; Via Colombo 36,
tel. 089/875-130, fax 089/875-595).

The pizzerias on the beach are a bit overpriced but
pleasant. Consider a balcony, terrace, or beach picnic dinner.

Sleeping in Amalfi, Atrani, or Agerola
(tel. code: 089)
If marooned in Amalfi, stay at the **Hotel Amalfi** (40 rooms,
Db-L100,000–170,000, includes breakfast, CC:VMA, no
sea views but on a garden; 20 meters from cathedral, Via dei
Pastai 3, 84011 Amalfi, tel. 089/72-440, fax 089/872-250) or
hike 15 minutes (or ride the bus) to the tiny beach town of
Atrani, and stay in **A' Scalinatella.** This informal hostel with
dorm beds, private rooms, family apartments, and a guest
clothes washer (L7,000/load) is ideal for a small-town Amalfi
hideaway without the glitz and climbing of Positano. The
English-speaking owner Filippo is friendly and helpful (17
beds, L30,000–35,000 per bed in D or T, D-L50,000–70,000,
Db-L80,000–100,000, all accommodations include breakfast
and spaghetti in Filippo's restaurant; near main square, 84010
Atrani, tel. 089/871-492). There's a tiny youth hostel in
Agerola on Piazza G. Avitabile (L15,000 per bed; catch bus
from Amalfi, tel. 081/802-5048).

CAPRI
Made famous as the vacation hideaway of Roman emperors
Augustus and Tiberius, these days Capri is a world-class
tourist trap packed with gawky tourists in search of the rich
and famous and finding only their prices. The 4-mile-by-2-
mile "Island of Dreams" is a zoo in July and August. Other
times of year it provides a relaxing and scenic break from
the cultural gauntlet of Italy. While Capri has some Roman
ruins and an interesting 14th-century Carthusian monastery,
its chief attraction is its famous Blue Grotto, and its best
activity is a scenic hike.

Tourist Information: The TI, at the ferry dock, offers a room-finding service (daily 9:00–13:00, 15:30–19:00, tel. 081/837-0424, 081/837-5308, or 081/837-0686). A baggage storage service is nearby.

Sights—Capri

Capri and Anacapri—From the ferry dock at Marina Grande, a funicular lifts you 500 feet to the cute but most-touristy town of Capri. From there buses go regularly along a cliff-hanging road to the still cute but more bearable town of Anacapri.

Blue Grotto—To most, a visit to the Blue Grotto is an over-rated "must." While the standard tour is by ferry from Marina Grande, hardy hikers save L7,000 by catching the bus from Anacapri and hiking briskly for an hour. Admission, by rowboat with a guide, is L15,000. (Those who hike dive in for free.) Touristy as this is, the grotto, with its eerily beautiful blue sunlight reflecting through the water, is impressive (daily 9:00 until an hour before sunset, except in stormy weather).

Hike down Monte Solaro—From Anacapri, ride the chairlift to the 1,900-foot summit of Monte Solaro for a commanding view of the Bay of Naples and a pleasant downhill hike through lush vegetation and ever-changing views, past the 14th-century Chapel of Santa Maria Cetrella, and back into Anacapri.

Villa Jovis—Emperor Tiberius' now-ruined villa is a scenic one-hour hike from Capri town. Supposedly Tiberius ruled Rome from here for a decade (in about A.D. 30).

Transportation Connections—Capri

By boat to: Sorrento (nearly hrly, L5,000 for 50 minute ride, L8,000 in jet boat), **Naples** (six hydrofoils/day, 45 min, L16,000). For an untouristy alternative to Capri, consider the nearby island of Ischia (easy boat connections from Naples and Sorrento).

POMPEII, HERCULANEUM, AND VESUVIUS

▲▲▲**Pompeii**—Stopped in its tracks by the eruption of Mount Vesuvius in A.D. 79, Pompeii offers the best look anywhere at what life in Rome must have been like 2,000 years ago. An entire city of well-preserved ruins is yours to explore. Once a thriving commercial port of 20,000, Pompeii grew from Greek and Etruscan roots to become an important

Pompeii

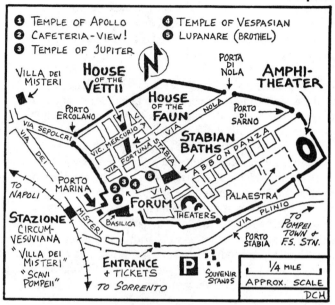

❶ TEMPLE OF APOLLO   ❹ TEMPLE OF VESPASIAN
❷ CAFETERIA-VIEW!   ❺ LUPANARE (BROTHEL)
❸ TEMPLE OF JUPITER

Roman city. Then, Pompeii was buried under 30 feet of hot mud and volcanic ash. For archaeologists this was a shake 'n' bake windfall, teaching them almost all they know about daily Roman life. It was rediscovered in the 1600s, and the first excavations began in 1748 (L12,000, daily 9:00 to an hour before sunset, 20:00 in summer, ticket office closes an hour before closing time).

Orientation: Pompeii is halfway between Naples and Sorrento, about a half-hour from either by direct Circumvesuviana train (runs at least hourly, you may save time by riding the normal train closer before catching the Circum vesuviana). Get off at the "Villa dei Misteri, Pompei Scavi" stop. (The modern town is Pompei, the ancient sight is Pompeii.) Check your bag at the train station for L1,500 or at the site for free. From the station, turn right and walk down the road to the entrance (first left turn). The TI, farther down the street (look for the "i" above the locked door) may have a Pompeii layout. The *Pompeii and Herculaneum* "past and present" book has a helpful text and allows you to re-create the ruins with plastic overlays—with the "present" actually being

1964; L25,000 price, but pay no more than L18,000. A guidebook is essential. Books are also on sale in Sorrento.

Allow at least three hours to tour Pompeii and consider
the following route, starting at the Porta Marina (town gate)
after the ticket booth.

Tour of Pompeii: When touring Pompeii, remember this
was a booming trading city. Most streets would have been
lined with stalls and jammed with customers from sunup to
sundown. Chariots vied for street space with shoppers and
many streets were off-limits to chariots during shopping hours
(you'll still see street signs with pictures of men carrying
vases—this meant pedestrians only). Fountains overflowed into
the streets flushing the gutters into the sea (thereby cleaning
the streets). The stones you see at intersections allowed pedestrians to cross the constantly gushing streets. A single stone
designated a one-way street (just enough room for one chariot)
and two stones meant a two-way chariot street. There were
no posh neighborhoods. Rich and poor mixed it up as elegant
homes existed side by side with simple homes throughout
Pompeii. With most buildings covered by a brilliant white
ground marble stucco, Pompeii in A.D. 79 was a fine town.
Remember, Pompeii's best art is in the Naples museum,
described above.

After buying your tickets, stop before the archway
into Pompeii. This was the **Porta Marina**—the sea came
right to Pompeii's door here before Vesuvius blew. There
would have been large public baths below. Approaching
the Porta Marina, notice two openings—big for chariots,
small for pedestrians.

From the Porta Marina, Via Marina leads to the
Antiquarium (first building on right, usually closed), contain-
ing artifacts and casts of vaporized victims. Back on the Via
Marina, walk ahead 50 yards and turn left to the **Temple of
Apollo** (Tempio di Apollo), surrounded by 48 columns. You'll
enter facing the altar. The Forum is just to your right.

The Forum (Foro), Pompeii's commercial, religious,
and political center, is the most ruined part of Pompeii. It's
nonetheless impressive, with several temples; the "basilica"
(Pompeii's largest building, used for legal and commercial
business); and some eerie casts of volcano victims displayed
with piles of pottery (behind the fence on the left as you
enter the Forum).

From the Forum, walk toward the volcano—past the convenient 20th-century cafeteria (decent value, gelati, over-priced cards and books, WCs with great rooftop views) down Via del Foro, and enter into the impressive **baths**, Terme del Foro, which have more casts of victims (on your left just after the cafeteria). Here, three rooms offered clients a hot bath (*calidarium*), a warm bath (*tepidarium*), and a cold plunge bath (*frigidarium*).

Exit the baths through the back door (onto Via della Fortuna), turn right and walk to the **House of Faun** (Casa del Fauno). The faun is still dancing just inside the door. One of Pompeii's largest homes, this provided Naple's Archaeological museum with many of its top treasures, including the famous mosaic of the Battle of Alexander. Wander through the many courtyards. Exit to the rear, turning right on to Viccolo di Mercurio, then left on the Viccolo dei Vetti (notice the exposed 2,000-year old lead pipes at ankle height as you turn left) and enter Pompeii's best-preserved home, the House of Vetti (Casa dei Vetti).

The **House of Vetti**, which has retained its mosaics and frescoes, was the home of two wealthy merchant brothers who were into erotic wallpaper (cover your eyes as you enter). An immediate right upon entering (open your eyes now) takes you into the slave's sleeping quarters and through to the kitchen. Enjoy the beautifully preserved rooms walking counterclockwise around the central courtyard. Some explanations are posted in English.

Leaving the House of Vetti, turn right onto the Viccolo dei Vetti, and peek into the Casa degli Scienziati. Then turn left onto the Via della Fortuna. From there a quick right leads down a curving street to the **bakery and mill** (*forno e mulini*). The ovens look like today's pizza ovens. Take the first left after the bakery onto Via degli Augustali, checking out the mosaics on the left at the Taberna Hedones (must be the tavern of hedonism), then turn right following signs to the **brothel** (*lupanare*) at #18. Wander into the brothel, a simple place with stone beds, stone pillows, and art to get you in the mood.

If you're tired after the brothel, you've seen the essentials and can head on out. Otherwise, Pompeii's last great sight is a worthwhile ten-minute stroll away. Exiting the brothel, turn right onto the same street you entered from, then turn left on the Via della Abbondanza which leads to the well-preserved

Stabian baths (Terme Stabiane—about 25 yards down on the left and worth the detour). At the end of Via della Abbondanza, jog to the right and see the huge, rebuilt **Amphitheater** (*anfiteatro*). This is the oldest (80 B.C.) and best-preserved Roman amphitheater in Italy. From the top, look into the giant rectangular Palestra, where athletes used to train. Retrace your steps all the way down the Via della Abbondanza to the entrance of Pompeii.

▲▲**Herculaneum (Ercolano)**—Smaller, less ruined, and less crowded than its famous big sister, Herculaneum offers a closer peek into ancient Roman life. Caked and baked by the same A.D. 79-eruption, Herculaneum is a small community of intact buildings with plenty of surviving detail (L12,000, open 9:00 until one hour before sunset; 15 minutes from Naples and 45 minutes from Sorrento on the same train that goes to Pompeii, turn right and follow the yellow signs, five minutes downhill from the Ercolano station).

▲**Vesuvius**—The 4,000-foot summit of Vesuvius, mainland Europe's only active volcano (sleeping restlessly since 1944), is accessible by car or by the blue Vesuvio bus (from the Herculaneum station, 45-minute ride, irregular, often five/day, often only taxis). The trip, with a two-hour wait on the mountain, costs about L12,000 (including the L3,000 admission). From the bus and car-park, you'll hike 30 minutes to the top for a sweeping Bay of Naples view, desolate lunar-like surroundings, and hot rocks. On the top, walk the entire crater lip for the most interesting views. The far end overlooks Pompeii. Be still and alone to hear the wind and tumbling rocks in the crater. Any steam? Closed when erupting.

PAESTUM

Paestum is one of the best collections of Greek temples anywhere—and certainly the most accessible to western Europe. Serenely situated, it's surrounded by fields and wildflowers and has only a modest commercial strip.

Note: The temples will be covered with scaffolding until the fall of 1998—maybe longer (call TI to confirm, tel. 0828/811-016).

Founded as Poseidonia in the sixth century B.C., a key stop on an important trade route, its name was changed to Paestum by occupying Romans in the third century B.C. The final conquerors of Paestum, malaria-carrying mosquitoes, kept the site wonderfully desolate for nearly a thousand years.

Rediscovered in the 18th century, Paestum today offers the only well-preserved Greek ruins north of Sicily (L16,000, separate L8,000 admission fees are charged for the museum and site, daily 9:00 until one hour before sunset, ticket sales end two hours before sunset).

Buses from Salerno (see Transportation Connections, below) stop at the "secondary entrance" that leads to the lonely Temple of Ceres, across from a good bar/café with sandwiches and cappuccino. Get a feel for the manageable scale of this three-temple set of ruins by looking through the fence, then visit the museum opposite the entrance.

The Museum: Orient yourself at the site plan. If you're not buying a guidebook, establish your sightseeing plan here. The large carvings overhead adorned various temples from the nearby city of Hera. Most are scenes from the life of Hercules. Don't miss the Greek sculptures in the ground-floor back room. Find the plans for the Temple of Neptune, the largest and most impressive of Paestum's temples, and notice the placement of the decorative carvings and the gargoyle-like heads behind you (tel. 0828/811-023, museum closed on the first and third Monday of the month).

Touring Paestum: Allow two hours, including the museum. After you pay the admission at the ticket booth, walk through the small rose garden to the Temple of Neptune. (You'll exit near the Temple of Ceres.) The key ruins are the impossible-to-miss Temples of Neptune, Hera, and Ceres, but the scattered village ruins are also interesting. After entering, you'll see the misnamed Temple of Neptune, a textbook example of the Doric style. Constructed in 450 B.C. and also dedicated to Hera, the Temple of Neptune is simply overwhelming. Better preserved than the Parthenon in Athens, this huge structure is a tribute to Greek engineering and aesthetics. Walk in, sit down, and contemplate the word "renaissance"—the rebirth of this grand Greek style of architecture. Notice how the columns angle out and the base bows up (scan the short ends of the temple). This was a trick ancient architects used to create the illusion of a perfectly straight building. All important Greek buildings were built using this technique. Now imagine it richly and colorfully decorated with marble and statues.

Adjacent to the Temple of Nepture is the almost-delicate Temple of Hera (dedicated to the Goddess Hera in 550 B.C.).

Near the exit is the imposing Temple of Ceres (a ten-minute walk from the Temples of Neptune and Hera).

With extra time, explore the traces of the old wall that protected Paestum. Faint remains of swimming pools, baths, houses, a small theater, and lone columns will stretch your imagination's ability to re-create this ancient city.

Sleeping near Paestum: Should you get stuck in Paestum, the **Albergo delle Rose**, which has a respectable restaurant, is just across from the main entry (Db-L90,000, includes breakfast, tel. 0828/811-070, NSE). **The Seliano Estate for Agritourism** offers spacious and spotless rooms on a farm which comes complete with horses, buffalo, a pool, and great cooking, run by an English-speaking baroness (Db-L100,000 with breakfast, L120,000 in August, near the beach, a mile from the ruins, tel. 0828/724-544, fax 0828/723-634).

Transportation Connections—Paestum

Salerno, the big city just north of Paestum, is your transfer point. From Naples or Sorrento you'll change buses or trains in Salerno for Paestum.

Salerno to Paestum: Several companies offer a Salerno–Paestum bus service from the same stop (2/hr, 70 min, buy L4,200 ticket on board, schedules are more difficult on Sunday). The Salerno–Paestum train (6/day, 40 min) is usually less efficient, but check schedules at the Salerno station. When leaving Paestum, catch a northbound bus from the far side of the street bordering the ruins. Flag down any bus, ask "Salerno?" and buy the ticket on board. Most buses stop in front of the Salerno train station.

Naples to Salerno by train: Hourly, one-hour trip.

Sorrento to Salerno by bus: The scenic three-hour Amalfi Coast drive (blue SITA bus, 12/day) drops you in Salerno, 75 yards from the Paestum bus stop (head toward waterfront) and 150 yards from the train station. Ask the driver to direct you to the station and/or Paestum bus stop.

Sorrento to Salerno by train: Ride the Circumvesuviana to Naples central station (hourly, 70 min), then catch the Salerno train (hourly, 60 min).

Drivers: While the Amalfi Coast is a thrill to drive, summer traffic is miserable. From Sorrento, Paestum is three hours via the coast and a much smoother two hours by autostrada. Driving toward Naples, catch the autostrada (direction:

Salerno Connections

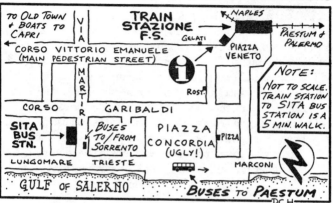

Salerno), skirt Salerno staying on the autostrada (direction: Reggio), exit at Eboli, drive straight through the modern town of Paestum, and you'll hit the ruins about when you're worried that you missed a turnoff. Along the way, you'll see signs for *mozzarella di bufalo*, the soft cheese made from the milk of water buffalo that graze here.

APPENDIX

Let's Talk Telephones

In Europe, card-operated public phones are speedily replacing coin-operated phones. Each country sells telephone cards good for use in its country. In Italy, get a phone card at any newsstand (rip off the corner before you use it). To make a call, pick up the receiver, insert your card in the slot in the phone, dial your number, make your call, then retrieve your card. The price of your call is automatically deducted from your card as you use it. If you have phone-card phobia, you'll usually find easy-to-use "talk now-pay later" metered phones in post offices. Avoid using hotel room phones, which are major rip-offs for anything other than local calls and calling-card calls (see below).

Calling Card Operators

Calling home is easy from any phone if you have a calling card. From a private phone, just dial the toll-free number to reach the operator. At a public phone, insert a coin or an Italian phone card, dial the operator, who will ask you for your calling-card number, and place your call. You'll save money on calls of three minutes or more. When you finish, your coin should be returned (or if using a card, no money should have been deducted). Your bill awaits you at home (one more reason to prolong your vacation). For more information, see Introduction: Telephones

	AT&T	**MCI**	**Sprint**
Italy	172-1011	172-1022	172-1877

Dialing Direct

Calling Between Countries: First dial the international access code, then the country code, followed by the area code (if it starts with zero, drop the zero), then the local number. To call Italy from the U.S.A., dial 011-39-area code (without the zero)-local number. To call U.S.A. from Italy, dial 00-1-area code-local number.

   Calling Long Distance Within a Country: First dial the area code (including its zero), then the local number.

   Some of Europe's Exceptions: In Spain, area codes start with nine instead of zero (just drop or add the nine as you would a zero in other countries). A few countries lack area codes, such as Denmark, Norway, and France; you still use the same sequence and codes to dial, just skip the area code.

International Access Codes

When dialing direct, first dial the international access code of the country you're calling from.

Austria: 00	France: 00	Norway: 00
Belgium: 00	Germany: 00	Portugal: 00
Britain: 00	Ireland: 00	Russia: 810
Czech Rep.: 00	Italy: 00	Spain: 07
Denmark: 00	Latvia: 00	Sweden: 009
Estonia: 800	Lithuania: 810	Switzerland: 00
Finland: 990	Netherlands: 00	U.S.A./Canada: 011

Country Codes

After you've dialed the international access code, then dial the code of the country you're calling.

Austria: 43	France: 33	Norway: 47
Belgium: 32	Germany: 49	Portugal: 351
Britain: 44	Ireland: 353	Russia: 7
Czech Rep.: 42	Italy: 39	Spain: 34
Denmark: 45	Latvia: 371	Sweden: 46
Estonia: 372	Lithuania: 370	Switzerland: 41
Finland: 358	Netherlands: 31	U.S.A./Canada: 1

Useful Italian Phone Numbers

Emergency (English-speaking police help): 113
Emergency (military police): 112
Road Service: 116
Directory Assistance (for L1,000, an Italian-speaking robot gives the number twice, very clearly): 12
Telephone help (in English; free directory assistance): 170

Rome's Climate

1st line, avg. daily low; 2nd line, avg. daily high; 3rd line, days of no rain.

J	F	M	A	M	J	J	A	S	O	N	D
39°	39°	42°	46°	55°	60°	64°	64°	61°	53°	46°	41°
54°	56°	62°	68°	74°	82°	88°	88°	83°	73°	63°	56°
23	17	26	24	25	28	29	28	24	22	22	22

Numbers and Stumblers
•Europeans write a few of their numbers differently than we do. 1 = 1, 4 = 4 , 7 = 7. Learn the difference or miss your train.
•In Europe, dates appear as day/month/year, so Christmas is 25-12-98.
•Commas are decimal points and decimals commas. A dollar and a half is 1,50 and there are 5.280 feet in a mile.
•When pointing, use your whole hand, palm downward.
•When counting with fingers, start with your thumb. If you hold up your first finger to request one item, you'll probably get two.
•What we Americans call the second floor of a building is the first floor in Europe.
•Europeans keep the left "lane" open for passing on escalators and moving sidewalks. Keep to the right.
•In Italian museums, art is dated with A.C. (for Avanti Cristo, or B.C.) and D.C. (for Dopo Cristo, or A.D.). O.K.?

Metric Conversions (approximate)

1 inch = 25 millimeters	32 degrees F = 0 degrees C
1 foot = 0.3 meter	82 degrees F = about 28 degrees C
1 yard = 0.9 meter	1 ounce = 28 grams
1 mile = 1.6 kilometers	1 kilogram = 2.2 pounds
1 centimeter = 0.4 inch	1 quart = 0.95 liter
1 meter = 39.4 inches	1 square yard = 0.8 square meter
1 kilometer = .62 mile	1 acre = 0.4 hectare

Public Holidays and Festivals
Italy has more than its share of holidays. Each town has a local festival honoring its patron saint. February is Carnevale time in Venice. Italy (including most major sights) closes down on these national holidays: January 1, January 6 (Epiphany), Easter Sunday and Monday, April 25 (Liberation Day), May 1 (Labor Day), May 20 (Ascension Day), August 15 (Assumption of Mary), November 1 (All Saints Day), December 8 (Immaculate Conception of Mary), and December 25 and 26.

Basic Italian Survival Phrases

Hello (good day).	**Buon giorno.**	bwohn **jor**-noh
Do you speak English?	**Parla inglese?**	**par**-lah een-**glay**-zay
Yes. / No.	**Si. / No.**	see / noh
I'm sorry.	**Mi dispiace.**	mee dee-**speeah**-chay
Please.	**Per favore.**	pehr fah-**voh**-ray
Thank you.	**Grazie.**	**graht**-seeay
Goodbye!	**Arrivederci!**	ah-ree-vay-**dehr**-chee
Where is...?	**Dov'è...?**	doh-**veh**
...a hotel	**...un hotel**	oon oh-**tehl**
...a youth hostel	**...un ostello della gioventù**	oon oh-**stehl**-loh **day**-lah joh-vehn-**too**
...a restaurant	**...un ristorante**	oon ree-stoh-**rahn**-tay
...a supermarket	**...un supermercado**	oon soo-pehr-mehr-**kah**-doh
...the train station	**...la stazione**	lah staht-seeoh-nay
...tourist information	**...informazioni per turisti**	een-for-maht-seeoh-nee pehr too-**ree**-stee
...the toilet	**...la toilette**	lah twah-**leht**-tay
men	**uomini, signori**	**woh**-mee-nee, seen-**yoh**-ree
women	**donne, signore**	**don**-nay, seen-**yoh**-ray
How much is it?	**Quanto costa?**	**kwahn**-toh **kos**-tah
Cheap(er).	**(Più) economico.**	(pew) ay-koh-**noh**-mee-koh
Is it included?	**È incluso?**	eh een-**kloo**-zoh
I would like...	**Vorrei....**	vor-**rehee**
...a ticket.	**...un biglietto.**	oon beel-**yay**-toh
...a room.	**...una camera.**	**oo**-nah **kah**-may-rah
...the bill.	**...il conto.**	eel **kohn**-toh
one	**uno**	**oo**-noh
two	**due**	**doo**-ay
three	**tre**	tray
four	**quattro**	**kwah**-troh
five	**cinque**	**cheeng**-kway
six	**sei**	sehee
seven	**sette**	**seht**-tay
eight	**otto**	**ot**-toh
nine	**nove**	**nov**-ay
ten	**dieci**	deeay-chee
hundred	**cento**	**chehn**-toh
thousand	**mille**	**mee**-lay
At what time?	**A che ora?**	ah kay **oh**-rah
now/ soon / later	**adesso / presto / tardi**	ah-**dehs**-soh / **prehs**-toh / **tar**-dee
today / tomorrow	**oggi / domani**	**oh**-jee / doh-**mah**-nee

For 192 more pages of survival phrases for your next trip to Italy, check out *Rick Steves' Italian Phrase Book and Dictionary*.

Italy's Public Transportation

KEY: —— RAIL   - - - BUS   •••• SHIP

NOT TO SCALE ⊙ OVERNIGHT STOPS (ON 21 DAYS ROUTE)

Train Connections

from . . . to	duration of trip	frequency	cost (2nd class)
Milan–La Spezia	3–4 hours	hourly	L20,000–L25,000
La Spezia–Pisa	1 hour	hourly	L6,000
Pisa–Florence	1 hour	hourly	L7,000–L9,000
Florence–Siena	75–120 minutes	hourly	L7,200
Siena–Orvieto	2–3 hours, 1 change	10/day	L10,000
Siena–Assisi	4 hours, 2 changes	5/day	L16,000
Assisi–Rome	2.5 hours, 1 change	9/day	L14,000–L20,000
Siena–Rome	3.5 hours, 1 change	8/day	L20,000–L25,000
Orvieto–Rome	1 hour	14/day	L11,000
Orte–Rome	40–80 minutes	20/day	L7,000
Rome–Naples	2–3 hours	6/day	L16,000
Salerno–Naples	1 hour	hourly	L4,500
Rome–Venice	5–8 hours	6/day	L50,000
Venice–Bolzano	4 hours, 1 change	8/day	L20,000–L28,000
Bolzano–Milan	4 hours, 1 change	2/day	L20,000

Faxing Your Hotel Reservation

Most hotel managers know basic "hotel English." Faxing is the preferred method for reserving a room. It's more accurate and cheaper than telephoning and much faster than writing a letter. Use this handy form for your fax. Photocopy and fax away.

One-Page Fax

To: _____ @ _____
                    hotel   *fax*

From: _____ @ _____
                    name   *fax*

Today's date: ____ / ____ / ____
                 day   *month*   *year*

Dear Hotel _____,

Please make this reservation for me:

Name: _____

Total # of people: _____   # of rooms: _____   # of nights: _____

Arriving: ____ / ____ / ____   My time of arrival (24-hr clock): _____
            day   *month*   *year*   (I will telephone if I will be late)

Departing: ____ / ____ / ____
             day   *month*   *year*

Room(s): Single___ Double___ Twin___ Triple___ Quad___

With: Toilet___ Shower___ Bath___ Sink only___

Special needs: View___ Quiet___ Cheapest Room___

Credit card: Visa___ MasterCard___ American Express___

Card #: _____

Expiration Date:_____

Name on card: _____

You may charge me for the first night as a deposit. Please fax or mail me confirmation of my reservation, along with the type of room reserved, the price, and whether the price includes breakfast. Thank you.

_____
Signature

_____
Name

_____
Address

_____
City   *State*   *Zip Code*   *Country*

Road Scholar Feedback for ITALY 1998

We're all in the same travelers' school of hard knocks. Your feedback helps us improve this guidebook for future travelers. Please fill this out (attach more info or any tips/favorite discoveries if you like) and send it to us. As thanks for your help, we'll send you our quarterly travel newsletter free for one year. Thanks! **Rick**

I traveled mainly by: ___ Car   ___ Train/bus tickets
___ Railpass   Other (please list _____)

Number of people traveling together:
___ Solo   ___ 2   ___ 3   ___ 4   ___ Over 4   ___ Tour

Ages of traveler/s (including children):

_____

I visited _____countries in _____weeks.

I traveled in: ___ Spring ___ Summer ___ Fall ___ Winter

My daily budget per person (excluding transportation):
___ Under $40   ___ $40–$60   ___ $60–$80   ___ $80–$120
___ over $120   ___ Don't know

Average cost of hotel rooms: Single room $_____
Double room $_____   Other (type _____) $_____

Favorite tip from this book:

_____

Biggest waste of time or money caused by this book:

_____

Other Rick Steves books used for this trip:

_____

Hotel listings from this book should be geared toward places that are:
___Cheaper   ___More expensive   ___About the same

Of the recommended accommodations/restaurants used, which was:

Best _____

    Why? _____

Worst _____

    Why? _____

I reserved rooms:

____from USA   ____in advance as I traveled

____same day by phone   ____just showed up

Getting rooms in recommended hotels was:

____easy   ____mixed   ____frustrating

Of the sights/experiences/destinations recommended by this book, which was:

Most overrated _____

    Why? _____

Most underrated _____

    Why? _____

Best ways to improve this book:

_____

I'd like a free newsletter subscription:

___ Yes   ___ No   ___ Already on list

_____

Name

_____

Address

_____

City, State, Zip

_____

E-mail Address

Please send to: ETBD, Box 2009, Edmonds, WA 98020

INDEX

Rick Steves' Phrase Books

Unlike other phrase books and dictionaries on the market, my well-tested phrases and key words cover every situation a traveler is likely to encounter. With these books you'll laugh with your cabby, disarm street thieves with insults, and charm new European friends.

Each book in the series is 4" x 6", with maps.

RICK STEVES' FRENCH PHRASE BOOK & DICTIONARY
U.S. $5.95/Canada $8.50

RICK STEVES' GERMAN PHRASE BOOK & DICTIONARY
U.S. $5.95/Canada $8.50

RICK STEVES' ITALIAN PHRASE BOOK & DICTIONARY
U.S. $5.95/Canada $8.50

RICK STEVES' SPANISH & PORTUGUESE PHRASE BOOK & DICTIONARY
U.S. $7.95/Canada $11.25

RICK STEVES' FRENCH, ITALIAN & GERMAN PHRASE BOOK & DICTIONARY
U.S. $7.95/Canada $11.25

Books from John Muir Publications

Rick Steves' Books

Asia Through the Back Door, $17.95

Europe 101: History and Art for the Traveler, $17.95

Mona Winks: Self-Guided Tours of Europe's Top Museums, $18.95

Rick Steves' Europe Through the Back Door, $19.95

Rick Steves' Best of Europe, $18.95

Rick Steves' France, Belgium & the Netherlands, $16.95

Rick Steves' Germany, Austria & Switzerland, $15.95

Rick Steves' Great Britain & Ireland, $16.95

Rick Steves' Italy, $14.95

Rick Steves' Russia & the Baltics, $9.95

Rick Steves' Scandinavia, $13.95

Rick Steves' Spain & Portugal, $14.95

Rick Steves' French Phrase Book, $5.95

Rick Steves' German Phrase Book, $5.95

Rick Steves' Italian Phrase Book, $5.95

Rick Steves' Spanish & Portuguese Phrase Book, $7.95

Rick Steves' French/Italian/German Phrase Book, $7.95

City•Smart™ Guidebooks

Albuquerque, $12.95 (avail. 4/98)

Anchorage, $12.95

Austin, $12.95

Calgary, $12.95

Cincinnati, $12.95 (avail. 5/98)

Cleveland, $14.95

Denver, $14.95

Indianapolis, $12.95

Kansas City, $12.95

Memphis, $12.95

Milwaukee, $12.95

Minneapolis/ St. Paul, $14.95

Nashville, $14.95

Portland, $14.95

Richmond, $12.95

San Antonio, $12.95

St. Louis, $12.95 (avail. 5/98)

Tampa/St. Petersburg, $14.95

Travel+Smart™ Guidebooks

Alaska, $14.95

American Southwest, $14.95

Carolinas, $14.95

Colorado, $14.95

Deep South, $17.95

Eastern Canada, $15.95

Florida Gulf Coast, $14.95

Hawaii, $14.95

Kentucky/ Tennessee, $14.95

Michigan, $14.95

Minnesota/ Wisconsin, $14.95

Montana, Wyoming, & Idaho, $16.95

New England, $14.95

New York State, $15.95

Northern California, $15.95

Ohio, $14.95 (avail. 5/98)

Pacific Northwest, $14.95

Southern California, $14.95

South Florida and the Keys, $14.95

Texas, $14.95

Western Canada, $16.95

Adventures in Nature Series

Alaska, $18.95

Belize, $18.95

Guatemala, $18.95

Honduras, $17.95

Kidding Around™ Travel Titles

$7.95 each

Kidding Around Atlanta

Kidding Around Austin

Kidding Around Boston

Kidding Around Chicago

Kidding Around Cleveland

Kids Go! Denver

Kidding Around Indianapolis

Kidding Around Kansas City

Kidding Around Miami

Kidding Around Milwaukee

Kidding Around Minneapolis/St. Paul

Kidding Around Nashville

Kidding Around Portland

Kidding Around San Francisco

Kids Go! Seattle

Kidding Around Washington, D.C.

Ordering Information

Please check your local bookstore for our books, or call **1-800-888-7504** to order direct and to receive a complete catalog. A shipping charge will be added to your order total.

Send all inquiries to:
John Muir Publications
P.O. Box 613
Santa Fe, NM 87504